THE CLUB KING

THE CLUB KING

*My Rise, Reign, and Fall
in New York Nightlife*

PETER GATIEN

Published by Little A, New York
www.apub.com

Amazon, the Amazon logo, and Little A are trademarks of Amazon.com, Inc., or its affiliates.

ISBN-13: 9781542015318 (hardcover)
ISBN-10: 1542015316 (hardcover)
ISBN-13: 9781542015301 (paperback)
ISBN-10: 1542015308 (paperback)

Cover design by Isaac Tobin

All photos courtesy of the author unless otherwise noted.

Printed in the United States of America

First edition

This book is dedicated to the amazing community of inspired souls who helped create my clubs over the years, the designers, artists, musicians, security personnel, door people, sound techs, lighting wizards, bartenders, barbacks, DJs, bussers, legal advisors, hosts, managers, bookers, interns, promoters, floor sweepers, dishwashers, and everyone else who had a hand in making the magic happen. As Bob Dylan said, "I've got nothing but affection for all those who've sailed with me."

Contents

PROLOGUE

Peruvian Tea at the Old Hindu Temple

Word had it that ayahuasca ceremonies possessed the power of intensive therapy, a decade of it, crammed into a single weekend. The whole enterprise sounded exhausting. No wonder I resisted.

For years, my daughter Jennifer had been proposing that I attend a ceremony and drink the bitter tea, to experience the ancient Peruvian rite of self-renewal. She often participated in ayahuasca ceremonies herself, and she swore by them.

But I didn't want to be transformed. I had endured enough changes in my life, enough forced renewal to last a lifetime. I'd grown accustomed to my rut, enjoying a peaceful existence in my downtown Toronto condo, living a private, serene, drama-free life, happy to be out of the limelight. But Jen was insistent. She began reserving spots for us at a secretive, invitation-only ayahuasca retreat. I would agree. Then, days before we were scheduled to leave, I'd back out. The cycle would repeat.

The thing about a rut is that, while limiting, it's also comfortable. As I headed into my early sixties, my days and ways had acquired a "Do Not Disturb" sign. I felt that all my human potential had been realized long ago. There just wasn't much left in my subconscious to uncover.

Don't get me wrong—I always like to push boundaries. As a club owner I had helped foster some of the most influential cultural movements of the past decades, devoting my energies to sharpening the cutting edge of popular culture. I had heard about ayahuasca in the sixties, when we called it *yagé*, and psychedelia pioneers like Timothy Leary and William S. Burroughs endorsed its benefits. Both Leary and Burroughs had hosted parties at my clubs.

But I tended to be cynical about the entire New Age trip—EST, transcendental meditation, channeling past lives, Burning Man, going vegan, and all the other trendy obsessions. I self-identified as a nightlife entrepreneur. My energies had always been directed outward, not inward.

Jen, though, would not relent. "This time you're going through with it, Dad," she told me, after securing a retreat reservation for the umpteenth time.

"I'm busy that week," I said.

"I haven't told you when I booked it for yet," she responded.

"I'll think about it."

In Joseph Campbell's *The Hero with a Thousand Faces*, this stage of a transformative quest is known as "refusal of the call." On a less grandiose level, I was rolling over and hitting the snooze button on my life.

"Dad," Jen said to me, steel in her voice that I recognized well, "if you don't come, if you don't show up *this* time, I'm going to stop speaking to you."

It was a threat that my daughter was perfectly capable of following through on. The Gatien family had a long-established tradition of the silent treatment. Jen and I had once gone two years without speaking to each other. It wasn't a dynamic I was eager to revisit.

A couple of months later I found myself lying on a mat alongside nineteen other questing souls gathered in a dimly lit, high-ceilinged room at an undisclosed location. The place had formerly been used as a temple by the Hare Krishnas. The surroundings had leftover mystic vibes and a faint smell of palo santo that complemented the altar of freshly cut flowers.

Jen was beside me. She had abstained from the tea so she could monitor my progress, to see for herself what condition my condition was in.

"Just stay on your own journey," Jen counseled me, "and don't let anything else be a concern."

I drank the tea, and, yeah, it was bitter and tasted like tar. The concoction, I knew, was prepared from sections of a kind of creeping vine, *Banisteriopsis caapi*, otherwise known as "the vine of death," a fact that didn't exactly flood me with optimism.

That was the last orderly thought I had for the next six hours. Our shaman guide, a medical doctor from Peru, conducted the entire ceremony in Spanish, a language I don't speak. It didn't matter. I understood everything.

The music began to guide me. I didn't know where the musicians came from and hadn't known what a pool of incredible talent they had in Peru, but it felt like the best concert I'd ever experienced. The reverberating pulse of the drums rose to match the beat of my heart.

I had approached the ceremony expecting a five-minute Six Flags fun ride and instead found myself shot into orbit. Moments from my past floated vividly into my mind, taking me over, to the point that I seemed to become my memories. My thought-dreams were real—more real than the former Hindu temple where my body lay in the dark, paralyzed by time. Scenes from my childhood rose and vanished. I felt, incredibly vibrantly, the moment on the parochial-school playground when I lost my eye—the violence of the blow, the wet blood on my cheek. I was with my parents as they sat by my hospital bed. My memories of the trauma had always revolved around my own feelings of pain and confusion, but in that moment, under the influence of the ayahuasca, I'd gained access to my mother's and father's emotions—their agony, their sense of loss. I stood in that room with my mother as she wept tears of regret for her son's injury. I wasn't visualizing her as a younger woman, I was *seeing* her that way beside me. I'd never experienced the moment so fully, understood the totality of it. A part of me wanted to stay, to witness all I could there by my mother and father, but the ayahuasca moved me on, through my first loves, the years I spent running popular nightclubs, the monumental crash-and-burn that happened later. On and on rumbled the caravan of my life, one image after another. I experienced trauma, success, excitement, trials and tribulations.

I stood posted at the entrance of the Tunnel during one of the club's groundbreaking Sunday-night hip-hop parties. It wasn't *as if* I were there—I felt like I really had been transported back in time and space. I could smell the wind off the river on Manhattan's West Side, the rain that had earlier washed the sidewalks clean of grunge, freshening the nighttime darkness. I checked out the eager club-goers waiting to get in, a line of a thousand-plus hopefuls that ran down the block and disappeared around the corner.

A solitary, ghostly presence, I glided inside. Young Biggie Smalls was onstage, debuting a new track in front of an audience crammed shoulder to shoulder, appearing to dance as a single ecstatic organism. Behind Biggie, skateboarders performed their hypnotic fall-and-rise moves on a half-pipe I'd had installed to the rear of the stage. Sunday-night regular Jay-Z was present, and Hova's rival, Puffy, as well as Lil' Kim, 50 Cent, and members of the Wu-Tang Clan—so many young artists who would go on to become rap royalty and together would revolutionize popular music. Making my way through the crowd of club-goers to the coed bathroom, I picked up the heady scent of sex mingled with champagne.

Then the scene changed and I was abruptly thrust into another of my clubs, Limelight, flashing through seminal moments there. I watched Whitney Houston give a flawless solo performance, her first public appearance in New York City. I saw Pearl Jam absolutely kill it with a crowd that had never before seen anything like the grunge band. A group of hired performers danced by, recreating surreal scenes from the movies of Federico Fellini. As soon as those visions faded, Prince emerged, remaining stubbornly apart, walled off from everyone by his security crew in the VIP room, talking to no one, solitary even as he let loose for hours on the dance floor.

The ayahuasca led me through a series of much less glamorous moments. There were the cocaine-fueled binges, being shut off in a hotel room for days, indulging in decadent parties, and degenerating into bouts of drug paranoia, when I was convinced there were interstellar aliens all around me. I stood in court, awaiting a verdict on charges that could send me away for twenty years. Throughout, I felt myself beset by conflicted waves of joy, longing, and regret. Beyond shattered moments of indulgence and freedom, there was a looming sense of darkness and danger, waiting to engulf me.

During the entire ceremony I left my shades on and attempted to keep it together. I remained stoic even though my thoughts were rattling around the universe like exploding stars. I was aware of Jen nearby, monitoring me, and felt desperately that I had to maintain an equilibrium in front of my child.

"You OK, Dad?" Jen asked as that first six-hour session finished up and we trailed out into the parking lot for some fresh air.

I nodded, mumbling that I was fine.

"So tell me, really, how was it for you?"

"Oh, you know me," I said weakly. "No high is too high."

Then my knees buckled and I blacked out.

I snapped to minutes later, with Jen leaning over me and people gathered around us.

"Mother Aya showed you who's boss," someone said, chuckling.

"I'm fine," I repeated.

I wasn't fine. I was cored out. "Mother Aya" had shattered my armor. The tea, the chants of the shaman, and the music penetrated my ego to a degree I had never before experienced. The ceremony threatened to break me wide open, forcing me to take stock and finally, at long last, come to terms with the truth of my life.

PART ONE: CORNWALL TO CHELSEA

CHAPTER ONE

Lilianne and Bernard

Long before I was ushering hip-hop stars like Jay-Z, Missy Elliott, the Notorious B.I.G., and Mary J. Blige into the Tunnel, or surveying the undulating crowd of club kids from the balcony of Limelight, I was just a provincial boy from the little Canadian town of Cornwall, Ontario. The first time my wife, Alessandra, visited the place where I was born and raised, we drove north across the US-Canada border and the Saint Lawrence River on the now-demolished Seaway International Bridge.

Welcome to my world, honey, I thought as I rolled up the car windows. Cornwall is a mill town, or at least it still was when I brought Alessandra there. One of the mills produced paper, and, as anyone familiar with a paper mill knows, the process gives off a god-awful stench—a sulfurous, rotten-egg fog. The stink, which was seeping its way in through the car windows and vents, comes from the kraft pulping process that employs "white liquor," a chemical brew that breaks up the cellulose in wood.

When you live near a paper mill, your sense of smell gets accustomed to the odor, until you don't notice it much. But newcomers like Alessandra get hit immediately. I had been away for long enough that I thought I'd have a similar reaction, but it's funny how something like that can work its way into your bones, into the fabric of your being. Cornwall isn't unique, and other towns are well known for their sulfur bouquet—the infamous "aroma of Tacoma" in Washington State, for example. Mayors of paper-mill towns are fond of grandly pronouncing "That's the smell of money" whenever anyone points out the odor.

My father, Joseph Bernard Maurice Gatien, managed to avoid working in the mill, but my uncles weren't so lucky, and my brothers eventually held summer jobs there. Most of the people in town were connected to the mills on the Saint Lawrence River somehow, punching their time cards at factories that pungently polluted the air and more insidiously polluted the water. The area's whole economy was based on the meager pay that mill owners doled out. But that's not all the local industry was responsible for: people always say Cornwall has one of the highest cancer rates in Canada.

Into this polluted world I was born in August 1951: Joseph Jean Pierre Gatien, a postwar boomer baby like so many others. In a lot of ways I had an idyllic small-town childhood. I came of age in the Canadian version of 1950s Eisenhower America—safe, sleepy, and boring. It was maybe a little rougher around the edges than life on the other side of the border, but it wasn't exactly Calcutta, either.

I grew up as Pierre, the middle child in a house full of brothers. The oldest was Maurice, who took on the nickname Moe as we headed into our teens. He was three years ahead of me and our clear leader. Ray was just a year and a half older, while the twins, Mark and Paul, completed the Gatien quintet a couple of years after I was born. There was always a lot of loose testosterone floating around the house.

We were all supercompetitive, sports minded, and rambunctious. Though they were only a bit older than me, Moe and Ray seemed to belong to a different generation. They were more serious, less infected with the rebellious spirit of the sixties. And on the other side, the twins were more or less removed from my sphere, just a pair of dismissible kids. Whether by circumstance or choice, I stood alone in the midst of the five.

My mother, Lilianne Annette Gatien (née Henri), proved more than equal to handling the family's masculine majority, and she did it with unfailing cheerfulness, warmth, and generosity of heart. While my father clerked at the local post office for forty years, my mother worked as hard or harder on the home front. She was the most industrious soul I have ever met, the standard against which I measure all other people.

Looking back, I can hardly conceive of the number of household tasks she took on. She sewed all our family's clothes, and when I say *all*, I am including our winter coats, our Halloween costumes, and whatever superhero cape was popular at the moment. She had mastered the art of the invisible stitch. Every year, she would start knitting in the fall and wouldn't stop until spring, churning out scarves, hats, gloves, anything and everything for her boys and husband.

But it would be wrong to pigeonhole my mother as the stereotypical doting housewife, waiting quietly at the door for my father to come home and take charge. My mother painted the house when necessary, inside and out, and maintained our family accounts. She learned the difficult craft of upholstery in order to refurbish our furniture. One year, when the family car rusted out from the heavy salt on Canadian roads, my father refused to spend the money we needed for the repair. So Lilianne found a body shop that was willing to let her use their facilities, and she enlisted all five of us sons to sand and patch the steel body. Then she spray-painted the car herself.

Maman was so adept and industrious because she had grown up a country girl, accustomed to hard work, born on a farm twenty-eight miles east of Ottawa in a backwoods hamlet called Clarence Creek. Her mother, my grandmother Francine, had Algonquin blood running in her veins, and her father was one of the last of the *voyageurs*, hunters and trappers who spent months in the wild.

Fred Henri, my grandfather, was pretty rough-hewn. He worked as a butcher, collecting game from area hunters, processing it, and transporting the meat to Ottawa for sale—in the early days by horse and cart, and later by truck. He met Francine at a dance in the small town of Pendleton, Ontario. The two married soon after, a native girl and her French Canadian beau, wedding young, as most people did in those days, their parents eager to get them out of the house to make room for the younger siblings. Fred and Francine settled in Clarence Creek, had eight children—among them Lilianne—and raised their family on country values, tough and resilient. Maman modeled those uncompromising ethics for us Gatien boys.

We lived in wartime housing, units that had been slapped together by the government for WWII veterans. With two bedrooms upstairs and one down, all seven of us in the household were served by a single bathroom. As Bob Hope reportedly joked, that's how I learned to dance, living in a house with a big family and one john. My penny-pinching father kept the hot-water heater off every day except Saturdays, our weekly bath time. I usually had to wash in leftover water from my brothers, just like I dressed in Moe's and Ray's hand-me-down clothes.

Don't get me wrong—I didn't consider any of it a hardship. When I was a child, my mother made Saturday night baths into a ritualized expression of her affection. Our house had a floor furnace, and she would toss my pajamas over the heating vent to warm them. I'd come out of the tepid water and she'd towel me down, then slip me into a pair of toasty pj's that she had sewn herself.

Sundays, in most of our neighborhood households, were devoted to a sacred-secular schedule: church in the morning, family dinner midday, and then, in the evening, TV. The morning and afternoon held little interest for me, but when the dishes had been cleared, we kicked off our family viewing with *Walt Disney Presents*, which led seamlessly into *The Ed Sullivan Show*. If I had been a particularly good boy that week—a rare occurrence—I was allowed to stay up and watch *Bonanza*. It was a wildly entertaining lineup chock-full of Western Civilization ideals like capitalism, consumerism, and a breakneck work ethic.

Those television shows served as my window to the south, and the vision of American domestic bliss they presented became an obsession. The sitcoms—*Father Knows Best, My Three Sons, The Adventures of Ozzie and Harriet*, and especially *Leave It to Beaver*—showed an idyllic vision of life. The Beaver came home from school to hot chocolate and loving conversations with his mom and dad. June always had on an impeccable dress, and Ward consistently wore a spotless pressed shirt and straight tie. The parents were kind, never yelled, were always in a good mood, and kept a home where everything had its place, polished and purposeful. The feckless but harmless Eddie Haskell was the closest thing that golden realm apparently had to evil.

That was what wealth looked like to me. Sitcom happiness was American and upper class, two qualities that were inextricably linked in my young mind. I bought into the hype, hard. Those episodes ought to have had warning labels, they were so addictive, seductive, and intoxicating, like cultural cocaine.

Recently, through the wonders of cable TV, I stumbled across a random episode of *Beaver* where Theodore "the Beaver" Cleaver won a gold necklace at a carnival and wanted to present it to his crush. June and Ward Cleaver painstakingly guided him through the emotionally loaded gifting process.

No wonder we were so hypnotized by a TV show, I thought, watching the paint-by-numbers plot unfold. There was no way I could ever have discussed with my parents anything so fraught and personal as young romance. Maman was too busy keeping our entire house together and corralling five sons, making our clothes, cooking our meals, fixing our car. Papa came home in his postal uniform, ready to kick off his shoes and relax. An exhausted Bernard Gatien was definitely not up for a conversation.

Neither of them had the time or interest to navigate their son's social anxieties. Not to mention, my parents were fairly strict Catholics and faithfully followed the Church's teachings and social directives. I wasn't supposed to have crushes on girls. I was supposed to work hard and, when the time came, marry a neighborhood girl without much courting. The Beaver's type of schoolboy puppy love wasn't possible in my universe, though it seemed to be a matter of course in this other, finer universe that I believed existed just across the border but far, far away.

Seeing the Cinderella castle sparkling with Tinkerbell's pixie dust every Sunday during the opening credits of *Walt Disney Presents* sent a clear message: if I wished upon a star, there'd be no harm or shame in forever expecting my dreams to come true. The truth was, that Disney castle that floated through our living room every Sunday could have been on the moon for all we knew. I couldn't imagine even asking: *Can we go there, Papa? Can we go to Disneyland?* I knew what the answer would be.

Eh, Pierre, are you stupid?

Our type of family vacation was much more subdued. On the rare occasion that we traveled, we didn't stay in hotels, much less fairy-tale castles. We camped, and the first time we ventured out, to Meacham Lake in the Adirondacks, we nearly froze to death. My parents had little idea what they were doing. Bernard had borrowed an army tent from a buddy, and we hadn't packed sleeping bags, only bed linens. None of us understood how different the weather would be in the mountains of upstate New York, compared to summery Cornwall. I still have a clear memory of my twin brothers whimpering, weeping through the night as they huddled with my mother.

On later excursions, we went a little better equipped, but we still never rivaled the elaborate setups of the American campers all around us. On those trips, my father met fellow postal workers from the US, and it was obvious to me, even as a child, that they were better off than we were. They possessed deluxe camping gear, had new cars— sometimes *two* new cars!—and novelties like Polaroid cameras, all the consumerist bells and whistles that my father and his fellow postal clerks in Canada lacked.

As far as I understood, my dad and these American guys did the same job, so their access to luxury baffled and fascinated me. The only way I could explain it was that something magical must be happening just across the Saint Lawrence River, something like ancient alchemy that could turn our leaden lives into gold. All of America had that new-car smell, while my hometown boasted a very different kind of odor.

Our most frequent trips took us farther away from American luxury, to Clarence Creek, Canada. Anytime my mother wanted to visit her aunts, we'd all pile in the car and head out to the original homestead. The conditions there were shockingly primitive. No electricity, no indoor plumbing, with the only luxury being the hand-pump-powered "running water" in the kitchen. For light, they used kerosene lamps. The ripped-apart catalogs stacked conveniently beside the toilet in the outhouse were a detail that set the place apart as a whole different realm.

Grand-Maman Francine couldn't read, write, or do anything that involved numbers. She didn't speak any English. But simply by virtue of her buoyant personality, she was one of my favorite people in the world. She had birthed ten kids, eight of whom survived infancy. When I would ask my mother what it had been like growing up with Fred and Francine in Clarence Creek, she shrugged as if to say that everyone had made do. As a child, my mom loved school so much that she never missed a day, tromping miles in winter darkness down unlit roads, exposing my complaints about walking a few blocks as a spoiled child's whining.

My mother's parents' dynamic somewhat mirrored her and Papa's relationship. Grandpa Fred was so tight-lipped it was like he was being charged by the word, while Francine was open, tolerant, and beyond kind. During the Depression, they moved forty-five miles south from

Clarence Creek to Cornwall, seeking the security of the mill economy. Growing up I saw my grandparents almost every Sunday, but each of their kids had gone on to raise such large families that if we all appeared at once it would have cleaned out the larder. We'd stagger our visits, and we only ate together a few times a year, on special holidays.

On those days we would all gather, rough genetic copies of one another. All the women were warm, open, and loving, the men gruff, closed off, and distracted—a contrast that informed the rest of my life. My mother told me how Francine would sit in the back seat of a rattletrap sedan with her brothers up front. Even though she wasn't a big drinker, and had seen the ravages that alcoholism had inflicted on her native people, she would cheerfully dip into a case of beer that sat beside her, popping bottles open and handing them up front whenever she was asked. As I said, she was a supremely tolerant woman.

When I drove my wife, Alessandra, over that bridge, we'd crossed over Cornwall Island, a part of the sprawling Mohawk reservation that spreads across both sides of the US-Canada border. My mother's heritage means that I am a quarter native Algonquin—a completely different tribe from the Mohawks, but, given the prejudices of the day, lumped into the same ethnic group.

Ever since the reservations were established, and especially over the last half century, the border around Cornwall ran hot. Disputes, friction, and outright violence between natives and government authorities convulsed Cornwall Island in particular. Native protests over violations of Mohawk sovereignty were answered by government accusations of drug smuggling, gun running, and cigarette bootlegging. In 2000, the Seaway International Bridge officially became part of Three Nations Crossing—the three nations being Canada, the US, and the Mohawk Nation.

With my background and the way I've lived, I can relate to the concept of being from three nations. I don't self-identify, like they say nowadays, as a native person, but the influence of my grandmother is there. First Nation people were everywhere in my childhood—on the streets of Cornwall and, of course, around Francine's home turf of Clarence Creek. But, oddly enough, no one in my family ever talked about being "a quarter Indian" or anything like that. Native heritage was something we simply did not mention. It was a secret that hid in plain sight, a quiet form of cultural apartheid. At my public high school, First Nation kids were bused in, it seemed, simply to take positions on the football team. They showed up, kept to themselves in class, played ball, and then went back home without mixing too much with the rest of the student body.

As I saw it, the things I inherited from my grandmother didn't have to do with being Algonquin; they were qualities that exemplified humanity. Through her, and through my mother, I learned decency. Francine exhibited no thirst for revenge, to my knowledge, over the historical wrongs done to the First Nation people; none for the prejudice she and her husband experienced from French Canadians; in fact, no anger toward any other person. She and her daughter Lilianne had not a mean bone in their bodies. They both loved to host social gatherings in their homes, bringing everyone together and filling the place with laughter, card playing, joking, and drinking.

If there were any mean bones in the Gatien clan, they came from the other side of our family. Papa was a somewhat sullen, practically wordless presence in our house. I didn't have to be a genealogist to trace the lineage of that vibe. Grand-Papa passed away when Papa was nine months old, so neither he nor I knew him, but Papa's mother was enough of a presence to make up for the lack of a paternal influence.

Alphonsine Gatien was maybe the least fun person on earth, with absolutely no sense of humor that I ever witnessed. Her principles were hard and fast: You shouldn't drink, you shouldn't smoke, you shouldn't play cards or laugh or be jovial. You might be able to find favor with the Almighty by becoming a priest. Otherwise, it was best to just sit and not do anything at all, apart from getting yourself to mass often and with abject humility in your heart. The single time I ever saw her laugh during my whole childhood was when my twin brothers were tussling, and one of them went down and cracked his head on the corner of a coffee table. It was a really harsh blow, but my grandmother thought the whole business was the most hilarious thing that ever happened.

Her son Bernard did his best to follow the straight and narrow path laid down by his mother, but there was no joy in it. Like a lot of men of his generation, Papa was molded by the Great Depression, a time when securing enough food, clothing, and adequate shelter required a constant grind. Bernard Gatien and every other adult male I knew growing up was tightfisted with money, not because they were miserly but because they knew what it was like to go without. Anyone who had endured the economic distress of the 1930s and then the hardships of WWII came out of those experiences tough as nails.

Bernard took on his duty as head of the household as though it were a life sentence, and, in his case, it was. There's a picture that Maman saved with each parent holding one of the twins. The expression on my dad's face is priceless, so clearly that of a set-upon man just barely keeping panic at bay, facing the firing squad. No to the blindfold, yes to the cigarette.

My mother, when pregnant with the twins, had been hoping for a girl to balance out our family, but Mark and Paul came along instead. Our tiny house on Vimy Avenue grew more crowded, and the wait for the bathroom got longer. Those were the days before disposable diapers, so I was often treated to the spectacle of a toilet full of cloth nappies waiting to be cleaned out.

"Ma!" I'd call out, needing to pee but blocked from going. "What am I supposed to do here?"

The yin and yang qualities of my parents often confounded me. Papa wasn't domestic, to say the least. It seemed impossible for him to express empathy. He wasn't a slob or prone to violence, but he had all the charm of a stone statue. My mom constantly filled the house with light, a lot of which was absorbed by the black hole that was my father.

"Why would you marry someone like that?" I asked my mom once, probably after some less-than-happy encounter with my esteemed progenitor.

"Listen," Maman said. "Dad doesn't drink, he doesn't beat me, and he gets a solid paycheck every week. You have no idea—a lot of women, including some of your aunts, their men go to the bar and cash their paychecks, and after they get done with their night of drinking there's not much left over."

She was right—at least Papa wasn't one of those guys. He always kept ten dollars a week for himself, bought a Jos Louis snack cake because he was a lunchbox kind of guy, and provided gas and maintenance for the car. The rest of his weekly pay, which amounted to about fifty or sixty bucks, always went to my mother. Out of that, she had to pay all the bills—everything from the mortgage to the insurance—and provide the whole family with groceries, clothes, and whatever other necessities arose.

Frugality was my father's most pronounced characteristic. He never willingly parted with money; it always had to be torn out of his closed fists. Our car muffler rusted out almost every winter. Even though I could hear my father coming from blocks away, the muffler half hanging off our car, he wouldn't repair it. It was embarrassing when the old beater banged and belched up to our house, the whole neighborhood taking notice.

Cars were the supreme marker of prestige in economically depressed Cornwall. There was a whole hierarchy. Driving a Buick, for example, automatically meant you were a step above the average wage earner, especially if your ride was a recent model. Witnessing what was out on the roads was like having a personal *Forbes* magazine wealth listing for my tiny little world. My parents never once purchased a new car, and the majority of the people in town drove rust buckets.

Gawking through automobile showroom windows at the sleek, hot-off-the-assembly-line models, we yearned for car-culture luxury. I religiously tracked the television ads during *Bonanza*, the ones that introduced the upcoming new model lines for Buick, Ford, and Dodge. I remember the moment when I first saw the flip-up headlights on the 1963 Corvette Sting Ray. As a ten-year-old, I knew cars like a seasoned auto mechanic and could tell the difference between a Ford Custom and a Ford Galaxy, say, and distinguish them each by year.

My father's uncle lived in the nearby town of Massena, in that better world across the US border. As kids, we loved to watch him drive up to our house in his brand-new 1957 Lincoln Continental. My brothers and I would rush out to marvel at the big land boat and sit on its hood, desperately hoping the neighbors would notice us. Having a Lincoln out front, we thought, meant we knew a rich person, that our world stretched beyond the limited circumstances of our parents. It gave me status among the neighborhood kids. All I had to do was mention my great-uncle's Lincoln Continental for an automatic boost in prestige.

I can still remember every single Gatien vehicle of my childhood, from the used 1936 DeSoto to the '67 green Pontiac with a black vinyl roof, a nice-looking car, even though we had to have been its second or third owners. Cars were one of the most important lenses through which I saw the world. Somewhere inside I ached for something better, finer, higher than what we had, to step out of our tiny home with too many boys and dirty nappies, and into a world like that of the lucky American family the Cleavers.

I was just three years old when I hopped onto my own vehicle, a secondhand tricycle, and ran away from home as fast as I could pedal.

"Forget this crap," I said to my barely-out-of-diapers self. "I'm not putting up with it anymore." Of course I don't recall what sent me running—a scolding from Maman? Maybe a lack of attention because the newborn twins took all her time?—but I do remember winding up at the local police station, where the gendarmes presented me with my very own can of 7UP. Somehow I'd found my way to an amazing prize, one that I had never possessed before. It was such an astounding piece of luck that, after my mother picked me up and brought me home, I ran away again the next day. My mother, in all her wisdom, figured out what was going on and caught up to me before I could grab my second free serving of bubbly bliss.

In my working-class world on Vimy Avenue, the neighborhood focused on the necessities of shelter, food, and clothing. Anything else was considered an extravagance. All purchases were agonized over, and when my parents finally did have to buy something, they sent the clear message to us kids that a new purchase was a bad thing, not a good thing, and none of us should be happy about it.

If I asked my father for a dime to go buy a comic book, some candy, or almost anything, for that matter, he had a stock reply, always delivered in a terse, grumpy tone.

"Je ne suis pas la banque à Jos Violon!" What do you take me for, the bank of Jos Violon?

The first time Dad dropped the name Jos Violon, my brother Ray and I exchanged a wordless look. I arched my eyebrows. Ray shrugged. Most French Canadian grown-ups used the line, but we kids never knew who the hell this Violon fellow was, only that he must have been very rich, since he evidently owned a bank. Years later I learned that Violon was a fabled French storyteller in the tales of Canadian author Louis-Honoré Fréchette. But to me, he was just one more reason why it wasn't worth asking for anything I wanted.

The most notable exception to that rule was Christmas, a time of pure, unbounded joy. For months before the actual holiday, my brothers and I pored over store catalogs, especially Eaton's and Simpson's, whose glossy full-color wish books were like our very own consumerist porn. I remember getting blown away at age seven when I opened my present and found a little $7.95 tool kit. I had seen it in the store catalog, so I knew exactly how much it cost. And that was that—we each got only a single, glorious present. And I was happy as shit. Every kid I knew looked forward to Christmas.

The season also brought high-spirited holiday dance nights, when my relatives gathered at our house. My parents rolled up the rug in the living room and threw talcum powder down to create a better slide on the dance floor. My grandmother had forty-six grandchildren, so there were a lot of us. We sang *chansons à répondre*, call-and-response songs that represented an expression of communal love and shared joy. It was like the beginning of Don McLean's song "American Pie": "A long, long time ago, I can still remember how that music used to make me smile."

My horde of cousins and I would all go down in the basement to play, and we'd look up to see the floor joists jumping with all the adults dancing and singing upstairs. Dust filtered down just like Tinkerbell's magic sparkles. When I'd venture upstairs, all I saw were happy, smiling people. As frugal as they were, when I saw my parents at those parties I knew they were filled with a generous spirit. Their guests were, without exception, people who led hard lives, but there they were, joking and laughing for hours. There was real joy in our house during the holidays.

As an adult, high on this or that illicit alkaloid, I never managed to achieve the elation and happiness that my family possessed in their hearts as they sang and danced together. But a few times, when I stood on a balcony at one of my clubs, the exuberant expressions on the dancers below reminded me of the wedding receptions, the card parties, and those homespun Christmas hoedowns of my youth.

Our house at 30 Vimy Avenue squeezed itself in between rows of almost identical 750-square-foot homes. None of them were plush or spacious, but they were the standard dwelling in our neighborhood. Many of our neighbors lived in even tighter circumstances than we did, with eight or nine kids squeezing into two bedrooms. My friend Billy Tyo lived a few doors down and had to share that same type of house with thirteen siblings.

Despite the close quarters, or maybe because of them, my brothers and I got along. We had the regular tussles, but we were never mean spirited. With the twins, I had to take two of them on at a time once in a while, just to demonstrate who was boss, but our fights never ended in blood or broken bones.

In a neighborhood teeming with other kids, I had a lot of options. Moe, Ray, Mark, and Paul weren't the only game in town. We all hung around in our separate crews, and then each of us was competitive in sports. There was hockey, of course—ball hockey in summer, ice hockey on the barely plowed winter streets—as well as football, lacrosse, and baseball.

The childhood activities of the neighborhood had a mysterious quality. Trends seized everybody at once, gripped us in an obsessive frenzy, then faded just as quickly. One day, I and all my friends acquired peashooters. The air filled with stinging green projectiles, and we were only as rich as the number of peas we possessed. Peashooter season lasted for about a month, before being abruptly replaced by yo-yos, or Hula-Hoops, or marbles, all of which enjoyed similar vogues. When every kid suddenly had to have a Davy Crockett–style coonskin hat, my mother dutifully sewed up a few pelts for me and my brothers. No logic seemed to dictate the crazes, but I was determined to keep on top of them.

I should have recognized a certain singular quality about myself as a kid, based on the fact that I always, *always* had to be the captain on any team I played for. I refused to have it any other way. No matter what I was doing, I had to be first or else I wasn't interested. Which was why, when it came to academics, I became something of a slacker. I was bright enough, and always got good grades, but the competition from my brothers was fierce. Maurice was so bright they skipped him up *two* grades. Raymond turned out to be a whiz, too.

The school often buzzed with some news like "Ray Gatien got a ninety-nine on the math test." I didn't know how I could compete with that. Even if I put in as much work as Ray did, I was always going to fall a few points short.

Second best was never going to cut it with me. I would not be outshone. My brothers and I were all overachievers, and since I would never surpass them in the academic realm, I lost interest. I had to find another way.

CHAPTER TWO

Frog

In May 1958, when I was six years old and in first grade, I noticed all the classes ahead of mine had a bat and a softball to play with during recess. My life could have taken an entirely different trajectory if I had just accepted that first graders are at the bottom of the elementary-school pecking order. They are *supposed* to be deprived. It wasn't up to pipsqueak me to question the order of the universe.

"Hey, Brother, Brother!" I wasn't calling to my brothers Moe or Ray, but was rather tugging on the sleeve of one of the ordained Catholic teachers who oversaw the playground of Saint Jean Bosco School. Named after "Don Bosco," Giovanni Melchior Bosco, who had dedicated his life to educating poor ragamuffin kids like me, my public school was run by nuns in habits and "brothers" wearing cassocks.

"Brother!"

The teacher turned a tired eye toward me.

"Can you get us a ball and bat? How come the other kids get them and not us?"

"Because you're too young to play baseball," responded Brother Playground Monitor, although the real reason was that the school had few resources, and the older kids had grabbed all the equipment.

Jean Bosco School was a French Canadian institution, so the whole exchange went on in French: *"Parce que tu es trop jeune pour jouer au baseball,"* said the brother.

"Frère! Frère!" I called, but he was already walking away.

Even at that young age I had an edge. It was torture for me to be overlooked.

"Hey, Brother! Brother!" I repeated every recess for three or four days.

Finally, just to shut me up, Brother Authority Figure found the most pathetic baseball in the world, one with the leather cover blown off and the string wrapping exposed. What a prize! But it was ours, and a half dozen of us scurried off to play a game like the big boys.

Bosco was coed, but the school grounds were strictly segregated by gender—girls on one side and boys on the other. If we ever snuck over to catch a peek at what the girls were doing on their side of the playground, the brothers would give us hell, so all our attention turned to the first ball game of the spring among the first-grade classmates.

We scavenged a broken broomstick for a bat. I took my place as starting pitcher. As I let loose the first toss, a shiny late-model car going by on the street distracted me. I turned my head slightly. The kid in the batter's box swung the broomstick and it slipped out of his hands, flying across the playground like a wooden javelin.

That sharp, jagged end of the makeshift bat tore out my left eye.

I never saw it coming. The stars had lined up perfectly: a cool car, a slight turn of the head, a swing at the ragged-ass ball that I myself had procured. All resulting in a bloody wound that left me one eye short.

I passed out. I remember coming to in an ambulance, then arriving at the hospital and being moved from a stretcher to a gurney to a hospital bed. My first thought was for the blood-soaked shirt the emergency-room nurses cut off me. My mother had bought the shirt only the day before at a rummage sale. *I'm going to get in real trouble,* I thought. Then I passed out again.

When I finally came to the next day, my mother was in the room. "How are you feeling?"

"My eye feels funny, Maman," I reported. "I can't open and close it."

"You don't have one," she responded through tears, unable to put a reassuring spin on the situation.

What is she talking about? I thought. *Don't have one what?* I could still blink my eye, sort of.

When I was six, I was too young to consider what effect an accident like that might have on my future. I'm a frigging kid, living in the moment—what do I know? Plus, I had fallen into a state of deep shock. There wasn't a lot of pain and there wasn't a lot of introspection. Both my parents were by my bedside, weeping hysterically. I couldn't understand why they were so upset.

"You lost an eye," Maman said, trying to break through my stupor.

I was hospitalized for two weeks. When I returned home, I was still waiting for repercussions, figuring that my father had to be mad, since the hospital stay was bound to cost a lot of money. But neither Papa nor Maman ever complained about it. I was much more worried I might be held accountable for the damage than I was about my future with the glass eye I'd acquired, which left me feeling cockeyed and uncomfortable.

Bernard and Lilianne's ire was aimed elsewhere. My simple, conservative, lifelong-Catholic parents took an astonishing action and brought a lawsuit against the parish. It's hard to convey how outlandish, how difficult and absurd it was for them to take that step. In those days we didn't know a single person in our community who had taken any legal action at all, and certainly not against the Catholic Church. To the public at large, suing a religious institution was the equivalent of poking God in the eye with a broken-off broomstick. Every cent of any potential settlement money would be snatched from the mouth of the Holy Mother Church.

My brother Moe remembers the scene at the school on the day of the accident. He was summoned to the offices of the sister superior. The principal of the school appeared, as Moe remembers it, "severe and intimidating in her nun's uniform." He felt that the holy woman's reaction to my injury was one of annoyance, as if the Gatien family had somehow disturbed her day.

"Now, what should be done here?" she asked, seeming eager to shift the responsibility onto the shoulders of my nine-year-old brother.

She initially suggested that Moe take me home. Luckily, he was smart enough to insist she call the hospital. That surly response from the sister superior set the tone for Saint Jean Bosco School's attitude in the incident's aftermath. Let's just say they didn't exactly do their namesake proud. The negativity on the part of the church rose to especially shrill levels when it became apparent that the Gatien family was seriously considering filing a civil suit. All of us boys changed schools after that.

There exist a surprising number of myths, proverbs, and anecdotes floating around that relate to the loss of an eye: "In the country of the blind the one-eyed man is king," of course, and "an eye for an eye," as well as the declaration that something is "better than a poke in the eye with a sharp stick." Homer relates the famous story of Ulysses and the one-eyed Cyclops. In dreams, Freud tells us, loss of an eye symbolizes castration. According to one scientific theory, two-eyed sight evolved in order to better detect the slithering movement of venomous snakes.

The whole incident serves as an easy parable about the twists and turns that life can sometimes take. When I think about the way that accident shaped me, I always come back to an old song by the sixties novelty group Sam the Sham and the Pharaohs, "Oh That's Good, No That's Bad." The lyrics tell of a guy who breaks his leg. Oh, that's bad. But his injury lands him an enormous insurance payment. So, no, that's good. It goes on that way, the guy's circumstances flipping, what's bad turning out to be good, what's good proving to be bad.

Losing an eye was, of course, bad—but as I got older, the wound was something that set me apart, gave me an identity. In high school I gradually switched from the glass eye to an eye patch, which I hoped would prove a cooler and more rebellious accessory. When I first started wearing patches, my mother sewed each one, fashioning them out of black suede, two and three-quarter inches by two and a half, tied with a string of black threaded silk. I instantly became a member of a select fraternity of eye-patch wearers, which included James Joyce, Bazooka Joe, Sammy Davis Jr., David Bowie as Ziggy Stardust, and Snake Plissken, the hard-ass hero of the movie *Escape from New York*. (More recently, Madonna occasionally dons one in her "Madame X" persona.)

Choosing the patch gave me armor as surely as if it were Captain America's magic shield. I was an instant outlaw, suave and hard, Johnny Danger, someone not to be fucked with. Without it, I was just a shy small-town boy who had absolutely no business attempting to conquer the world of big-city nightlife. With it, I was Peter the Pirate. The patch became an instant image, and the image became something I could hide behind.

Over the years, there have been a number of articles that claim a "hockey accident" supposedly caused my eye loss when I was thirteen. The American media gobbled up the tale because it fit with the time-worn "Canada equals hockey" formula. In truth, the spread of the tale is not entirely this or that reporter's fault. When I started getting publicity after opening the second Limelight, I was looking for someone to handle my PR. I ended up hiring John Carmen, who was Grace Jones's road manager when I booked her in 1976.

Carmen was, like all good flacks, an outrageous liar. I recall cracking up, eavesdropping on his phone calls when we shared an office.

"I gotta put you on hold," Carmen would say, "Liza's on the other line and she's having a breakdown." Then he'd make a call, not to Liza Minnelli but to the deli across the street, order a sandwich, and then hop back on with the person he'd put on hold. "Wow, that woman is a real piece of work," he'd exclaim, while I tried to contain my laughter.

Carmen was responsible for inventing the hockey-injury story. I had given John a bunch of vague replies whenever he asked me about my eye. I just didn't want to get into it. As it turns out, truth is a flexible concept in public relations. I made no move to correct John's fabrication. There was a mystique that John helped create around me, an extension of that cool, rebellious character I'd been trying to create in high school.

Underneath all that there is still a lot of sadness, and way more vulnerability than I'd like to admit. I sometimes cry, still, when explaining the accident, tears from one eye shed for the ghost memory of the other. I allowed John's story to supersede my own, because I wasn't keen to revisit the image of my parents standing heartbroken beside my bed. I wasn't ready to think about them taking on the Church, an institution that they revered. I wanted an unencumbered story more than I wanted the truth.

Losing an eye. Oh, that's bad. Wearing an eye patch. Oh, that's good. The coin flipped from one side to the other many times.

Two circumstances, poverty and bigotry, dominated my early days. The first caused my prickly awareness that my family was poor, that other families had more money, and that the impoverished town we lived in had few paths toward prosperity. The defining tensions of my young life were the day-to-day grind of poverty, and my desperate desire to not be poor.

When I grew up, I decided simply to refuse to be broke. I rejected my father's frugality, which struck me as small minded. No matter that my father's penny-pinching attitudes and my mother's ingenuity were born of necessity. Emotionally, poverty made me feel like someone was squeezing all the air out of my lungs. Mine wasn't a joyful, Buddhist sort of frugality. It was the sullen sort.

On one occasion, a couple of years after my jailbreak by tricycle, I took a turn as Vimy Avenue's resident thief. I rifled through the pockets of my mother's best coat, a respectable rabbit-fur number for the harsh winter cold. Deep inside a pocket I discovered treasure: a Canadian dime.

"God bless the Queen," I whispered to myself, seeing the image of Elizabeth II on the face of the coin. The enticing mirage of a bottle of Orange Crush hovered before me. I had enough to buy my soda and still have a penny left over from the pilfered dime. With impeccable childhood logic I took the dime but hid the coat, on the theory that if my mother didn't wear the coat, she wouldn't discover the coin was missing.

I stashed the garment beneath the bed. My mother, of course, could not find it, and she proceeded to search the entire house, to no avail. In those days the dry cleaners would actually come to a customer's house to pick up clothes. They had been by that afternoon, so suspicion naturally fell on them. My father phoned the police. Meanwhile, my mother happened to glance at me, and one glance revealed all. Guilt was written all over my face.

"Did you have something to do with it?" my mother demanded.

"No, Maman, no! Nothing at all!"

Despite my best efforts, my gaze strayed to the fur coat's hiding place beneath the bed. My mother spanked me all the way up the stairs, driving me toward imprisonment in my bedroom.

The hidden rabbit-fur coat remains in my mind as a cautionary tale of how poverty can lead directly to crime. Entering into adolescence, I developed a slightly more convincing poker face, but I also decided that pilfering dimes from random pockets wasn't going to get me where I wanted to be. I turned, begrudgingly, to honest work.

When I was about six, I took on a paper route. I kept that job until my teens, but right up until the day I relinquished my route, that bulging canvas bag I toted around felt more like a badge of poverty than a sign of enterprise and independence. I obsessed over the images of newsboys from the movies, scruffy, dirty-faced kids scrambling for every nickel. I imagined hearing the sneers of passersby: *Look at that boy delivering papers—man, he must come from a really poor family!*

Nonetheless, the gig represented a path toward pocket money. As a byproduct, I glimpsed the private lives of the residents on my route. The view wasn't always pretty. There was a man who stood six feet four, a scary Freddy Krueger type, complete with a beat-up fedora and long yellowish nails. Part of my job was to collect forty cents from each household every Thursday. Instead, Krueger insisted on paying by the month.

"Here's your paper, mister," I'd say. "You owe me two dollars."

"Wait a minute, sonny-boy. Why don't you tell me how many weeks there are in a month?"

Somehow I knew it didn't matter that the last billing cycle had been a spillover month, with five weeks in it. All I could do was stare mutely back at him.

"There's four weeks in a month," Krueger growled. "Everybody knows that."

I remained silent, too intimidated by his frightening presence to come up with a response.

"Here's a dollar sixty—now beat it." I dutifully obeyed. For years, Freddy managed to pay for forty-eight weeks a year rather than the full fifty-two, essentially shorting me almost two bucks annually. Since that was my profit margin per house, it meant I was delivering the guy's paper for free.

I was disgusted. Everywhere I looked when I was growing up, people seemed to be cutting corners and performing mean-spirited acts, simply because there wasn't enough money to go around. Generosity was a luxury. I wanted to live in a better world than that.

My father put in his daily grind of consistent, honest work. Though he was eventually promoted to supervisor, he spent a majority of his working life standing in front of wooden cubbyholes, sorting mail into one little box or another. Day after day, month after month, year after year. There was a nobility and integrity in this approach to life that, I'm embarrassed to say, was completely lost on me.

One summer, when as a teenager I had finally outgrown my paper route, I was offered a temporary position at the post office. After just a few hours of performing the same job my father did five days a week, I felt my legs turn to concrete. I suffered through and saved up my paychecks to splurge on an outlandishly loud, twin-barreled street racer. The car had been painted black with a side decal of a cartoon mechanic and the vehicle's name, "Tinker's Toy." It didn't bother me that I wouldn't qualify for a license until my next birthday.

After I brought it home, a battle between me and my father ensued that, as brief as the tiff was, meaningfully shaped me. Bucking my old man was not something any of us kids did without consequences, since conflict impacted not only the culprit in question but my father's mood, which in turn affected everyone in the whole house. It was the summer of 1967, when the world was divided into crew cuts and longhairs. I had grown my hair down to my shoulders, forcing Bernard to lay down the law: "Either you get your hair cut, or I won't sign the papers for your driver's license."

A license meant everything to me—mobility, respect, independence. As far as I was concerned, it wasn't optional. I had to get my license as soon as humanly possible, on the day of my sixteenth birthday.

But I sure as hell wasn't going to give in to my father and get a buzz cut. My spur-of-the-moment purchase of Tinker's Toy brought the conflict to a head. After absenting myself from home for three days of unlicensed joyriding, I pulled up in front of the house with my outlandish new obsession.

Papa was not happy. "I'll make you a deal," he said to me. "You don't have to cut your hair, and I'll sign so you can get your license, but you have to get rid of that friggin' monstrosity of an automobile."

I came out of the experience with long hair and a driver's license, which, to me, seemed like a win. I always questioned authority more than my brothers did, and the Tinker's Toy episode was yet another in a series of clashes. Without my racer, I kept my freak flag flying, and instead co-opted an Austin Cooper 850 that had belonged to my older brother, taking over the car by sheer force of will, insisting that it be given to me and not sold by my parents. Then I accessorized it with a sonic-boom-level sound system.

But the job at the post office had given me more than a path to a nice car and long hair that whipped in the wind as I drove it. I finally understood how Papa felt every night, how he had developed the varicose veins that ran up and down his legs like a mess of escaped earthworms.

Not for me, I swore to myself. But options in Cornwall were limited, featuring crushing boredom and presenting all manner of dangers. My mother told stories about working at Courtaulds silk mill when she was fourteen. Courtaulds was a *Norma Rae*–style factory where a hand that accidently brushed against a fast-spinning mechanical bobbin could easily result in the loss of multiple fingers. I wasn't keen on the prospect of losing any more body parts.

Not for me.

My uncle Sugar, one of my mother's brothers, worked rotating shifts at Courtaulds, a hellish, disruptive job schedule that made it pretty much impossible to live a normal existence. Just when your body accustomed itself to the five-to-twelve swing shift, here comes the midnight-to-eight schedule, the aptly named graveyard shift. He took that job at age sixteen and didn't retire until a half century later at age sixty-five, then died after three years of cancer. What a life!

Not for me.

But the message the town of Cornwall was sending me and every other teenager was that yes, indeed, it's the mill life for each of us. Who was I to believe I could avoid it? The mills, the post office—it all amounted to the same thing, an existence of unremitting drudgery. Such was my hometown's birthright.

Our strained economic conditions went together with a second circumstance that ruled over my childhood. As a Catholic French Canadian in a society that heavily favored the ruling-class English Protestants, I was a second-class citizen. *Orangiste*, we called our overlords, from the favored color of their flags and banners, and they controlled the whole country—socially, economically, and politically. English Protestants dominated the poorer underclass of Catholic French Canadians, balancing on top of us, to lift a phrase from Bob Dylan, like a mattress on a bottle of wine.

When I signed up for a kids' football league in town, I remember the Anglo-Canadian registrar scrunching up his face in a theatrical effort to pronounce my name. "Pee-air?" he asked, examining my filled-out application. "Gah-gah—what is that last name, sonny? Gah-tee-un?" The guy nearly swallowed his tongue making sure I understood his disdain.

Rebelling against the working-class future that seemed to be stretching out ahead of me, and looking to shed the stigma of my French-Canadian roots, at age fourteen I decided to drop "Pierre" and go by my English name, Peter.

Cornwall was pretty clearly divided between the east end, where the French neighborhoods were, and the west end, where the English lived. The four-street enclave around my home on Vimy Avenue was mixed but predominantly English, since the wartime housing had attracted veterans and war brides.

"Vimy" itself commemorated WWI's Battle of Vimy Ridge, a famous triumph of the Canadian Expeditionary Force. The officers in that force, all the brass from the Field Marshal Viscount Julian Byng down to the lieutenants and sergeants, spoke English. Most of the enlisted men below them were French-Canadian francophones.

Twenty years after Vimy Ridge, when my father served in the Royal Canadian Air Force for four years during WWII, the social dynamics remained stratified. The officers giving the orders were Orangiste, and those on the receiving end were most often French Canadians. Civilian life followed the familiar pattern. The two largest local mills were owned by British companies, and the foremen were invariably Anglo-Canadian while the laborers were French Canadian.

Prejudice and bigotry sneak up on you when you're a kid. I certainly wasn't aware of my second-class status when I was a toddler. But eventually, simply by a process of social osmosis, reality filtered in. I began to hear the word *frog* thrown in my direction. The slur was loaded with prejudice and social discrimination, and it stung each time I encountered it.

Driving with my father one day, we passed an imposing building, the Cornwall headquarters of the Orange Lodge, the Grand Order of British America. "What's that, Papa?" I asked.

"It's like a club," he answered dismissively.

"A club," I repeated, catching his tone and turning his response over in my mind. "Why aren't we members?"

"They don't want people like us."

People like us.

The situation improved during the Quiet Revolution in the 1970s, and especially with the rise of Prime Minister Pierre Trudeau in the 1980s, helping to elevate the social status of French Canadians. But even in the 1950s and 1960s there were glimpses of light in the darkness. Predictably, the breakthrough in Canadian equality came via the national pastime of hockey. When I was just a kid, a high-scoring superstar forward from Montreal, Maurice "Rocket" Richard, was out-spoken in his criticism of social bigotry.

The same two-tier class system existed in hockey as it did in Canadian culture as a whole. The Montreal Canadiens was the team of French Canada, while the Toronto Maple Leafs were favored by the Anglos. But Richard, a fiercely physical player, challenged his coaches, other players, even opposing fans on their ingrained prejudice. He played a generation before my time, but his legend lived on. Like me, he had First Nation ancestry, and I gloried in his take-me-as-I-am attitude. He insisted his coach speak to him in French, for example. He was an icon of our proud heritage, and my father, my brothers, and I idolized him, as did every French Canadian we knew. Rocket Richard was both our Rev. Martin Luther King Jr. and our Jackie Robinson, with a little of Muhammad Ali thrown in for good measure.

During the 1954–55 season, a violent altercation on the ice led to local police attempting to arrest Richard after the game. NHL President Clarence Campbell, a stiff-upper-lip Brit if there ever was one, slapped a season-long suspension on Richard. On the first Montreal home game after Rocket Richard returned, thousands of demonstrators gathered and waved "*Vive Richard*" placards. Campbell had the gall to attend, and was punched in the face by an outraged fan. Outside the arena, French Canadians battled police, injuring a dozen cops during a looting rampage that culminated in fires, overturned cars, and almost a million dollars of damage to downtown businesses.

I was too young to remember the riot, but I heard about it time and again growing up. Rocket was the hero of the family and of the neighborhood. Hockey was a religion just behind Catholicism. The whole country slowed to a stop every Saturday night to watch the hockey game of the week on TV. Watching Rocket play represented an act of defiance when people like us were getting the social shit beat out of them elsewhere in the culture. Tuning in to see a French Canadian wailing on Orangiste ass felt like its own type of freedom.

But the joy of watching Rocket didn't stretch much beyond the weekly match, and the Saturday high gave way to Sunday doldrums. My parents, devoted and observant Catholics, attended mass often and made sure their sons did, too. I served as an altar boy, trudging through the freezing cold Ontario mornings for six-thirty mass and then staying to attend seven o'clock mass, collecting fifty or sixty cents a week for my trouble.

I also attended Catholic schools, where catechism was always the first subject of the day. After grade school, up to ninth grade, I attended a Jesuit institution, College Classique de Cornwall, where all the teachers were members of the order of the Society of Jesus. The Jesuits were pious and intellectually rigorous. Math and science were taught in English, and everything else was in French.

"Give me a child by the age of seven and I will mold him for life," runs the maxim of the Jesuits, but I might have been the exception that proves the rule. They taught old-style fire-and-brimstone Catholicism, traditional and strict. I was once even punched in the head for laughing in class. It was as if the liberalizing influence of Vatican II had never penetrated their enclave, and I'm sure some of the conservative priests would have preferred saying mass in Latin. Satan was a very real presence, and so were the fires of hell. If you weren't Catholic, you weren't going to go to heaven to sit beside Jesus. The heartlessness of that arrangement never sat right with me.

When I was ten I asked my mother, "Maman, if you aren't Catholic, the priests say you don't go to heaven. Doesn't that mean that all the other people who aren't Catholic go to hell?"

"I don't know anything about that," she said. "But do you know Mrs. Mallion?"

I nodded. Winifred Mallion was a nice English Protestant war bride who lived two doors down from us. She always had a smile and kind word for me.

"All I can tell you is that, in my opinion, Winny Mallion is going to heaven."

I was surprised to hear my mother break with the doctrine I was getting at school. Looking back, that might have been the first crack in the brutal logic of the faith, the first sign that questioning the teachings of the Church could be an option.

But what really knocked the Catholicism out of me was the tribulations of the Lebruns, my uncle's family. The whole Lebrun clan was beyond religious. There were portraits of Jesus all around their house, prayer candles burning twenty-four hours a day, and compulsory attendance at mass every morning, without fail.

Beyond their piety, the Lebruns were known as "a good family," without the usual problems with drinking or carousing—a little boring, but always kind, respectful, and decent. One of my Lebrun cousins became a priest, and I was sure that if anything could earn you favor with the Lord, it would be having a clerical collar in the family. But none of that seemed to matter. Trouble assaulted them at every turn. The family simply could not catch a break. When Cornwall flooded, which it did from time to time, the Lebrun house got hit the worst. If everyone else got the flu for a week and then recovered, the Lebruns came down with pneumonia and spent weeks in the hospital.

On and on went the catalog of misery, as if the trials of Job were being rained down on them. My uncle's wife died of a sudden illness when she was just forty-four. Then, a short time later, my uncle was roasted within an inch of his life in a steam blast during a mill accident. After an incredibly painful six months of burn treatments, he recovered and immediately got into a front-end collision with a drunk driver, a horrifying crash that killed him and paralyzed his young granddaughter for life.

Jesus, I thought, witnessing all this from afar and brooding on how moral and observant these people were. *If there is a God, I don't want Him to know that I'm alive.*

It was the 1960s, and the entire world seemed to be questioning authority. As a Catholic boy in the process of lapsing, I had a good jump start on what was happening in the wider culture. I left the Jesuits behind to enroll in Saint Lawrence High School, which, despite the "saint" in the name, was a public institution. My high school was more secular than any educational institution I had ever experienced. It was also fully coed—no separating out the boys from the girls on the school-yard. I felt as though my world was splitting wide open.

Because of my eye injury (oh, that's bad) my parents had received a substantial monetary settlement (oh, that's good). Saint Jean Bosco School paid up to the tune of around thirteen thousand dollars, the equivalent of almost a hundred grand today. My mother banked the money, spending only a little on my clothes and on tuition to College Classique while I attended there. She saved the rest for me once I became an adult.

Things were looking rosy for me. The day I turned eighteen, I would legally be able to access the settlement fund. The promise of that cash—the type of money my parents had never seen in their lifetime of work—was, as they say, better than a poke in the eye with a sharp stick.

CHAPTER THREE

In My Little Pond

Growing up in a small town, I had severely limited horizons. The prevailing wisdom was that if we didn't finish high school, we'd "wind up digging ditches," a particularly apt warning for a mill town that thrived on manual labor. In Cornwall, even those of us who managed to get a high-school diploma were still most likely to wind up toiling at the mills.

When my older brothers started talking about college, my father dismissed the idea. "We're French Canadians—we don't go to college."

My mother responded gently, "Oh, Bernie, come on."

"That's our lot!" Papa insisted.

Options? We don't have no stinking options! My dad had followed a narrowing career path, but we all knew that it had led him to an unhappy adulthood, working a mind-numbing job at the post office, putting in extra hours just to keep his family afloat. All my brothers rejected his model. Encouraged by our mother, we aimed a little higher. Our hope was that going to college would broaden our opportunities. With diplomas, we might become "professionals," which in our minds meant being either a lawyer, a teacher, or a doctor.

So the choice was to join the mills or take up a profession. But that was as far as our imaginations took us. By the time I reached high school, I knew it wasn't in the cards for me to follow my older brothers into a profession. The idea held absolutely no appeal. Moe aimed for law school, and Ray would be a doctor, but their futures appeared too regimented, too safe, too square. More than that, there was too much discipline and sacrifice required, and I knew myself well enough to know I wasn't going to put in the work.

I dreamed about a wider world, where people had multiple options. They could become almost anything—scientists, broadcasters, financiers, authors, cellists, or movie stars. It seemed to me that there was a whole universe of lives and lifestyles outside Cornwall, but careers such as those simply did not occur to anyone around me. Even if I made it as a professional, that life struck me as just another version of the hamster on the wheel. Timothy Leary characterized middle-class life as "the assembly line of school, college, career, insurance, funeral, goodbye."

Coming out of my Jesuit school and heading into public high school, I knew I wanted to break out of the trap that was so carefully set for young French Canadians of limited means. The settlement money gave me a leg up, but I knew a kid who received a similar windfall after a car accident and who immediately pissed the whole thing away on massage-parlor masseuses. That's a hell of a lot of happy endings, but I swore that I would put my little grubstake to better use. And yet, the first thing I did with my newfound wealth was buy a used muscle car.

I had owned other cars, but the muscle car that I bought with my settlement money, a canary-yellow 1967 Camaro SS 396 convertible, was the first vehicle that really felt all the way mine, when I was old enough to enjoy it. I was eighteen and wanted to drive fucking fast. The twisty roads along the river seemed to have been laid down just for me, having called out their invitation since my tricycle days. The Camaro, I reasoned, would also smooth my way with the opposite sex. I was too shy to be much of a ladies' man, but I desperately wanted to find a girlfriend, especially one who might elevate my social status. I had dated around a little, and had one longer relationship with a nice girl, the daughter of a local judge, but I wasn't the most confident guy. The car, I reasoned, would set me apart from the pack.

I had turned sixteen during the Summer of Love, and even in backwater Canada, eddies of social transformation were swirling around. Soldiers returned from Vietnam and brought back a lot of high-quality Asian hashish. Some of it wound up in Cornwall, along with a new drug, LSD. My older brothers were close in age, but we seemed to land on different sides of the generational divide. They were intent on developing their professional careers. I was too busy getting swept up in the sixties. Moe and Ray appeared oblivious to the Age of Aquarius, but I grew my hair out and embraced all that it had to offer.

My friends and I took more than a few trips on hallucinogens. I'd already tried LSD a few times when a schoolmate of mine, a part-time drug dealer nicknamed "Screw," secretly dosed a pitcher of orange juice with a dozen hits of high-quality LSD-25. Not realizing it was dosed, I drank the whole pitcher and spent the next two days sailing in a lysergic hurricane, messed up out of my mind.

I walked the banks and canals of my hometown, walking and walking throughout the night. Connecting with what I was sure were cosmic but chaotic truths, I found myself unable to share them because I had somehow lost the power to speak. I recall feeling profound sadness that I'd never be able to talk with my parents or brothers again. I spent two days and nights wandering mute before I felt the drug slowly releasing its grip. After that experience, I swore off LSD forever.

The Summer of Love came and went, but as far as I was concerned, the summer might have been great, but the love had been elusive. The sexual revolution was happening elsewhere, in New York and San Francisco—anywhere, it seemed, but wherever I was. Getting at all intimate with a girl was possible only after months of going out as a couple. A blow job was a totally unimaginable act, an emblem of perversion even amid the feverish back-seat fumblings of teenagers.

I noticed a pretty girl one grade behind me at Saint Lawrence High. Sheila Abraham stood out in the tiny dating pool of Cornwall. She was smart and confident, if a bit of a Goody Two-Shoes. At least those shoes were expensive, I noticed, and I saw that Sheila seemed to have an endless supply of fashionable sixteen-dollar sweaters.

I knew the Abrahams by reputation as one of the wealthiest families in town. Sheila's Uncle Richard, known as "the Duke," drove a conspicuous series of snappy cars: a fire-engine-red Buick Wildcat, a 1966 Riviera, and a 1963 Corvette (the model with pop-up headlights that I had lusted after when it first hit the streets). As a young kid on the loose in downtown Cornwall, I used to watch the Duke drive by in those cars with my tongue hanging out.

The Abrahams lived in a large house in the second district, the nicest part of town. They owned a hotel, a bowling alley, and one of Cornwall's tallest buildings, an eight-story office tower. They also owned their own boat and a vacation cottage, both out-of-reach luxuries to me.

She might have caught my eye initially with the showy upper-class trappings of the Abraham family, but once I got to know her, Sheila's intelligence and personality eclipsed her social standing. We fell in love and became a steady couple. In my last year of high school, we were both contemplating a life together. We found ourselves wondering what it would be like if we got married and settled down.

When I looked into the future, all I knew was that I didn't want a blue-collar job. I had seen the exhaustion on my father's face, the toll it took on his body. I knew what had happened to my Uncle Ainèe Lebrun in that horrific mill accident. I was surrounded by hardworking men and women, and I admired them, but I knew I wanted to escape joining their ranks.

I graduated from high school, moved out of Cornwall, and enrolled at Carleton University in Ottawa. I lived in a high-rise apartment building with a couple of my high-school classmates, excited finally to be away from Vimy Avenue. Once classes started, though, I almost instantly realized I'd enrolled in college only because I didn't know what else to do. My heart wasn't in it and, moreover, I found that my mill-town education had left me woefully unprepared for higher education. I remember scoping out a college course catalog and coming across a listing for "Anthropology." *What the fuck is that?* I wondered.

Instead of book learning, what I really studied was the counterculture. To anyone who didn't personally experience the sixties, it's difficult to convey the degree of upheaval going on in the world just then. The old order got demolished, uprooted, transformed. Everything seemed to be in flux all over the world: social conventions, politics, race relations, fashion, art, music—*everything*.

Peace and love. Question authority. Tune in, turn on, drop out. The slogan from the student riots of May 1968 in Paris resonated with me: "*Sous les pavés, la plage.*" Beneath the paving stones, the beach. I believed that if I could just smash through the hard crust of overcivilized behavior, I would discover the freedom of going barefoot in the sand.

Music became my true college major. The Stones, Uriah Heep, Santana, Bob Dylan. I inhaled rock 'n' roll, the blues, B. B. King, Sly, Three Dog Night, CSNY, Ten Years After, Jethro Tull, Jimi Hendrix. Mick Jagger was my ultimate rock hero. I'd crank the amp up to eleven, smoke a little hash, relax, and float downstream. I followed Tim Leary's advice faithfully, tuning in, turning on, and then, inevitably, dropping out. Carleton University seemed not to notice my absence. I stayed on in our hippie apartment and still pretended to attend class, but after a couple of months, I left college and returned to Cornwall.

Right back to square one, and back to Sheila Abraham.

When I hit my hometown on the rebound, most of my high-school friends were already working at the mills or stuck in other dead-end jobs like truck driving. Because I had lost my eye, the mills wouldn't hire me, even if I'd applied. I looked around the mean streets of Cornwall, desperately wanting to make my mark doing something, anything—to use my accident settlement to try for a more prosperous life than my parents.

During a quick stretch of time at the end of the sixties, being too ambitious was considered crass and bourgeois. But the antimaterialist concepts of the day never sank in with me. I always had an inner drive. *Be first or be nothing.* That attitude was both a curse and a blessing.

Apart from high achievers like my brothers—whom I constantly sought to outdo—the only other successful people around seemed to be businesspeople. Sheila's family had a lot of irons in the fire, and during this period I got to know them a lot better. The Abrahams became my anti–role models, with Sheila's father and three uncles serving as examples of how not to succeed in business. I studied them accordingly.

For a long time, I didn't realize that the Abraham empire was built on sand. All their holdings were heavily leveraged; every property they had was mortgaged to the hilt. I'd come to discover that the family didn't actually own anything—the banks did. I was too green to know what leverage even was. Over the course of a few years, as I continued to date Sheila, I witnessed the Abraham house of cards crash down, as one by one their holdings were ripped away from them.

Even so, I never questioned their methods. I idolized them. Sheila's father, Ted, and his brothers dashed frantically from enterprise to enterprise, always moving, never standing still. They were almost fiendish in their efforts to develop new schemes to prop up the old. The lesson I took was that the true essence of the capitalist was the hustle, not the score.

I entered the Abraham kitchen one afternoon to find Ted, Uncle Ness, and Uncle Sammy present and plotting. The room was filled with steam, like a sauna. As soon as I walked in, Sam quickly tossed a towel over a huge pot bubbling on the stove. They were fiercely private about their latest idea, but they eventually revealed that they were boiling water to steam wood and shape lacrosse sticks, aiming to corner the market.

I made what I considered to be an obvious observation. "Um, don't the First Nation tribes pretty much have the lacrosse market all sewn up? They've been making the sticks on the rez for like a hundred years. It's a Native game, after all."

The Abrahams didn't listen. No amount of negativity was going to harsh their mellow.

I blundered on. "I wonder how many lacrosse sticks are sold, anyway—say, in an average year? You know, what would be the total annual market in lacrosse sticks?"

Again, it was as if I were a mosquito buzzing in their ears. They didn't even bother to swat me away. The three of them focused on bending steamed wood. Lethal shards of birch began to fly across the kitchen. Having some history with wooden projectiles, I got the hell out of there.

The lacrosse scheme burned hot and fast for a time, and I never saw an actual Abraham-made stick, but I had to appreciate the absurdist quality of it. They moved on to shaping wood for violins, with the announced intention of competing with Stradivarius. The family's fortunes continued to diminish, though never for lack of trying. Push, push, push, never say die, pedal to the metal, balls-out effort always—such was the Abraham creed. And they communicated the capitalist virus to me.

Ted Abraham also handed me another priceless gift: giving his daughter to me in marriage. Sheila and I got hitched in the church her family favored. A French-Canadian Catholic kid and a girl with a vaguely Middle Eastern background said their vows in a Protestant house of worship.

Now the head of a household, I clutched the remainder of my settlement money a little tighter and looked around for opportunities. For a while I built houses with Ted, putting in full days on the construction site. But what I really wanted to do was open my own business. I liked the Abrahams' wholehearted embrace of the capitalist dream, even if their specific practice left a little to be desired.

I decided I would apply the Abraham style of fervor to my own ideas, just as soon as I could settle on one. So I started to search the town for opportunity. The year I graduated from high school, blue jeans were still forbidden in class. In the early fifties, blue jeans had the stigma of the working class, and anyone wearing them could be denied entry into a high-end restaurant or a supper club. In the sixties, though, that shit went out the window. The no-jeans rule was rescinded. Working class was cool, everything old was new again, and the fashion dictates of the period meant that every respectable teenager had to wear jeans, preferably Levi's, and preferably vintage denim that was faded and soft.

The two main clothing retailers in town were run by ancient shop-keepers who hadn't kept up with the times. They sold "trousers," and they always recommended proper cuffs, offering to calculate inseams with the paper measuring tapes that hung around their necks. I identified an untapped market, saw my opportunity, and grabbed it. Putting down a few grand of my own, I borrowed ten thousand dollars from my uncle at 15 percent annual interest. In spring 1971 I opened a jeans store I called the Pant Loft.

The times were indeed a-changing in the changing rooms of the Pant Loft. The pent-up demand for denim was so great that the place took off like a rocket. I paid off the loan from my uncle in six months and watched as the cash flow steadily, magically increased. I had a cool shop, as hip as hip could be, or at least as hip could be in Cornwall. I burned incense, played rock 'n' roll, and bought my own clothes at wholesale.

So I was set. I had something I'd long dreamed of—my own business. I could have just continued on, with my future as a prosperous clothier ensured. But restlessness set in, an agitated sense of incompleteness that would become familiar. Soon enough, I began to sour on the Pant Loft. I remember when the breaking point came, one afternoon when I was trying to sell a pair of jeans to a mother and daughter.

"I want these!" the fourteen-year-old girl was insisting, whining in a voice that was like fingernails on a chalkboard.

"They're too tight," her mom responded, poking and prodding at her child's waist.

"They're perfect!" the teen screeched.

"Can we have the next size up?" Mom asked.

"Nooo!" wailed the girl, tears brimming. "I . . . want . . . these!"

"They're too tight, and you look like a hussy!" Mom snapped. "I'm not buying them for you!" She turned to me. "I'm right, aren't I? The trousers don't really fit well, do they?"

Right then I saw my life rolling out in front of me. Sure, I would be a secure provider, but I would also have to endure an infinite number of scenes like this one. Jeans were not exactly a passion. While Pant Loft was a cool shop with plenty of music and atmosphere, for all I cared, I might as well have been selling plumbing fixtures. I had started the business because I saw opportunity, but the day-to-day life of a denim salesman grated on me.

I cast around for an alternative idea. What did I enjoy? What did I love? What did I have a passion for? Well, I had always liked going out at night and having a good time.

Alec Baldwin has a passage in his memoir, *Nevertheless*, where he fantasizes about alternate lives he would have liked to have lived. One such life is that of a nightclub owner. "I'd surround myself with a cast of lovably quirky characters. All men would envy me. Women, against their better judgment, would throw themselves at me nightly."

I've come to identify this image as the Alec Baldwin Fantasy of Club Owning, and I would eventually realize just how unreal it was. But back then, Alec and I might have had the same kind of stars in our eyes, because I decided to leave blue jeans behind and open a nightclub.

There were two types of liquor licenses assigned in Ontario. The standard government license was heavily regulated and had last been available in the 1940s. Those licenses were highly sought after and became available when a shop owner decided to sell. But there was a second kind of license, one that was granted solely to hotels. Taking over an existing liquor license was the only way anyone could realistically break into the hospitality business. If I was going to flee the mother-and-daughter horrors of the rag trade, I'd have to buy into an existing hotel license.

I was purchasing blue jeans at four dollars and selling them for eight. That's an OK profit margin, but I knew the bar business had a much better one. A draft beer that cost you maybe a quarter could sell for a dollar twenty-five, a fivefold markup. I suppose there were other businesses I could have turned my eye on. I simply wanted to compete with my brothers, to find some way to rival them in terms of success.

I scoped out the competition in Cornwall. *Sleepy* didn't suffice to describe the state of nightlife and entertainment in town. It was more like narcoleptic. For people in their twenties, the only live music available came via local cover bands that churned out the hit parade of the day. There was a bar called Northway Hotel, which had a strip club on the lower level and a dance floor with live music, but only on the weekend. The owner was a middle-aged Yugoslavian immigrant who favored Elvis cover bands.

Then there was the Lafayette House. Located in a run-down section of town, the hotel-tavern combo did its best to drag the neighborhood down even further. A squared-off bin of a building on First Street East, a block off the river, Lafayette was devoted to helping mill workers along their way to cirrhosis of the liver. The dive bar smelled of piss and whiskey and broken dreams. Pedestrians shivered as they walked by the door. The "hotel" part of the establishment was shabby and cheap, and only two of the eighteen rooms had their own bathrooms. The rest resembled single-room-occupancy lodging, more like a rooming house than a hotel, attracting transients and drunks.

The Lafayette enjoyed the worst reputation in town. My parents would never have been caught dead stepping through the door. The only form of entertainment was the drunken brawls that erupted almost every night. As forlorn as the joint was, it had what I wanted, which was a liquor license.

I poked around some and found that the proprietor wanted out, probably envisioning his golden years in a Florida beachfront condo. Selling the Pant Loft to a friend of mine, who went on to develop it into a successful chain, I used the proceeds to demonstrate my solvency to a bank, qualifying for a small-business loan from the Canadian government. I put $100,000 down on a $250,000 sale and bought the Lafayette House, lock, stock, and beer barrel. I was suddenly the proud owner of the land, the building, and—most important—the liquor license.

I showed up at the place one afternoon in the spring of 1973, the new twenty-one-year-old owner of the premises, looking to make big changes. The mood in the place was drunk and sullen, with happy hour just about to turn sad. At first, the mill workers in the place paid me no mind. "All right!" I called, my words swallowed up by the seedy surroundings. "Everybody's got to get out!" I was scared shitless.

The clientele—the ones who didn't have their foreheads glued to the bar in front of their half-finished beers—looked up, their eyes bleary and unfocused. *Eh? Why, you little punk . . .*

"Now!" I added, shouting in an attempt to impress my will on the dozen or so drunks. "New ownership! We need the barroom cleared!"

The room erupted. They barked their protests, but none of them bit, and eventually they left for bleaker pastures, staggering past me into the washed-out light of an Ontario afternoon.

With my in-laws and friends helping, I embarked on an intense thirty-six-hour makeover, painting the walls black, installing new bars, and extending the existing ones. There were two separate spaces: a main room, which had an occupancy of three hundred, with the three bars and a stage, and a smaller one, which held about a hundred. As a crowning touch, I hung a mirror ball over the dance floor.

I rechristened the place the Aardvark, after a character in the *Ant and the Aardvark* Saturday-morning cartoons, an anteater whose voice sounded like Jackie Mason with a corny Borscht Belt shtick.

In the previous month I had paid several visits to Toronto, checking out the music scene. I hooked up with a booking agent named Ron Scribner, and he guided me on a search for a band to open my new place. Word had it that an explosive, newly formed blues group was blowing the roof off of clubs all over town.

"These guys just got an album deal, coming out next spring," Ron told me. "After that vinyl hits the record stores, they won't come so cheap."

Rush had emerged from the city's Willowdale neighborhood with a hard-edged rock sound that brought to mind earlier power trios like the Jimi Hendrix Experience, Cream, and James Gang. Listening to Rush, you could not understand how a simple guitar-bass-drums threesome could possibly create that decibel roar. Guitarist Alex Lifeson, drummer John Rutsey, and the screaming lead singer, bassist Geddy Lee, would morph later on into one of the most popular bands in the world, changing their sound and lineup over the years. But in spring 1973 they were relative unknowns outside the Toronto area.

I signed them for Aardvark's opening and made sure the roof shingles were firmly nailed down. I traipsed into the offices of sleepy Cornwall's only newspaper, the *Standard-Freeholder*, trying to buttonhole whoever was responsible for covering entertainment. Turned out, nobody was. But I wound up talking to a tired-looking newsman my father's age.

I blurted out my scoop: "I'm doing this new club and we're bringing in a Toronto band called Rush for the first week." The guy didn't exactly shoot to his feet and yell "Stop the presses!" I had no idea that media outlets like the *Standard* sold ads to businesses looking to promote. For my unschooled efforts, the Aardvark got a tiny write-up, a couple of inches of copy tucked away in the local news section that went all but unnoticed.

But luckily for me, in a small town like Cornwall, word gets out. Just as it had with the Pant Loft, pent-up demand from area youth ensured that my first foray into the nightclub business was a monster success from the start. That first week, Rush packed them in, then blew them the fuck out. Geddy Lee's vocals reminded me of Led Zeppelin's Robert Plant, but in my opinion, Rush's front man was the better singer.

I knew from that first week that I had a hit on my hands. Aardvark was filled to its four-hundred-person capacity all six nights it was open. After Rush inaugurated the stage, I continued to bring in groups that were a cut above the local cover bands. We drew acts out of Toronto, Montreal, and Vancouver that were touring Canada. For midlevel acts—which were the only ones I could afford, given the bar's limited size—the Aardvark became a recognized stop on tour. I'd cycle the bands through, keeping things fresh, booking them for one-week gigs.

One month in, I was floating on air. I knew most of the people who came into my place. Nothing, I thought, could be better than hanging out and drinking with friends. I bartended when necessary, and glad-handed the clientele the rest of the time. I had put in a couple of bumper-pool tables in the smaller room, and I became something of a shark at the game, playing for rounds. That was a win-win situation for me, since it was my alcohol the losers were buying. Even away from the pool table, the shots always came at me fast and furious.

Soon enough, my lack of experience rose up and bit me in the ass. Aardvark might have been a success, but I actually didn't know what the hell I was doing. After that first month of partying hearty with my customers, something wasn't right. The place was crowded, the drinks were flowing, but somehow my payroll checks started to bounce, and I couldn't afford to buy groceries. I realized that while I was doing shooters with customers all night, the business tended to drift, like a ship without a captain. I swore off drinking on the job and paid attention to the till, and the ship began to right itself.

Sheila was excited about the Aardvark's success, but she preferred domestic life to the crazy tilt and chaos of nightlife. Our schedules clashed, and I never came home until she was long in bed. Imperceptibly, we began to drift slowly, too, in separate ways.

There was no real club competition within a fifty-mile radius. I pretty much exclusively booked rock bands, paying the acts $600 to $1,000 per week and charging a cover on weekends. From my scouting trips to Montreal and Toronto, I noticed a shift in the music scene. It was the mid-1970s, and the first hints of the disco revolution had started to appear. I preferred rock 'n' roll, but there was something powerful that happened when disco was booming over the sound system; the insistent beats got everyone up and dancing.

From a business perspective, I had to admit that disco made sense. Bands were more expensive than DJs, whom you could hire for fifty dollars a night. Aardvark's entertainment began to follow the trend, relying more and more on turntables rather than live bands. I watched from the bar as dancers got lost in the music. They hit the bar more often, flushed and excited, and stood passively listening less. Showing off their moves put a smile on everyone's faces. I remembered the magic of those *chanson à répondre* parties my parents threw around the holidays—the basement ceiling threatening to collapse, the talcum powdering the floor.

Even with the understanding that I was only a not-that-big-a-fish in a very small pond, I felt great. I was twenty-two years old and tooling around town in a Mercedes. I had married my whip-smart, beautiful high-school sweetheart and owned the hippest, most happening club this side of Toronto. What more could I want?

As happy as I was, I couldn't say I was content. That fabulous realm right across the southern border was so close that I could almost see it from the front door of my club, the magic-dust world of Disney and Polaroid cameras and two-car garages. A sad voice wouldn't stop whispering in my ear.

Ah, little Pierre, what chance would a French-Canadian nobody have in America? They'd eat you alive over there. Stay close to home, mon petit chou, *stick to your own kind.*

I was too restless to listen.

CHAPTER FOUR

Florida

By all accounts I should have been securely settled in the mid-1970s. In June 1974, Sheila and I greeted our first child, Jennifer, and her birth was one of the most singular events of my life. Like any proud papa, I was thrilled. I was transformed.

I remember working my tail off at the club, then returning home to a sweetly sleeping daughter at four o'clock in the morning. Without disturbing my wife—Sheila no doubt would have disapproved of the practice—I used to rouse Jen from her crib just for the delight of playing with her. *Don't wake the baby* is a universal rule of parenthood, but I couldn't resist.

A year and a half later, we welcomed another baby girl, Amanda, whom we always called Mandy. I was over the moon. My mom finally had the little girls she'd always wanted. The Aardvark was a success, and I felt confident I could support my growing family. I embraced the typical masculine formula of money equaling love, spoiling my daughters with the kinds of gifts and outings that would have been impossible dreams for me as a child. I brought them to Disney World on their birthdays so they could visit the fairy-tale castle I had fantasized about.

I made sure they always wore brand-new clothes, a luxury I had never even considered during my hand-me-down childhood.

Caught up in my nightly hustle, I didn't grasp the fact that being a good father involved much more than providing material comforts. *Jen and Mandy will be better off than I was,* I thought. *They will never suffer the indignity of poverty.* I thought I'd fulfilled my fatherly duties and then some. But I was young and emotionally unsophisticated. I didn't realize that my late nights and erratic schedule were taking a toll on the family.

From the beginning, I understood that part of my job as a club owner was to stay current, ride the trends, keep my finger on the public pulse. Maybe it harked back to my peashooter/yo-yo/Hula-Hoop days, but I intrinsically understood that there was always something new on the horizon, and I'd better be ready to get out in front of it. I wanted to be first, and I wanted to be best. *If you aren't the lead dog, the view never changes* was an expression I took to heart.

For better or worse—and much of it was for the worse—what was happening in culture in the 1970s was disco. With the European influence in Quebec, Canada embraced the pulsing music and flashing lights slightly earlier than America. The term *disco* went beyond music and dictated a sense of fashion and style, a total rejection of sixties political seriousness in favor of a "just wanna have fun" ethos. Disco has since become a synonym for shallowness and empty-headed hedonism, but as a club owner I witnessed what the music could do, jolting a dance floor alive as if an electrical current were running through the crowd.

I continued to haunt the clubs of Montreal and Toronto, making monthly forays in search of anything fresh and new. Plus I began to consume whatever cultural reportage I could scrounge up, reading everything I could get my hands on—newspapers, magazines, tabloids, xeroxed fanzines—sifting through it all in an attempt to break out of my provincial mind-set. Back then, *Rolling Stone* was still considered something of an underground publication, and I pounced on every issue.

I also subscribed to *Billboard*, the bible of the music industry, studying it religiously. In early 1975, I came across an advertisement for the first-of-its-kind *Billboard* National Disco Convention, which was scheduled to be held in a midtown Manhattan hotel. *Billboard* magazine was a bastion of rock 'n' roll, and its recognition of disco signaled that dance music was here to stay.

I turned that ad over and over in my mind. I had never visited New York City. I should have been terrified at the prospect of joining a collection of sophisticated music-industry professionals in one of the cultural capitals of the world, but my innocence served me well. Fools rush in, as they say, and, following my foolhardy impulses, I rushed right into places and situations where I barely belonged.

So I signed on for the conference and flew into JFK. It was springtime in New York. Stevie Wonder had a hit out called "Living for the City," and I was a perfect stand-in for the wide-eyed boy hero in the song: "Wow! New York, just like I pictured it—skyscrapers and everything!"

Taking my place among the assembled club owners, booking agents, DJs, and music-industry types, I initially felt as out of place as an altar boy at an orgy. Naïveté might have gotten me through the door, but it didn't help once the door swung shut behind me. At the opening-day lunch I sat next to Jay Rizzo, owner of 2001 Odyssey in Bay Ridge, Brooklyn. That was the club where, in just a couple of years, the dance-floor scenes from *Saturday Night Fever* would be filmed.

But when I looked around at the supposed geniuses attending the conference, I realized to my great relief that I could hold my own in the room. They were just ordinary people—hustlers, yeah, and with different accents than I was used to. But they put their pants on one leg at a time like the rest of us, even though their pants were flared extravagantly and made of white linen. *Fuck that,* I told myself, *my mother could sew those damned outfits, no problem.*

The main theme of the gathering was basic and straightforward: *In disco, the customer is the show.* The focus in the club scene, the conference organizers declared, had shifted from the acts onstage to the patrons on the floor. That message, as spot-on as it seemed to be, felt a little stale to me. I'd witnessed that shift and used it to my advantage. I didn't need a room of presenters to tell me that nightlife was changing. I couldn't help but wonder if everyone at the conference was riding a wave that was already cresting, and the disco trend might be flattening out. Peashooter season might still be happening, but by next week I had a feeling everyone would have moved on to the yo-yo.

I made my way through the events of the conference one after another. The caliber of the nightlife entrepreneurs there inspired me, sure, but they also ignited a competitive flame in my gut. Meeting those so-called music moguls and cultural curators, I realized I needed to expand my horizons in order to compete with them. I had to set my sights beyond Cornwall, with its obvious limitations, and find my motivation from something other than competition with my brothers. I dreamed of doubling down on the dance-club business, taking a risk on a *Titanic*-size discothèque that made the Aardvark look like an actual anteater. To go big, I had to think big.

Anyone else would have glanced at the ad in the Business Opportunities section of the *New York Times* and dismissed it as "too good to be true" before turning the page. I didn't. I had never looked at a copy of the *Times* in my life. But on one of my last days at the conference, an ad caught and held my interest.

"Fantastic Miami-Area Nightclub Discothèque! Thirty thousand square feet! $600,000 lighting array! $300,000 sound system! Capacity 2,000!"

I've always thought that using a lot of exclamation points is like laughing too hard at your own jokes. In small print at the bottom of the ad came the kicker, the price: $400,000, along with the helpful note, "Terms!"

Florida was a fantasy realm to me. In Canada, wealthy people relocated to Miami to avoid the frigid winters. I didn't know a single person who lived there year-round. The idea of moving my family to the Sunshine State indicated I was moving on up in terms of class status, the kind of great leap forward that instantly attracted me.

For months, I had been wondering what I could do to pump up the action at the Aardvark. I had considered enlarging the place, but at best I could only double the capacity, making it eight hundred instead of four hundred, though I might be able to squeeze in a thousand in a pinch. But the problem ran deeper than square footage. The club-going population of Cornwall could not consistently fill a larger place. The demographics wouldn't support it, and the market just wasn't there. As long as I hung around my hometown, my ambitions had a built-in limit.

So there were logical explanations for a career move to a bigger city, but they only served to cover up my real reason: I was restless. I've encountered this motive again and again throughout my life. I'd conquer a mountaintop only to scan the horizon for a taller peak to climb. A sense of been-there-done-that afflicted me whenever I accomplished a goal.

Restlessness caused me to read the *Times* ad over twice, three times, then once again. *You're good where you are,* the voice in my head insisted. *You pulled in over a hundred grand last year, and there's more where that came from.* Sheila and my daughters were safe and happy in Cornwall. Kids are little conservatives and hate to be uprooted.

Those were sober-minded, quite valid considerations. Ranked against them was a wild combination of big-city energy, disco-conference confidence, and my standing as probably the most naïve person in New

York City. I decided not to scurry back home after the conference as I had intended. Instead I booked myself on the first flight to Miami. I wasn't exactly making a blind leap. At least I had my one eye wide open.

As you travel north from Miami International Airport, the towns of South Florida merge seamlessly into one another, so you are never sure exactly where Fort Lauderdale ends, say, and Pompano Beach begins.

I had never been to Florida before. Of course, like every other Canadian citizen, I had visions of the place as a realm of sun and sand and warmth. South Florida was the anti-Canada, well endowed with everything my own homeland lacked. The sunlit spring landscape appeared beautiful, just as the tourist brochures had advertised. But I also glimpsed the American Dream's underbelly. A huge influx of Cuban immigrants was just beginning. I passed encampments that had been set up beneath the highway interchanges, packed dense with hundreds of refugees.

It turned out that the "Fantastic Miami-Area Nightclub Discothèque!" at 1001 North Federal Highway in Hallandale had a seedy underbelly of its own. The ad copy was total garbage. That "$600,00 lighting array" the *Times* ad boasted about was antiquated shit. The expensive and fabulous sound system was also outdated. Lighting and audio technology advanced so quickly in those days that what was cutting edge one year inevitably became worthless only a few years later. I would have to start all over from scratch.

Even the name of the club sucked. Rum Bottoms had been created by a half dozen Greek and Italian businessmen from Long Island. They named the Hallandale place after their flagship nightclub back in Massapequa. The dudes were behind the times, proudly claiming to have unleashed the band Twisted Sister upon Long Island and the waiting world. The owners were all in their midforties and almost comically at each other's throats. I walked into Rum Bottoms to discover two of them in the midst of a fistfight.

The Florida venue had taken over a German beer hall that special-ized in drag shows. To my mind, the name Rum Bottoms called up the idea of "bottom feeders," and that seemed to be the type of patrons the place attracted. The club logo was of a dancer striking a disco pose next to a palm tree. The old owners let me examine their books and it was clear that, as a nightclub, the place just wasn't making it. Fluctuations in Florida's seasonal population made winter the only time of year they made a profit. Barely.

But I wasn't interested in buying someone else's vision, or even someone else's clientele. I thought of the transaction as "buying the box"—purchasing the club's structure, the physical plant, the location. In that sense, the box was solid, the box was good, and it came with one other necessary piece of the puzzle: a liquor license. As soon as I walked into the building, my mind raced with ideas for a makeover. Thirty thousand square feet—six times what I had in Cornwall. Visions of a disco inferno danced in my head. What I could do with thirty thousand feet!

Once you exited the box, the location proved to be great, too. There was a lot of action at area nightclubs, especially at smaller cover-band venues like Pete & Lenny's, which had been packed the few times I vis-ited. I was certain that the South Florida nightlife scene could support a megaclub like the one I was envisioning. Two of the area radio stations had just switched to all-disco formats. The area had clear potential.

Just to take over the lease on the place, I bargained the owners from their original $400,000 asking price to $340,000. Looking back, I probably should have paid even less. I put down a couple hundred grand up front and negotiated an option to buy the building outright for $600,000. The deal was the equivalent of nearly $3 million dollars in today's money.

Things were moving fast. I had so many delusions of greatness clouding my vision that I didn't talk over the move with Sheila. It wouldn't have mattered. Any consultation with my family would have been pure window dressing. There was precious little that could have stopped my ambition. There was nothing for Sheila to say, really. It was clear that I'd made the decision without her input. She was resigned, if not supportive.

We moved into a North Miami Beach rental, but she felt lonely and isolated in Florida. To be honest, her hometown was the only place on earth where Sheila seemed to be truly comfortable.

To satisfy my wife's Ontario longing, I purchased the best house in Cornwall that I could lay my hands on. But at the same time I also bought a three-bedroom townhouse on the canal in Hallandale for $120,000. The two homes symbolized my split-personality life. I had one foot in the past and one in the present. Sheila and the kids spent time at the Hallandale townhouse, but the scene wasn't exactly domestic. She retreated to her hometown nest during the week, flying back down with Jen and Mandy only on weekends.

For myself, Canada was fast receding in the rearview. I unloaded the Aardvark, and the new owners installed a restaurant and tried to keep the club going, but it died the good death a few years later. I went back to Cornwall often enough at first, but less and less as time passed.

Instead, I focused on realizing my vision in Florida. Right away, I brought on board a lighting-and-sound designer from Montreal, Paul Sciotte. His business was growing as fast as mine was. He had done lighting installations in Montreal and Quebec clubs that were impressive for their day—strobes, spinning mirror wheels, "meteor chasers," trippy stuff like that.

Exploiting a program designed to support small businesses, we convinced the Canadian government to grant a million-dollar loan to Paul's Montreal-based company. In the interest of stimulating the national economy, and not caring that the loan would actually be used to remodel a club in America, Ottawa handed us the money, amortized over five years at over $16,000 a month. I put most of the million into lighting and sound, creating the most up-to-date nightclub infrastructure anywhere in the South.

Paul brought along a friend of his, Brian MacGuigan, who would eventually go on to become my indispensable right-hand man. With a few former Rum Bottoms employees who proved to be great finds, our team was coming together. Bob Lombardi was an employee who had been wasted at the seedy club, revolutionizing the art of deejaying with the use of "carts," or tape cartridges, instead of vinyl discs. He could set up a set list for a whole night on just a few cassettes. Long before it became the standard for EDM, or electronic dance music, Lombardi was experimenting with the beats-per-minute approach to programming music.

My operations manager was also a Rum Bottoms alum. Functioning as operations chief but without the formal title, Fred Levin put his nose diligently to the grindstone without any pressure from me, logging as many hours at the club as I did. I took care of the music and ambience, while Fred handled pretty much everything else. He was the kind of superdedicated employee who appeared to have no life at all outside of work.

I have a bedrock-basic business principle: I know what I don't know, meaning I'm aware of my own limitations, so I have to find employees who can fill in the gaps. I don't have time to be good at everything. That rule had served me well at Aardvark, and I applied it even more rigorously in Florida while creating the new, much-larger club. I kept my staff small and employed that core crew to optimum effect.

Everything seemed to be falling into place. I had the basic box of the old Rum Bottoms buffed up and refurbished, with state-of-the-art lighting and sound systems installed courtesy of the Canadian government. I also put in a killer dance floor fabricated out of brushed steel. The only thing left was to come up with a name. By that time, I had more or less abandoned the whims of youth, along with the idea of naming a club after a cartoon character, so Aardvark was out of the question.

The fundamental principle that I had taken away from the disco conference kept coming back to me: *In disco, the customer is the show.* In the theater world and in cabaret, there's something called a solo spot or a follow spot, a tight spotlight that tracks a single performer around the stage. I wanted the dancers who came to my club to have that feeling, that the focus was all on them. Paul Sciotte understood the concept immediately, and the lighting arrays he installed had the capability to single out people on the floor. It seemed like a huge selling point, and I wanted to telegraph it with the name. I considered calling the club "Spotlight" but it sounded generic, too literal.

But what about Limelight?

The word *limelight* had nothing to do with the citrus fruit, but rather referred to limestone—or, more specifically, calcium oxide, which was used in the lighting technology that had been invented in the 1830s. The phrase "in the limelight" meant being the center of attention. It was perfect, evoking visions of club-goers busting out their signature moves on the dance floor.

So the old Rum Bottoms became the new Limelight. At the very least, I thought, the name change represented a step up. I thought we were finally ready to throw open the doors. I had my core team lined up—me, Fred, a part-time receptionist, and seven security people. Bartenders and barbacks could be rotated in and out.

I figured that I could get away with a bare-bones security staff—essentially one security person per 280 people, give or take—because to say that the local police were in our pocket would be an understatement. I made it a priority to set up a friendly relationship with the Hallandale police force, getting to know them personally and offering them preferential treatment at the venue. I felt sure they would smooth over any problems and keep the lid tightly screwed down on the whole area.

As it turned out, the local cops came cheap. In fact, they didn't require grease at all, beyond the literal grease contained in the bar foods we offered them. To my northern eyes, they were all Southern good ol' boys. When they came to the club as customers, in plain clothes, they humbly paid their own way in.

But before I took over the lease and officially made the place my own, I received a slap-in-the-face introduction to another dominant feature of South Florida culture. The old Rum Bottoms owners had a couple of upcoming events already in place. The biggest was an awards night for the local queer community, modeled on the Oscars, handing out prizes for the best drag costume, best wigs, best shoes—an event that was half joke, half deadly serious.

"Hey, it's a big party," one of the owners told me. "It always makes a lot of money."

He handed over the keys and I kept the party on the books. The crowd that evening wound up blowing the provincial mind of *petit Pierre* from Ontario.

At that point I had only the vaguest notions about the queer community. In Cornwall, homosexuality was still padlocked in the closet. My mother and her generation couldn't even bring themselves to believe that Liberace was gay—they kept waiting for him to meet the right woman. The way I grew up wasn't really steeped in prejudice, but rather in a near total lack of experience with and understanding of queer culture.

When I walked into the club that night, a raucous crowd of two thousand greeted me, wearing everything from fishnets, ball gowns, and feather boas to chaps. Most of the men were bare chested. The bouffant hairdos on the drag queens towered two feet tall. I thought I'd stepped into a Fellini film set crossed with a Mardi Gras carnival.

I was shocked and couldn't figure out how to act. I was thrilled to have the club packed, but I sequestered myself in my office for much of the night, just trying to puzzle out what I'd gotten myself into. South

Florida in the seventies was the recognized winter refuge of every gay person in America. From the snowy north they came, and from small towns everywhere, places where, if they stayed, they would be mocked and tortured.

When timid Peter Rabbit finally emerged from hiding and walked out among the partiers, I encountered crazed energy, pure happiness, and not a whiff of negativity or violence. The crowd was exuberant, the vibe was full of celebration and acceptance, and right at that moment I felt the ground shift beneath my unsophisticated feet. The awards night reemphasized a basic lesson in humanity for me: there is no "them," only us. The people in the club were my people, dancing and partying and enjoying their lives. My new philosophy became *Whatever floats your boat, God bless you—at least it works that way for you.*

I would soon learn that a flamboyant clientele didn't even register on my list of worries. All during the run-up to the opening, I kept waiting for the mythic violent American dark side, the America of *The Godfather* and *Mean Streets*, to appear at my door. But things were pretty tame—no gangsters, no Mafia, no muscle. Between the constant police presence and the absence of the barroom brawls I'd had to ward against in Cornwall, Florida seemed to be a dream. The only thing we had to watch out for, I thought, was overindulgence and sloppy behavior.

Late one night, when I had just taken the keys from Rum Bottoms, I told one of my security guys to eighty-six a customer who was drunk and acting up. That night Sergeant Shep, a thick-necked local cop, was posted outside the club.

"Get rid of him," I said, imagining the drunk customer would be escorted to the parking lot and sent on his way.

Instead, my security guy, Nicky, a big bouncer with hands like catchers' mitts, gave the troublemaker a stiff backhand slap. The drunk crumpled to the ground. I was appalled. The guy rose up screaming, appealing to Sgt. Shep.

"Did you see that?" he shouted. "I got assaulted!"

"I know what I saw," Sgt. Shep responded mildly. "I know if you aren't out of here in thirty seconds I'll run you down to the station."

Welcome to South Florida. I concluded that I might have to establish some guidelines about removing unruly patrons from the club. No sucker punches allowed.

The other events remaining on the Rum Bottoms books came off without a hitch. The renovations were in place. Now I needed to build a fan base for parties at Limelight. These were the days before invitations, guest lists, and promoters in charge of getting warm bodies into the club. I exploited other approaches.

Announcing the debut of Florida Limelight would be the first and only time I ever bought ads on local radio. It was also the first and only time I used aerial banners—airplanes flying along the beaches, trailing massive ads for the venue. I now presided over the largest nightclub in South Florida, at thirty thousand square feet. Legal capacity was two thousand people, five times what my old club in Cornwall could handle. In a pinch I could squeeze in twenty-five hundred or even three thousand. Those numbers gave me the cash flow that enabled booking big acts.

On the new club's official opening night, I suffered an acute attack of insecurity. *What was I thinking? This is America, this is the big leagues. Lucky that I kept my home base in Cornwall,* I thought. Gauging my chances of success on a scale of one to ten, I gave myself a one. But as had happened at the Aardvark and even with the Pant Loft, there was a long line waiting when we threw open the doors. Somehow, via radio, airplane banners, or word of mouth, the news had gotten out. Limelight packed them in.

But the line didn't alleviate my anxiety. I was too busy to bask in my success. And, let's face it, you can take the boy out of Cornwall, but there's no way to totally eradicate Cornwall from the boy. Those first nights running a nightclub in Florida opened my eyes to a lot of things. Cocaine, for one. It was the first time I'd ever seen the stuff. We had a game room in the venue, and there was a guy in there chopping up white powder with a credit card on the glass top of a pinball machine.

"What's he up to in there?" I asked one of my security people, who shot me a look of pure pity, as if I were some kind of babe in the woods.

Again, welcome to South Florida. Soon enough, Miami would be buried in the white powder, and *snowbird*—a Canadian who flew to Florida for the winter—would take on an entirely different meaning.

Ninety-nine percent of success is being in the right place at the right time. I was the owner of a megaclub in South Florida the year John Travolta in *Saturday Night Fever* hit America like a Mack Truck in platform shoes. If disco had been headed for a slump, it now reconquered the world with a vengeance. All I had to do was ride the wave.

Booking acts wasn't exactly rocket science, but you had to have a gift. It took a lot of time, finessing, and research, getting a feel for what was going down before it happened. I simply relied on my instincts, somehow summoning the chutzpah to follow through on them. I kept telling myself that I was the guy who'd booked Rush before they broke big.

Limelight's liquor license allowed us to stay open until six a.m. In the booking contracts for the club, I specified two sets a night, the first at twelve thirty or one o'clock, and a second an hour or two later. I was always pushing to have the last show come on as late as possible, in order to keep the crowd beyond the first set. But that was a struggle, since most of the acts just wanted to get their appearances over with and head home. Regardless, we were packing them in and keeping them late.

Our biggest break came when I booked Village People, four months in advance of their actual appearance at the club. Their *Macho Man* album hadn't dropped yet when I signed them, but I knew that the cowboy/hardhat/cop/leather-man gimmick was great, simply because everyone likes dress-up. From the beginning, the act had perfect crossover appeal between the queer and straight worlds.

Four months later, when Village People finally hit Limelight, "Macho Man" was in nonstop rotation on local radio, and I had the hottest act in the country. The song was so ubiquitous on the airwaves that I remember people asking me what the hell was going on. "What's the secret—does your uncle own the radio station or something?"

Lightning struck not twice, but again and again. The Trammps had appeared at Limelight in 1977, the week before Easter, when "Disco Inferno" was in such heavy rotation that it was being played every tenth song. Eventually I booked every top disco act with the exception of Donna Summer, who was too big for the venue. But we had Grace Jones, Two Tons O' Fun, Sister Sledge, Gloria Gaynor.

Limelight was an instant hit.

CHAPTER FIVE

Atlanta

In fall 1978, I found myself increasingly restless. The voice of reason spoke to me once again: *Peter, what are you thinking? You have this fabulous club operating full tilt in one of the greatest nightlife markets in the world, in a state that draws more people than pretty much anywhere else—and you're not happy?* My response was to book myself on a flight to Houston so I could check out the potential for a club there.

Part of the trouble was that I never really liked Florida. I missed the seasons. Other factors figured in. Narco violence was just beginning to rear its ugly head. Miami was a huge market, and that had a downside in increased traffic and crowding. A thousand people moved to Florida every frigging day. They couldn't all be wrong, could they? But *Fuck 'em*, I thought. It was time for me to set my sights on a new horizon.

Ever since opening, I routinely had patrons telling me how a club like Limelight would really blow up big in a place like (fill in the name of a midsize city here—Cleveland, Minneapolis, Charlotte, Houston, etc.). What none of them understood was the thing that made a club work was a pool of hip, creative people, the kind of scene-makers who could inject a little life into nightlife. Eager to mount a new venture, I was willing to chase down any lukewarm tip. I spent a week in Cleveland one night, as they say. Day or night, I couldn't find a pulse.

I flew to Houston. There was certainly a lot of money lying around waiting to be plucked up. America's oil-and-gas industry was steadily pumping black gold from the ground and funneling it into the pockets of Houston plutocrats. But therein lay the problem. The whole town was full of fat cats in cowboy hats and bolo ties, and those were not the customers who would supercharge the kind of club I envisioned.

A side trip to Dallas made a slightly better impression, but I still wasn't convinced. There's a Texas saying about poseurs being "all hat and no cattle," and I couldn't imagine either one, Stetsons nor livestock, on my dance floor. The queer population in the city seemed to be closeted or running scared, and if you don't have a healthy percentage of gay people in a nightclub, it turns into a boring hetero meat market.

A real-estate broker in Dallas took me around to potential properties. She showed me the Texas Theatre, where Lee Harvey Oswald was arrested after he murdered JFK.

"This place has a real kind of historical value," she said.

The wrong kind, I thought, and I left the state without discovering any prospects.

Then I had a casual conversation with a barback kid at the Florida club, who told me tales of the great nightlife scene in his hometown of Atlanta. At that point, I had such a hair-trigger sensibility that it didn't matter where the input came from, a professional broker or a twenty-year-old bartender's assistant. I was on the next plane to Georgia.

In 1978, Atlanta was climbing out of a real-estate slump that had hit the town a few years earlier. The local economy was on the upswing, but there were still a lot of empty properties to choose from. It turned out the barback kid had lied. There was no real nightlife in Atlanta. The whole of downtown emptied out at six o'clock, with everyone retreating to outlying districts. Still, there was something about the place that held my interest.

I found a failing dinner theater, the Harlequin, in the fashionable-but-sleepy Buckhead neighborhood of "uptown" Atlanta. It didn't matter that the area was suburban, well beyond the city center, and altogether out of the way. Long before I ever saw the movie *Field of Dreams*, I had an attitude of "If you build it, they will come." The interior of the abandoned Harlequin had a spooky *Phantom of the Opera* feel, with a greenroom that was still full of old show costumes. I applied my "buying the box" logic and, in this case, concluded that the box was large enough to suit my purposes.

I thought the theater's old orchestra pit would serve as a great sunken dance floor. Back then, every club owner had the same idea about how a disco should look, spun directly out of their *Saturday Night Fever* fantasies. In the movie, John Travolta struck his iconic poses on a glass dance floor, and the lighting underneath the glass had shown off the dancers to great effect. I found the aesthetic boring and already passé, and I sought to advance beyond the routine glass-and-lights formula. In place of the usual bank of spotlights, there had to be something else that I could put beneath the new Limelight's dance floor.

My mind buzzed. *What would be cool? What would be cooler than cool?* I'd always been haunted by one of my earliest childhood memories, when I encountered a neighbor's black cat, its back arched, fangs bared, spitting evilly. It was one of my first interactions with an animal, and it left a terrifying impression. That memory came back to me, and I couldn't help wondering what a cat might look like, roaming around underneath a glass dance floor.

Not a housecat, of course, but how about a very big, very scary cat? The more I thought about it, the more I set my heart on finding a panther for hire. A sleek, long-clawed, dangerous-looking panther. There had to be one in some zoo or wildlife sanctuary that I could borrow.

In America, you can get anything you want for a price. The owner of a private menagerie had a panther that had been trotted out for show at basketball games, car-dealership openings, and similar events. We would build an enclosure below the dance floor deep enough so the panther could move freely.

As we underwent renovations, I started to talk up the idea. I hired a New York publicity firm for the Atlanta opening. The effect was electric. Every inch of newspaper coverage, every mention on the five o'clock news programs included my plans for a disco panther. *I gotta see this* was the universal reaction.

Not every response was positive. The Georgia chapter of the ASPCA got wind of the plan and took me to court to prevent it. I immediately transformed back into the trembling kid from Cornwall, terrified of authority. I worried I might be arrested and given the heave-ho back to my native country. With a measure of fear and loathing, I hired a lawyer and showed up to face off with the ASPCA.

Through the real-estate broker who showed me the Harlequin, I met a lawyer named Jay Block, an elegant Southern squire who knew the judge from previous legal cases. As we headed into the courtroom, Jay asked if I was worried.

"I can't lose," I responded, putting on a brash face.

"What do you mean, you can't lose?" he asked. "It could go either way."

"It's about publicity, Jay," I responded, coming off as the know-it-all adult I was desperately trying to be. "If the judge rules in our favor, I get to keep the cat, and there's obvious publicity value to that. But if the ruling goes against us, that's free publicity, too."

Jay shook his head, an old-school attorney gaining insight into the topsy-turvy realm of nightlife. He already thought I was a little crazy to open Limelight. A giant disco would never succeed in Atlanta, he predicted. The city was too traditional, too set in its ways.

Whatever he thought about our chances of success, Jay was in top form arguing my case. He pointed out that the panther in question would have a familiar handler nearby at all times, and that it had already been shown at dozens of events.

"It's accustomed to the public eye, Your Honor," Jay said, keeping his tone even. "That's how the animal makes its living." The more strident voices came from the other side, with the ASPCA lawyers predicting the big cat's death by heart attack.

"Well . . ." The judge began his decision on whether to grant an injunction. "I used to have an old hound dog." He spoke in a grits-thick Southern drawl.

"That old boy, well, we lived near some railroad tracks, and he would raise a darn howl to beat the band every time the B&O freight went by and blew its whistle. He'd *a-rooo* like it'd be the death of him. But just a tick of the clock later he'd be all settled down to his noonday nap, sweet as sugar."

The judge slammed his gavel down and denied the ASPCA's request for an injunction. He'd let the club open with the animal in place, he announced, and have someone monitor the situation after the first night.

So I got to keep my big cat, and more than that, I had found myself a steadfast friend, mentor, and advocate in the person of Jay Block. I could have lost to the ASPCA, and the entire episode would still have been worth it because of Jay's influence on my life from that time forward.

When we had our grand opening, a full-size panther roamed beneath the glass dance floor, my childhood nightmare come to life. There didn't need to be any deep psychological strategy here, as though I were caging my youthful fears in order to tame them. Sometimes a panther is just a friggin' cool panther.

In hindsight, I realize the panther wasn't such a great idea. In terms of publicity, yes, it served a function extremely well. But my empathy for animals has developed a lot in the decades since. Back then, I considered the big cat to be a showbiz professional. I was paying a fee for a booking, and the creature duly put on a show. Today, I cringe at the whole concept, but the animal was neither spooked nor overly impressed by the whole herd of human bipeds thundering above it. The cool cat spent most of the time under the glass fast asleep.

Either by the disco panther or simply because Atlanta lacked night-life, the hook had been well set. Outside the club, the line to get into the most talked-about new venue in town stretched for blocks down Piedmont Road. An overwhelming sense of excitement mixed with the homegrown scent of magnolia blossoms. Atlanta saw itself as a bur-geoning metropolis, and the demand for big-city-style nightlife didn't disappoint. The club had over five thousand entries that first night.

I had another smash hit on my hands. When Jay Block showed up on opening night, I tried to keep the "told you so" smirk off my face. He was delighted to be proven wrong about a big disco in his hidebound hometown.

Due to the splashy opening and the efforts of the New York PR firm, Limelight didn't remain just a local phenomenon. It became a national one. I had sent invites to several tastemakers, people I thought of as "lead horses," whom the rest of the herd would follow. These were celebrities I knew from the Miami club, such as Grace Jones, and a few new ones, like Tina Turner and Rod Stewart. But the camera flashes flared brightest for the lead stallion of them all, the Pittsburgh-born son of Slovakian immigrants, Andrew Warhola, better known as Andy Warhol.

Among a certain sector of the population, and certainly in the opinion of the fashion and society *beau monde*, Andy Warhol's presence at the Limelight meant that I had arrived. In fact, Andy had agreed to cosponsor the event. The invitation to the club opening read "Peter Gatien and Andy Warhol invite you . . ." His presence ensured the opening would be covered by the must-read gossip column, *New York Post*'s Page Six.

Ever since I'd entered the nightclub business, I'd had to remind myself of the fact that patrons never came out to see me. I put a lot of energy into making a product, creating an environment. Gratified as

I was by the acclaim that I received personally, I realized no one was showing up to hang out with Peter.

Some club owners took a different approach. It was the era of Studio 54 and Steve Rubell, who became his own kind of celebrity by throwing himself into partying with his patrons. The media labeled me "the anti-Rubell," which was not exactly a compliment. To journalists and cultural commentators, I was "stiff," "aloof," "holier-than-thou." As Mick Jagger once noted, if you don't do interviews, if you don't willingly self-promote and play along with the fame game, then the press derides you as arrogant.

Yes, I was an elusive presence, on my way to earning the nickname "the Ghost" from my staffers, mainly because I tended to behave like one. Popping up here and there throughout the evening, I would vanish back in my office almost before anyone noticed me. Busy running my clubs, I kept my private life carefully veiled, shielding my persona behind my eye-patch façade. Which was probably a good idea, since in the personal sphere my life had been crumbling for some time.

If you'd like to know the story of my first marriage, check out Bruce Springsteen's song "The River." It tells a story about life in a small factory town much like Cornwall, where "they bring you up to do like your daddy done," and a sad relationship between high-school sweethearts who married too young.

That was Sheila and me. We got hitched when we were teenagers, before we had figured out the direction our lives would take, how we wanted to live, where we'd set down roots. We had an enormous amount of change and transformation ahead of us. As with all too many young marriages, we didn't have the tools to make it.

Running clubs meant that I consistently kept late-night hours. The moment when the real fissure cracked open was when I had an affair during my Aardvark days. To my young, unenlightened male mind, I considered it meaningless. But Sheila found a letter that had evidence of my dalliance. She never really trusted me again. In her eyes, I'd broken our partnership. In retrospect, it was a fair conclusion for her not to trust me. My priorities had shifted. My real love, from Miami onward, was Limelight, nightlife, or what Billy Strayhorn once labeled the lush life. How could the domestic sphere compete with the energy, exuberance, and endless possibilities of that?

My rival, when it came to Sheila, was Cornwall. In this world, there are those who strive to leave their hometowns and those who don't. One choice isn't better than the other; they're just two separate desires. The small villages of the world probably owe a debt of gratitude to New York, London, Paris, and all the other great metropolises, for siphoning off the troublemakers and keeping the backwoods sleepy and peaceful.

It was clear to me, from the moment I flew to New York, that my life would happen outside Cornwall. When Sheila and I got married, I'm sure she assumed we would set up a life in our hometown and live near her family. The point is, we simply didn't talk about our diverging goals, because they weren't fully formed yet. To me, our future had seemed so open, so limitless. To her, our future had boundaries set by community and family.

My brash attempt to transfer my family from Canada to South Florida never really happened. By the time I opened the second Limelight in Atlanta, my marriage was over. Sheila and I had been living apart for some time. In 1978, we divorced. I had started a relationship with a bright, simpatico woman named Adrienne Norman, and she moved with me to Atlanta.

Almost as soon as I left, the Florida Limelight became a bridge that literally burned behind me. I should have seen the fire coming. I had sold the club in September and it became a smoking ruin three months later. According to the terms of the deal, I kept the deed to the building and leased the place to new owners for $900,000. They paid $300,000 down. Newbie businessman that I was, I hadn't spelled out terms as to liability in case of fire. Soon after the ink was dry, the former Rum Bottoms burned to the ground.

When the place went up in flames, the insurance company labeled it arson and refused to pay damages. The new owners managed to lose the case in court, and I saw over a half million dollars in equity vanish like smoke. Still possessing the deed to the property, I managed to sell the land later for $550,000. So in the end I didn't take too much of a bath, but the entire fire and its aftermath represented a pesky distraction.

Luckily, I was really coming into my own with the Atlanta club. A smash opening was one thing, but keeping the momentum going on a consistent basis was another. From the start we got top-notch media exposure, but what really had patrons coming back for more were the creative strides we made. I became obsessed with continually refreshing the club environment. A credo came together in my mind, defined by the phrase "Clubs create culture." I began to repeat that phrase to my employees.

What's next? What's next? What's next? was my constant inner refrain. After a single appearance, I retired the panther. I remember giving the beast its walking papers as it sprawled, purring, atop the desk in my Limelight office, the handler by its side. It really was a tame pussycat. I mentally thanked the magnificent animal for generating such a huge opening-night buzz.

My crew proved to be a collection of construction wizards, taking only a single day to install a large saltwater pool in place of the panther cage. I hired a troupe of topless mermaids to float alluringly below the dance floor, but their shifts had to be limited or they would turn into total prunes.

Out with the . . . In with the . . . I wound up stocking the tank with sand sharks, and, surprisingly, liked them even better than the mermaids. Somehow, the movement of the creatures seemed to match the pulse of the music above them. Patrons used to pull up and stand stock still on the dance floor, mesmerized by the show below their feet. Meanwhile, the ASPCA didn't raise objection, their jurisdiction evidently limited to big cats and other species higher on the evolutionary ladder than sand sharks.

The house DJs pumped music through the club's monster 100,000-watt audio system, leaning heavily on European disco. I felt dance music from the continent was a little more advanced than the American brand, with groups such as ABBA and Arabesque breaking into the mainstream. What came to be called Euro disco was busy giving birth to house, space disco, and techno. That sound eventually morphed into EDM, the winner and still champion of the current nightlife world.

Homegrown artists contributed their fair share of tracks, too, especially the women. Blondie's "Heart of Glass," Chic's "Le Freak," Anita Ward's "Ring My Bell," and Donna Summer's "Bad Girls" were all topping the charts. Michael Jackson's *Off the Wall* album dropped in 1979, and we played the shit out of "Don't Stop 'Til You Get Enough."

The late seventies was the absolute greatest period to own a club—pre–herpes contagion, pre–AIDS plague, when the DEA's War on Drugs hadn't yet reached the heights of madness it saw in the 1980s. People were doing coke back then, but nobody lost their minds, their jobs, their souls to the stuff. In that era, the drug's reputation was more playful than evil. I blasted the Atlanta club two or three times a night with confetti that fell from the ceiling and looked like snow, a *wink-wink-heh-heh* reference to cocaine.

On weekends, along Piedmont Road, there was an hour or hour-and-a-half wait to enter. A grocery store next door came to be known as "Disco Kroger," because so many tricked-out, platform-shoe-shod club-goers ducked out of our place and into the grocery for beverages. Before we opened, the neighborhood of Buckhead had been a tad stuffy, snooty, and upscale, with a lot of ostentatious mansions lining the residential streets. The conservative matrons of Buckhead didn't know what hit them. Not through any pronounced intent, we contributed to the neighborhood's transformation into the hipper high-rise shopping mecca it is today.

Atlanta Limelight was large enough, and the money flowed freely enough, that, for the first time in my career, I could really allow my imagination full rein. We did crazy-ass shit, lowering dancers from the ceiling to the dance floor in chains, setting up cabana tents in place of VIP rooms, throwing monthly events when we would perform a complete, multithousand-dollar makeover on the whole club to bring the décor into line with an established theme.

Right out of the box, the most successful theme night was Bare as You Dare. The Cornwall boy in me was shocked at how enthusiastically Atlanta embraced the concept. The city might have been located in the American Bible Belt, but that belt unbuckled pretty damned quickly. I saw more skin on Bare as You Dare nights than I would have in a strip club. Atlantans *loved* letting it all hang out.

From the street-level entrance to the club, a grand stairway led down to the dance floor, but in the anteroom or foyer at the top of the stairs I had art installations that changed every week. People could walk in and think they were entering an entirely new club. I paid K. P. Hendry, an employee who had experience as an artist and set designer, $5,000 a month to curate the space. In the spirit of "knowing what I don't know," I let her do whatever she wanted with the top-of-the-stairs minigallery.

K. P. was a wonder. She produced tableaus that were by turns funny, surreal, and disturbing: strange disco automatons called Glitter Bots, glamour-girl marionettes, a "white trash" panorama, plus seasonal stuff like a food fight between pilgrims for Thanksgiving and a Christmas set off *The Nutcracker*. All of it was sexy and impeccably stylish, and it served well as a calling card for the club.

Down on the dance floor, we showcased a troupe of dancers that I recruited from our regulars, terming them "exciters." My staff insisted on calling them "twinkies," telling them the term was short for "twinkletoes," but I suspected that it referred to the soft Hostess snack cakes. Whatever term they went by, they functioned as club kids before club kids existed, showing up every weekend, dressed to the nines and fiercely loyal to the place. In exchange for me waiving the nominal door charge, they essentially provided free entertainment, dancing atop six-foot-tall speakers on either side of the floor, or prancing along a black-and-white keyboard-style platform we had installed against one wall.

The exciters were as much of a draw as the music and the atmosphere. Human beings are a gregarious species. Even though no one readily admits it, the mundane reason anyone comes out to a club is for people-watching. The dancers atop the speakers were eye candy. One male dancer, Arturo, always stood out, wearing an all-leather outfit festooned with every buckle, snap, and chain known to man. Speaker dancing is actually a difficult feat, busting interesting moves within a space the size of a small kitchen table.

No one had ever before brought queer and straight crowds together in a city that was one of the capitals of the Deep South. No one in the whole state dressed like some of the gay patrons who came into Limelight. My experience in Miami allowed me to reinvent and integrate nightlife in Atlanta. Once I did, the two camps stared across the segregated divide at each other and decided they liked what they saw—or at least weren't threatened by it. Atlanta came out, in both senses of the phrase, at a new nightclub in what was once fusty old Buckhead.

Atlanta Limelight rose to the level of a cultural phenomenon, as much as anything can be a phenomenon in the America that exists outside the confines of NYC and LA. For a quick minute we were known as "The Studio 54 of the South." On almost a weekly basis we'd land in Page Six or get a line or two in the syndicated columns of gossip doyennes Liz Smith and Cindy Adams.

Andy Warhol's presence in the club always helped. After he showed up at the opening, he returned every month or so, a gnomic, sphinx-like presence in public, but personable and friendly one-on-one. What outsiders often don't get about Andy is how funny he was, as ahead-of-their-time, whip-smart people often are. He could make everybody laugh.

"Well, I do like chest hair," he commented once during a conversation about actor Burt Reynolds, who also frequented Limelight. Reynolds was then notorious for his *Cosmopolitan* magazine centerfold, where he posed nude on a bearskin rug, a stroke of genius by editor Helen Gurley Brown. "Burt doesn't need a toupee *down there*," Andy added, and the whole table of his sycophants laughed hysterically. Reynolds was a favorite target of Warhol, who once asked the man's paramour, Lorna Luft, what Burt was like in bed. Luft politely refused to answer. Warhol's wit was biting, but he brought the club together, and his jibes were more warm and playful than mean spirited.

Whenever a celebrity or wannabe celebrity hit Atlanta, they showed up at Limelight. Madonna, Tom Cruise, Ali MacGraw, Isaac Hayes, Ann-Margret, Debbie Harry, Eartha Kitt, and Farrah Fawcett all cycled through. When actor David Hasselhoff showed up, he was not yet *Baywatch* hot, but he was popular in the South because of his supercar-crime-fighter TV show, *Knight Rider*. At the club he always went around accompanied by a trio of female "bodyguards"—more body than guards, if you know what I mean.

The biggest media clusterfuck exploded when Anita Bryant came out—in the most literal sense. The peppy, up-with-people orange-juice spokeswoman was then the public face of homophobia, a high-profile, ardently conservative, overtly religious voice raised against the various kinds of excess on nightly display on Limelight's dance floor. She was white bread through and through, originally a singer of middle-of-the-road, easy-listening, Lawrence Welk–style music.

I could never understand how this cardboard cutout had become popular, but she was widely admired by self-proclaimed "decency" advocates, once headlining a rally condemning Doors singer Jim Morrison after he'd dropped his leather pantaloons at a concert. Bryant also acted as the public face of a bogus "Save Our Children" crusade aimed at killing a civil-rights ordinance in Dade County, Florida, one that prohibited discrimination based on sexual orientation.

This was the paragon of virtue who showed up at Limelight for an afternoon tea dance in the summer of 1981. She had made a strange choice for a dance partner in Russ McGraw, an evangelist who was well known as a gay activist. Bryant's presence sent a buzz through the club. My house photographer, Guy D'Alema, snapped a photo of the odd couple out on the dance floor, and it was a shot seen round the world, on the front pages of tabloids the country over.

In the end, it turned out that hypocrisy didn't pay. Bryant's sponsors, the Florida orange-juice-industry group, were confronted with a boycott. Screwdriver cocktails were suddenly off the menu at every club in the country with a queer clientele, including Limelight. Facing declining sales, the group fired Bryant, who wound up going bankrupt. In a final indignity, she found herself shunned by the very moral-decency people she had courted, when she committed the high crime of divorcing her evangelist husband. I took no joy in her downfall, seeing her as a pawn in a game played by opportunistic politicians.

Whether the boldface name in question was an albino trendsetter in a bad wig or a fear-mongering Christian orange-juice shill, I rejected the role of star-fucker. I often didn't even glad-hand the celebrities who came into my club. I never joined them in those mythical VIP cabanas that lined the back walls at Atlanta Limelight, where activity went on behind the closed tent flaps that would have raised the hair on Anita Bryant's perfectly coiffed head.

I had a business to run, thank you very much. I got a lot more enjoyment from—and was much more deeply influenced by—the non-celebrity friends I hung out with in Atlanta. As far as I was concerned, they were the trendsetters, the ones pushing artistic limits, unfettered by the influence of public opinion. They were a lot more interesting than any face in a gossip column could possibly be. And they were the ones who kept me one step in front of the next trend.

If I was a ghost, I was a pale one, with a complexion that rivaled Warhol's. Adrienne Norman, my constant companion in those days, had skin that was a beautiful shade of olive brown, a heritage of her Lebanese background. At times our appearances in public reminded us that, although Atlanta billed itself as "The City Too Busy to Hate," we were still in the Deep South. Several times people thought it was their duty to tell us that race-mixing was not OK.

Most Atlantans were much too cool to care. The city floated like a tolerant, happily diverse island in a redneck sea. Drive thirty miles out of town and it was *Deliverance* country. I had a foreman overseeing construction at the club who proudly displayed his Ku Klux Klan medallion to me. There were parts of American culture, I was learning, that *Leave It to Beaver* hadn't highlighted.

But other Southerners proved a great deal more evolved. Jay Block, who'd become my go-to lawyer after he fended off the ASPCA in the panther case, was raised in Thibodaux, Louisiana, former site of one of the largest slave plantations in the state. He had an openhearted, supremely unbigoted soul.

Much more than that, Jay opened up my provincial mind to the possibilities of the wider world. I remember him once taking me out to La Côte Basque, an upscale "ladies who lunch"–style restaurant on the Upper East Side in New York City. Jay ordered a $200 Bordeaux without blinking an eye. At that point in time, I was still a TGI Fridays kind of guy, and I'd clawed my way up to that chain restaurant from the even more limited dining options in Cornwall. My idea of wine was a four-buck bottle of Blue Nun. After my lunch with Jay, I immediately embarked on a crash course in wine appreciation.

Jay really modeled everything I liked about the South. He was smart and personable, cultured but laid back. He worked hard and he also knew how to relax. Once, when the kids were visiting from Cornwall and he took us all sailing, we got pulled over for a minor traffic infraction. The ticket didn't ruffle a single hair on Jay's head. We continued on our way, went out in the boat, and enjoyed ourselves as if the whole incident never occurred.

This was astonishing to me. If anything like that would have happened to my father, he would have turned around, gone home, and remained mired in a bitter funk. I recall my mother once getting a three-dollar parking ticket that put a dark cloud over the whole household for days.

Enjoy yourself. There's a rich tapestry of life out there. Don't flinch, don't duck, don't shy away. Those were the lessons Jay Block taught me. He helped guide my nightclub empire as it expanded, a constant steadying hand on the tiller.

I tried to take those lessons into both my professional and personal life. I endeavored to surround myself with people I trusted, and not worry about the small stuff. Adrienne was wonderful with my two kids when they spent holidays and one weekend a month with us. Truthfully, they spent the time with Adrienne, not me, since I worked eighty-hour weeks during that period.

Adrienne didn't normally accompany me to the club. I was of the opinion that if I were a bricklayer, say, my significant other would probably not visit me on the job. I was at Limelight to work, so I thought it was inappropriate to have Adrienne hanging around the club once our relationship became serious. She was just fine with that arrangement. Nightlife had never been her passion.

I assembled a second family of sorts, a core of dedicated staffers around me, a collection of misfits, geniuses, and misfit geniuses. I came to think of them as a street crew, tight knit, loyal, fiercely fun loving.

The crew was headed up by jack-of-all-trades Brian MacGuigan. With my heart in my throat, I once watched as Brian balanced a 150-pound klieg light on his shoulder while climbing a teetering A-frame-style ladder. Witnessing him take apart an amplifier component and put it back together with a pair of tweezers was a thing of beauty. He could do anything, and accomplished it all with humor and bonhomie.

Over and over again I've heard this or that former staffer describe their gig at Limelight as "the best time of my life." My employees were usually on their way to some other career, some other goal. I wasn't hiring Harvard graduates. They were artists, actors, musicians, architects of castles in the air. But for the period we spent together, we engaged in a gigantic co-conspiracy to build this club, to orchestrate this experience, to pull everyone together and have as much fun doing it as we possibly could. One of the byproducts of a cocreator mentality was having a fucking good time.

The most interesting soul I encountered in the entire quarter century that I owned clubs was Tony Pelligrino. I'd met Tony when he casually dropped by the club one afternoon, saying he had been in Limelight the night before and liked the vibe. After he mentioned that he had mustered out of the US Marine Corps with the rank of major, I immediately hired him as an assistant security manager.

"Honorably discharged as a major—that's pretty good, isn't it?" he asked rhetorically. "Especially for someone whose uncle was Carlo Gambino?" The New York Mafia kingpin allegedly didn't want his nephew to be involved with organized crime, so Tony went another way.

That was pretty typical of my Atlanta crew. Some energetic, talented person would come to the club and feel like they wanted to be a part of it. That's not to say every person who showed up to party and tried to flip that into a paycheck was the next employee of the month. I could usually suss out during a ten-minute interview who had ideas and talent. Those were the people I wanted. It was my job to figure out what they were best at and then fit that skill to the proper role.

The real job of running a nightclub is done during the day. I always thought my job of club owner resembled a theater director who casts the parts, works like a dog in rehearsals, but then leaves and never returns once opening night happens. By then, the director's job is done, because the cast and crew know what to do. If I took care of my business completely and correctly during the day, the nights should have taken care of themselves. But most of the time I didn't really manage to clear out before closing. I always wanted to stick around to see the show.

Since I was protective of my productivity in the afternoons, I didn't suffer fools coming around and eating up my time. Tony was an exception who schmoozed his way inside. He was a really pleasant guy—a little older than the rest of my immediate Limelight circle, who were mostly in their twenties. I hired Tony on a whim, simply because I liked him. With his military background, I thought he'd do well working with the security crew.

We had a small office in the back of the club, and Tony installed himself there. The next day I ducked my head in and saw he had covered one of the walls with pictures of himself—Tony posed with Richard Nixon, Tony next to Henry Kissinger, Tony palling around with different generals and other military brass. That was my first whiff that this whimsical hire I'd made might turn out to be something other than an average, everyday employee.

For a military-theme party we threw at the club, the former Major Pelligrino showed up in full dress whites, complete with medals and commendation ribbons—not exactly the kind of getup you could rent at a local Halloween costume store. Tony made up for his air of mystery with a pronounced ability to produce results. One afternoon, he squired Jen, Mandy, and me around Six Flags amusement park. I watched, spell-bound, as Tony absolutely crushed it at the shooting gallery, winning so many huge stuffed animals that the carny finally told him to get lost.

I began to wonder about the guy's background. To this day, I'm still relatively in the dark about Tony Pelligrino. Who was he? CIA? Black ops? A fabricator of his personal mythology? I couldn't tell you, and no else could, either. In the end, apart from being an enjoyable storyteller and friend, I know only what he represented to me. He was our fixer.

If you wanted something, anything at all, Tony could get it for you. To me, it felt like magic. If I wanted a suit, Tony would get me a great suit. If I asked for theater tickets, I'd wind up fourth row center. If I had wanted a swimming pool, a crew would have shown up with a backhoe and been digging up the yard the next day.

"Hey, Tony, can you get me a good deal on a limo?" I asked him once.

Two days later he showed up with a sleek $30,000 limousine for a bargain-basement price of $16,000, brand-spanking new, legit papers, fully stocked bar, all the bells and whistles. By virtue of that particular accomplishment, he became my driver.

Somehow the guy had special clearances, or possessed some sort of super ID card. In those days I flew into Atlanta's Hartsfield International Airport from Canada two or three times a month after visits with my family. Picking me up, Tony would pull right out onto the tarmac beside the plane. No terminal hassle, no baggage claim, no security checkpoints. Fuhgeddaboudit! He'd just slap a blue bubble atop the car and we would speed through all the bullshit like I was fucking POTUS. I was approaching thirty years old, still a young punk. I thought the whole business was hilarious.

The last weekend of every month, my daughters flew into Atlanta from Canada and stayed with me for a few days. At a time when gold was going for a thousand bucks an ounce, Tony would always greet them both with small gifts of gold—necklaces, charm bracelets, earrings. That was a sure way into a little girl's heart, and Jen and Mandy loved him. One weekend in 1979, my parents came down. My dad had never been to an NHL game. Back then, the local team was called the Atlanta Flames (great ironic name in a town that was burned to the ground by Sherman!). Tony got Bernie and Lilianne ice-level seats, then took them back to the locker room afterward. They, too, fell in love with the guy.

Tony had a generous way with everyone, including me. He once presented me with a Girard-Perregaux watch. My Jay Block finishing-school lessons hadn't been completed yet, so I would've had no clue what that watch meant if I hadn't just read Ian Fleming's *From Russia with Love*, wherein a character gets killed over a Girard-Perregaux timepiece. I was pretty thrilled just with the association, but when I had the watch appraised at $17,000, I understood the true magnificence of his gift.

And, with all the gifting and driving and special favors, it's astounding that Tony had time or energy left over to handle club security, too. One day a loser wise guy showed up at the club demanding an "envelope," which was Mafia-speak for an extortion payment.

"Wait right there, will you?" Tony asked him. He jumped on the phone and launched into a blizzard of Italian. I understood not a word, but I watched the poor man's face turn pale, then take on a sick shade of green. He turned on his heel and practically ran out the door without another word.

The insane thing was that Tony wasn't doing any of this work for the paycheck. He was pretty much set in that department. "I've got my own Cadillac," he used to say, dismissing my offers of bonuses or raises. He dressed well. He wasn't a druggie and didn't traffic in the stuff, either. He didn't even drink at the club. He never shook me down for anything. He was ex-military, a covert-ops type of guy, but he wasn't doing any gunrunning on the side. Tony Pelligrino simply liked being around the action at Limelight.

That was the kind of place we created. There was hard work to be done, and late nights, but we all mostly hung around for the action, for the thrill of experiencing what we created. Atlanta Limelight felt enchanted in a way that Miami had never quite achieved.

Life was pretty swell. Adrienne and I were solid as a couple; Atlanta was consistently packed. True to form, though, after a couple of years

I felt myself becoming distracted. By the time the second or third Bare as You Dare theme night came around, I realized I was jaded. The secondary gratifications of living in Atlanta—the houses, the cars, the travel—made for a life that I had never dreamed of living. But it still wasn't good enough. My gaze strayed northward. Not back to Canada, nope, not that far. Just 746 miles north, to be exact.

The media had labeled Limelight the Studio 54 of the South. I found that infuriating. I didn't want to be the Studio 54 of anything. That particular scene was over. I wanted to create a new nightlife experience, one that every other club would be measured against, and I wanted to do it in the cultural capital of the world.

CHAPTER SIX

I'll Take Manhattan

The church, when I first walked into it in 1983, was an unholy mess. A thick layer of grime covered every surface. Leave a building abandoned for long enough, and dust and dirt take over. In the shuttered former house of worship on busy Sixth Avenue in Manhattan, each step I took was muffled by grit.

Beautiful old mahogany pews were scattered every which way in the main sanctuary. Everything was cobwebbed and silent. The plaster had come off the walls, and water damage warped the wooden floorboards. The stained-glass windows were among the only things that remained intact, and they looked out of place amid the filth, like flowers blooming in a garbage heap.

The church's interior was a maze of hallways, chambers, and stairwells. As I passed through one empty room after another, rats sprinted away into darkened corners. Since I'd arrived in New York I'd been informed, several times, that more rats than people lived in the city—a five-to-one ratio, residents said, citing the statistic with a grim sort of glee. It turned out the truth was something like four-to-one the other way, but the myth felt pretty accurate.

Dirt, vermin, and all, I thought the former Church of the Holy Communion was magnificent. The 139-year-old edifice had been built in the Gothic revival style, a holdover in Manhattan's modern Chelsea neighborhood, dominating the corner of Sixth Avenue and Twentieth Street. Abandoned by a dwindling congregation in 1975, the place had been officially deconsecrated by its Episcopal overlords, and the vestments, collection plates, and Eucharist wafers packed up and taken away. The brick-and-mortar shell eventually sold to the highest bidder, a drug-rehab organization, Odyssey House. When Odyssey moved on, the splendid old rock pile had been left empty.

For a long time, the vision of owning a New York venue had ruled my imagination. Though I might not have dared to dream that big while playing bumper pool in the Aardvark game room, somewhere deep inside, the American dreams of my youth still held sway, and those dreams zeroed in on the national epicenter of New York City. I meditated upon the possibilities of Manhattan continually, making grandiose plans in my mind, ones I wasn't bold enough to announce publicly.

By the dawn of the 1980s, I thought I was ready to take the leap. As at a high-roller poker table, it required a hefty stake to buy into a seat in the New York nightlife scene. Awash in cash from Atlanta Limelight, I had amassed more money than I ever thought I would possess. I had the buy-in I needed.

First I had to settle on a location. Nothing average, nothing run of the mill, would do. I needed a building that stood out. Something that would function in and of itself as a calling card.

I had been scouting New York quietly for as long as I'd been in America. On one 1980 visit, I remember being impressed but not blown away by Studio 54. By then, the club was well past its prime. Studio had flamed out in a tax-evasion prosecution, and then reopened under a new owner. Despite the fading reality, the freewheeling scene that had been created by Steve Rubell and Ian Schrager remained etched in people's consciousnesses. The public still viewed the club as the very definition of *fabulous*. On my undercover forays I was a spy in the house of the glitterati, visiting two or three times just to see what was what.

The place was smaller than I had expected. I knew I could create a better lighting system and a better sound system than Studio. But I had to consider how to accomplish the feat. I didn't think installing three miles of neon tubing rather than the two miles at Studio was going to cut it. The chrome-and-neon era had peaked. I couldn't push it any further, so I had to find another direction.

The Stones song "Gimme Shelter" had always been one of my favorites, with its mesmerizing "It's just a shot away/It's just a kiss away" fade-out. I was determined to take a shot of my own. For anyone with ambition, Manhattan was the Emerald City of Oz. If I can make it there, I'll make it blah blah blah. After that early scouting foray, I returned to Atlanta and bided my time. From then on, I always kept an eye on New York. Well, one eye was all I had.

I realized that a successful assault on the city's nightlife would require not only a pair of brass balls but also a certain amount of ingenuity. I had logged enough time in the business to know that clubgoers displayed a voracious hunger for novelty. I sought to cater to that hunger.

Art and architecture were emerging as new and vital elements in the early 1980s, seizing the public interest in a way they had never done before. Almost overnight, a wave of storefront galleries opened in the East Village. A lot of them were improvised, often run by artists themselves. I once had dinner in a restaurant off Tompkins Square and watched as a crew of movers came in with oversize paintings to transform the place into an art gallery right before my eyes.

Keith Haring, Jenny Holzer, Jean-Michel Basquiat, and Jeff Koons all came out of that scene. A parallel explosion was happening in photography, with young turks like Robert Mapplethorpe, Annie Leibovitz, Peter Beard, and Bruce Weber joining the established guard of Helmut Newton, Scavullo, and Avedon, pushing the limits of the art.

For my purposes, the artistic ferment indicated a renewed level of public obsession with aesthetics. Art, photography, and architecture, I realized, were like the yo-yos, peashooters, and Hula-Hoops of my childhood, trends that would flare up and blaze across the sky like meteors.

I wanted to be in on it.

"I have to be different," I had told the real-estate broker handling my search for a club venue. "Give me something that is architecturally really interesting, a large space like a church or a museum. I want high ceilings, as few columns as possible, and I want a lot of entry points and exits."

We toured the city together. The broker showed me the Beacon Theatre on the Upper West Side. I immediately concluded that the place was too big. And besides, another theater wasn't going to cut it. Anything that might feel like a knockoff of Studio 54, which was located in an old opera house, represented stale territory. I needed to make it new, make it fresh, make it different. I'd already seen how eager the press was to compare any new club to the legendary Studio.

"Find me a church," I said again, growing surer of my direction. I had to hold myself back from demanding a Disney-style castle, but that was what I wanted, some sort of edifice covered in fairy dust in the middle of New York. The broker headed downtown, rumbling along the traffic-choked West Side Highway. Heading east to Sixth Avenue, we pulled up outside an abandoned house of worship.

The former Church of the Holy Communion and the former Joseph Jean Pierre Gatien represented a match made, if not in heaven, then at least in purgatory. For one thing, the neighborhood represented the exact Manhattan sweet spot for me. If the three rules of real estate are location, location, location, Chelsea was a nightclub owner's dream.

In real estate, anything below Twenty-Third Street in Manhattan was considered downtown, the locus of the creative community that I hoped would become my customer base and constitute my workforce.

Chelsea was developing into the center of the New York queer world. From my experience in Miami and Atlanta, I understood how much I needed a queer clientele. Gay people were the straw that stirred the drink of the straight world.

Oddly enough, the church proved to have no real neighbors apart from industrial buildings and Garment Center satellite shops. By six p.m. the streets would empty out and the area would become a virtual desert. Nowadays you can't toss a rock in the neighborhood without hitting a restaurant, but back then there was nothing. Along the former Ladies' Mile shopping district on Sixth Avenue, huge mercantile buildings that were destined to become a Bed Bath & Beyond and a Barnes & Noble stood abandoned.

For the sake of simple visibility, being situated on an avenue was ideal. To get anywhere in Manhattan, the traffic has to be routed along the main north-south thoroughfares, not the smaller cross streets. Jimi Hendrix had already taught this Canadian boy what he needed to know, that all crosstown traffic does is slow you down. Sixth Avenue would give me a steady flow of eyeballs rolling past the club, and the church's conspicuous nature would make an impression.

With the former Church of the Holy Communion, I could swoop down upon an architectural prize lying empty and discarded in the middle of heartless Manhattan. Personally, I was drawn to the place both as a Disney child and as a lapsed Catholic. I had spent a lot of time in churches. Now I was buying a church of my own, using my Atlanta profits for the $1.6 million purchase price and socking in another $2.5 million for renovations to the crumbling structure.

When a church is deconsecrated, it loses its religious affiliation and becomes just another building. Churches, synagogues, tabernacles, and mosques had been turned into condos, artist studios, offices, and flea markets. I tend to think that a structure is defined by what people do in it. If they pray and worship, it's a church. If they go to twelve-step programs, it's a drug-rehab center. If they lose their minds and dance like no one's watching, then it's a nightclub.

I didn't go in for a deep analysis of my motivations behind the purchase. Because of my strict Catholic upbringing, did I have some grudge against organized religion? Was I a former altar boy acting out? If you insist, Dr. Freud. But really, things were less complicated and more straightforward than that. Churches are designed and built as places for human assembly, with lots of exits and large open spaces in their floor plans. It was as if the building had been designed with me in mind.

The logistics made sense, and opening a club in a church was a mischievous move, one that shot out sparks every which way. A disco church represented a great publicity hook. I was banking on people coming to the club just to take a look at the place. A panther beneath the dance floor wouldn't cut it—been there, done that. I was more interested in the attraction of a Holy Ghost up in the rafters.

To some, putting a disco in a deconsecrated church will always be a poke in the eye of the Almighty. The reality of deconsecration faded in the face of the appearances. It was undeniable. No matter what kind of shingle hung outside, the structure on the corner of Twentieth and Sixth telegraphed as a church. If you asked a kid to draw a picture of a place of worship, the place on Sixth is what they'd come up with.

I wasn't totally naïve about the risk—just naïve enough, and just bold enough, to go through with it.

New York City should have been an intimidating next step for me, but I was hot off of a massive success in Atlanta. Each club I opened had taught me something new, and I had built up to this, believing that I could compete in the boldface, big-town big league of the City. The numbers were in my favor. Eighteen million people lived in the imme- diate metropolitan area. There would always be enough warm bodies to fill any number of dance floors. Even more important, New York's creative community was second to none. Countless musicians, artists, and other overachievers in almost every field of human endeavor flocked to Manhattan.

But mere numbers weren't enough. Even though the customers were out there, businesses failed in the metropolitan area all the time. It's a thickly populated place, but a cruelly Darwinian one. The city has a way of brushing aside the timid and clueless. It's a crucible of great success, but also of staggering failure.

I was very well aware that as a club owner, I was in the business of show. Image was everything. I knew that most people didn't see me as a businessman but rather as a freebooting buccaneer. I had chosen to project an aura of mystery instead of extravagance. Taking that approach allowed me to play to my strengths. I was shy in front of the press. I didn't want to be out on the dance floor leading the charge. I wanted to be the ghost, present but unknowable. The small-town provincial kid from Ontario, Pierre, disappeared behind the eye-patch façade. That was a key aspect of my success. In New York, a little mystery and a unique look made you someone to pay attention to. I intended to leverage that for all it was worth.

Through late summer and early fall 1983, I started to build the buzz. We worked to repair, refurbish, and rehabilitate the premises. Since New York City had declared the exterior a landmark in 1966, I couldn't touch the outside of the building. But I would never have wanted to alter the crenellated tower that looked, for my money, like it was waiting for Rapunzel to let down her hair.

The interior, on the other hand, needed a lot of massaging. We broke through and created a passageway from the main building to the nearby rectory. There was a room with great-looking built-in wooden bookcases where the minister formerly had his library. It would serve perfectly as a VIP enclave. The church's multiple entrances and exits meant fire inspectors would allow a high occupancy rating, which I needed because I was intent on drawing crowds.

The building had been designed with a lot of intersecting spaces, including a smaller chapel as well as classrooms, halls, and offices. In the early eighties, disco wasn't dominating as it once had, and music began to evolve into different subgenres. Michael Jackson's *Thriller* was huge, but New Wave and postpunk were both having a moment. Heavy metal experienced a resurgence, hip-hop was a rising force, and house, techno, and synth-pop swirled into the mix, too. The intricate floor plan of the church allowed me to install multiple sound systems, with different areas in the club devoted to different styles of music on the same night.

The interior featured elegant ecclesiastical details, like the milled wooden beams that arched above the main sanctuary. I left intact the gorgeous stained-glass windows, which the broker assured me were created by Louis Comfort Tiffany, though we found out later they were actually crafted by his competitor, John La Farge. We also retained some of the old pews for seating and used others to construct a bar. I scrounged up a set of organ pipes, had them painted gold, and installed them behind where the altar used to be, as a backdrop to the stage and the DJ booth.

Every theatrical producer understands that putting a "Banned in Boston" censorship label on a play will bring in the crowds. When word got out that the former church was slated to become Limelight nightclub, its deconsecrated status mattered not at all. I received a three-word, worth-its-weight-in-gold review from the Right Reverend Paul Moore Jr., the Episcopal bishop of New York:

"We are horrified."

Our debut night, November 9, 1983, featured traffic jams on Sixth Avenue and lines down the block. *Interview* magazine sponsored the evening. Andy Warhol declared the opening to be "the party of the year." I was getting my first hint of Manhattan fabulosity, and it tasted sweet.

I stood at the door for the opening, surveying the tumultuous scene. Two or three protesters lingered at the edges of the crowd, with one carrying a placard that read "Don't Dance on My Religion." A performance artist in a Jesus-style loincloth approached the club, hauling around a huge wooden cross. The crowd, made up of celebs, fashionistas, and the merely curious, as well as the random black-clad Goth or pink-haired punk, became increasingly giddy.

Clearly the circus had come to town, and I had assigned myself the role of ringmaster.

Nightclubs are like marriages. Anyone can get married, and anyone can open a club. In both cases, the real trick is to keep it going beyond the honeymoon period. Most nightclubs flame out after a year. Almost by definition, they cater to a jaded clientele. A frenzied crowd of trendoids seem always to be rushing around New York City, ever in search of what's new, what's hot, what's now.

So, yeah, I'd made a big splash opening New York Limelight. I'd managed to hit during something of a lull in the City's nightlife. Studio 54 was over. No new megaclub had arisen to take its place. Smaller boutique clubs like the World, the Pyramid Club, and especially the world-class Area were great, and I admired what they were doing artistically and creatively. But their capacities were limited to a thousand people, many times even less.

Soon after New York Limelight opened, we nabbed the booking for the seventieth birthday party of *Naked Lunch* author William S. Burroughs. Madonna, then just breaking big, sat alongside the former heroin addict and perennial gun-nut birthday boy, who as a favor to us left his assault rifles at home. It was hectic, it was a trial by fire, but we pulled it off. New to New York as I was, I already understood how to do this stuff. I knew how to organize and throw a party. I had been doing it all my professional life.

From there on out, Limelight attracted a huge percentage of Manhattan's literary and social elite, making each one of them feel as though they were getting an exclusive, unique experience. I may have been the new kid in town, but by some miracle of timing I also came in as the last man standing. Many of the other major nightlife venues had closed.

Indirectly, at least, I owe a debt of gratitude to Studio 54. It had gripped the public imagination so completely, and had become such a huge, globally recognized phenomenon, that all nightclubs afterward benefited from its notoriety. The media apparatus that had gone into overdrive for Studio 54 now took a look at New York Limelight and knew exactly what to do. The tabloids descended like a flock of hungry crows. I took out token ads, mainly to support small, niche gay publications, but I got so much free publicity that mainstream advertising proved unnecessary.

From hard-won experience in Cornwall, Miami, and Atlanta, I understood that I could only be as good as the crew I gathered around me. I had to create a community of sorts, a collection of simpatico workers to help me operate my club. The atmosphere around New York Limelight was so frenzied at the beginning that hiring was like inviting people to board a runaway train. Jack-of-all-trades Brian MacGuigan came along from Atlanta Limelight, and Jay Block journeyed north to run legal interference for the opening. Tony Pelligrino chose to stay behind in Georgia, a decision that sucked a bit of magic from my life.

I sold my interest in the Atlanta club to my brother Moe. From its early days as a roman candle streaking across the Georgia sky, the club eventually fizzled down into a wet firecracker. I was almost, but not quite, too busy to notice.

I did learn that nepotism has its limits. I had my four blood brothers, and then I had my other family of brothers and sisters, the creative community who helped make my clubs a success. In society, no matter where you are, out-of-step souls exist who are simply not built for office work. They echo Melville's Bartleby the scrivener: "I would prefer not to." Call it personality, background, or an imbalance of brain salts, a large sector of the populace can't cope with regular nine-to-fives. These were my people. And New York had them in droves.

I developed a great deal of fondness for the quirky, streetwise lineup of hipsters, artists, hustlers, strivers, and stoners that I employed, representatives of all races, creeds, sexual orientations, and upbringings. More than a few of them were graduates from the school of hard knocks. For the most part, staffers in my New York club, just as in Atlanta and Miami, possessed only short-term career goals. Limelight was a transient gig, a stepping stone to whatever bright futures they imagined.

One employee became a celebrated fixture: Fred Rothbell-Mista, the memorable host of the VIP Room. Fred had a magical touch with bringing people together. The evening might start out with rockers in one corner of the VIP inner sanctum, art gallery sophisticates in another, fashionistas next to them, and by the end of the night everyone was socializing, talking to each other. The ultimate schmoozer, Fred had a flamboyant energy that kept New York Limelight's VIP room popular for over a decade. In the midst of the AIDS crisis, he made the club-within-a-club into a second home for the embattled denizens of the downtown scene. What was once the library of the church's minister became their refuge.

Because we were such a motley crew, I was forced to devote a lot of time to settling disputes from the clash of strong personalities in my employ: tiffs and friction between promoters and door personnel, bartenders and busboys, security people and everyone else. It was by no means a gathering of saints. But we managed to make a community of it, a family that was, like a lot of families, somewhat dysfunctional. I would gaze out at members of my workforce and muse about their long-term life prospects. Talented as these people might've been in their own rights, I didn't think there were many other businesses where they stood to thrive the way they did with me.

And how odd were the people who worked for me, really, or how motley? Spend enough time with anyone and the tattoos, piercings, drag, and outrageous hairstyles fade into insignificance. Conversely, spend time in the straight world and the people there begin to seem deeply weird. Rudy Giuliani once hired a straight-arrow police chief, Bernard Kerik, who wound up a convicted felon. Through the right lens, there's a lot of motley out there in the mainstream. In court I once heard a US prosecutor declare club-goers "disgusting" because of their "freakish" appearances. My attorney replied quickly and accurately that my people were not disgusting, merely different.

It's only the ignorant who consider the nightlife underbelly to be populated with degenerates, freaks, and losers. The thing straitlaced critics fail to understand is that those "freaks" are exactly the kind of people who make New York City the blazing cultural capital that it is. I've seen what the daylight world has to offer by way of human character, via my history of collisions with the political and judicial realms. From that perspective, I can testify with utter certainty that, as a class and by a long shot, the people who worked in my clubs were more decent and honorable than half the politicians I've encountered.

Mixing a gay crowd with a straight crowd made for the best dynamic out on the dance floor, so we never balked at hiring an openly gay crew. In the summer of 1984, when New York Limelight was just hitting its stride a half year after it opened, Stonewall was only fifteen years in the past. Mixed crowds of queer and straight remained a novelty to many. Nightlife has always been a realm of social experimentation, where taboos are trampled and segregated groups become integrated. The logic held that part of the reason people take the trouble to leave their homes for the nightlife is to see what kinds of other people have done the same. People-watching was what made the straight-gay interchange so powerful. Straights watched the gays, who watched the straights watching them. Both elements acted out a bit more, flew their flair flags a little higher, and displayed their moves to better effect. The result was a live-wire energy.

Atlanta had proved the importance of attracting a queer clientele in many different ways, one of which was the proliferation of Sunday-afternoon tea dances, which had evolved out of the Fire Island gay community in the late 1960s. Unbelievable as it might seem today, in the sixties there were still laws on the books preventing serving alcohol to homosexuals, and against same-sex couples dancing. Serving tea instead of beer skirted the first issue, and the newly common practice of dancing apart got around the other. At Atlanta Limelight I was astonished to see tea dances draw huge crowds of two or three thousand people. The packed dance floors at three o'clock on a Sunday afternoon stuck with me.

More than the patronage, the queer subculture's vibe was one that I intrinsically tapped into. Energy, exuberance, insouciance. A brazen "I'm still here" attitude that pushed back at all the small-minded bigots out there. Above all, happiness. It was a feeling of being released from constraints. Although my parents, aunts, and uncles might not have appreciated the comparison, for me, the joyful letting go on the dance floor struck the same note as those Cornwall holiday parties.

Two years and four months before I opened New York Limelight, on July 3, 1981, the *New York Times* ran a small article buried on page twenty. Not a lot of people noticed it. I surely didn't, caught up as I was in running the Atlanta club. "Rare Cancer Seen in 41 Homosexuals," read the tiny, single-column headline. It was the first hint in the mainstream press that something very bad was happening in the queer community.

The rare cancer was Kaposi's Sarcoma, an opportunistic disease that took advantage of human immune systems weakened by HIV. Soon Kaposi's became not so rare and all too common. In the middle of the 1980s, while I was busily trying to build my club in New York, the plague hit the city with the force of a tsunami. Death cut down whole swaths of nightlife culture and sought out many of the people who worked for me.

The night would never be the same again.

CHAPTER SEVEN

New York, London, and Chicago

In the ominous year of 1984, at the height of Reaganism and after years as a common-law couple, Adrienne Norman and I married. My young daughters adored her. Jen and Mandy were living in Cornwall with their mother, Sheila, attending the same kind of schools I had gone to three decades previous.

I didn't have anything against Cornwall, but I felt a burning need to provide them with the kind of education they could receive in Manhattan, both in school and out. A bunch of doors would be open for them in New York City, so I pushed hard for them to make the transfer. I never wanted my kids to feel like I had growing up, shy and provincial and ill prepared for the journey of life.

I arranged the move with Sheila and set up a home in New York City that had ample room for the girls. Adrienne became pregnant and we had a child of our own, my third daughter, Hunter. Adrienne was superb at creating a warm home life and getting the trains to run on time, so to speak—clothing, feeding, and loving the children while making it all look effortless. But while I was trying to pull together the varied strands of my domestic life, New York Limelight had me spending fewer and fewer hours at home.

Working hard and banking enormous paychecks, I maintained the common breadwinner's fallacy of believing that making money was all there was to being a husband and father. After all, everything I did, I was doing for my family. I didn't understand why I should be home for evening dinners, birthdays, or putting the kids to sleep with bedtime stories. As far as I was concerned, a great provider made for a great dad. Period.

Because I was so totally focused on business, I had become something of an emotional loner. Adrienne and I loved each other, Sheila remained cordial, and I had three beautiful, rambunctious daughters. But I didn't spend enough quality time with them. Many nights, I came home to sleep and that was all. My children suffered, though I rationalized that they hadn't even noticed their dad's absences. I saw myself as a ringmaster, coming home from the circus. It wasn't easy to slip back into the realm of school activities, sibling rivalry, and domestic togetherness.

Even at work, shyness and arrogance proved to be two sides of the same coin, and I used my natural standoffishness as a defense against the countless people who wanted a piece of me. I like to think I'm openhearted, but more and more during this period, favor seekers began to approach me with fear in their eyes. I prided myself on being a self-made man, needing no one. I told my door people that whoever tried to drop my name to gain entry was almost certainly lying.

"If they come to you saying they're a friend of mine, just tell them that I don't have any friends." A group that virtually acted as our house band, Fun Lovin' Criminals, used to boast they had "more friends than Peter Gatien," but they were being sarcastic, since every other person bellying up to the bar in my clubs proclaimed themselves blood brothers to me.

I never once took on partners. A nightclub owner without partners is practically unheard of, tantamount to being a solo trapeze artist. Other nightlife entrepreneurs—Eric Goode, formerly of Area, for example, or Ian Schrager of Studio 54, among others—were always

shocked at my lack of associates. In such turbulent skies, they believed
that flying without a copilot was difficult and, at times, dangerous.

They did it their way and I did it mine.

Given its history and reputation, the world of Manhattan nightlife
could conceivably have sent crews of wise guys to muscle in on my
business. Organized crime had long been a presence in the city's late-
night scene. Vito Genovese, among other mob bosses, used to control
a vast percentage of nightclubs throughout the city. At an early meeting
with a real-estate broker for Limelight, I brashly stated an imperative:
"If I'm going to have any issues with the mob, you guys should tell me
right now."

"I'll tell you what you do," the real-estate agent spoke up. "Get this
guy Angelo Ponte's firm as your commercial sanitation service, and I
guarantee that you won't have any problems."

"Angelo Ponte?" That was the name of the gent from New York
who had bought my Hallandale townhouse in Florida when I moved
out—but I didn't believe it could be the same person. There had to be
a million guys with that name.

Turned out it was indeed the same Ponte. He remembered me,
and I hired his trash-hauling business right away. If I'd known who he
was when I was haggling with him over furnishings in the townhouse,
I would have offered him a better deal. In fact, I might have given him
the couches, curtains, and chairs outright. But in all the years I worked
with Ponte, his people couldn't have been nicer—never overcharging,
never strong-arming, never abusing the relationship. When the Pontes
came to my club, they stood on line, paid for entry like everyone else,
and never asked for special favors.

I tried to stay out of the figurative limelight, but the spectacular
success of the real Limelight came with a higher public profile than I'd
ever had before. Not all the press was favorable. My notices sounded
a now-familiar theme, describing me as a remote, unknowable figure.
"Isn't the life of the party but knows how to throw one," said the *New*

York Times. "Gatien remained largely out of sight," *New York* magazine reported, "a provincial money man who didn't make the scene but made his fortune on it." "A bit of a cold fish," sniffed the *Village Voice*. I was "stony-faced," stated freelancer Frank Owen, and "taciturn and awkward," "old school," "ungiving," according to others.

I had opened the biggest club in the greatest city in the world. I'd begun to think of myself as a real New Yorker, as belonging to and being in the middle of the cultural mix. But I didn't like glad-handing, showboating, or grandstanding. I kept my head down and my nose to the grindstone. The press inflated the mystery and painted me as a slightly sinister character. The image played well in the gossip pages.

I didn't recognize my picture in the media, but the figure portrayed there would grow more real as time went on, a doppelganger that the press created and then recycled over and over again. I considered it pointless to attempt correcting it. Image became reality.

Instead of battling the big-city press, I decided to invade Russia, so to speak, by embracing my Napoleonic empire-building ambitions. I wanted to capitalize on the New York club's success by opening Limelight outposts in other cities. The AIDS plague was kicking the stuffing out of New York City. The mid-1980s was a time of incredible fear and uncertainty about the disease. No one was sure whether AIDS could be communicated by a kiss, by drinking from the same glass, or even by shaking hands. New York had become a sad and ruptured place.

The memory of that period still chills me. The whole population was devastated, but the club-going population in the city turned especially frantic and terrified. New York and San Francisco represented twin ground zeros for the epidemic. Some Grim Reaper stalked the streets with his scythe, cutting down the young and careless. The ranks of people in the arts were decimated, including actors, writers, dancers, and musicians. These were my people, and I was losing numberless colleagues.

A massive lid of grief and fear had slammed down on the nightlife, snuffing out much of the energy and exuberance. It's difficult to have a good time when you're living in fear. Limelight might have been doing the same numbers in 1986, '87, and '88 as when it opened in 1983, but the mood had changed. There was pretty much zero gay presence, and without it, the scene missed an essential element, like a glass of champagne gone warm and flat.

I had already spent a few years looking for a place to land in Chicago, but the search had so far proved fruitless. I toured the downtown neighborhoods and trendy Lincoln Park, but nothing seemed quite right. I knew the town's population could support a megaclub, and there was nothing—no existing nightlife quite like what I had in mind—in the whole metropolitan area.

With notoriety from the buzz surrounding New York Limelight, I revived the effort to find a home in Chicago. On my visits, I started to notice a somewhat surly attitude on the part of the residents. As a middle child I understood the feeling of being overlooked and overshadowed. I wasn't the first to detect a chip on the City of the Big Shoulders. Chicagoans accepted the "Second City" label, as if acknowledging the town's status as an also-ran. When I visited, I saw posters with "NYC" printed in a circle with a slash through it. It reminded me of the funny title of a country-western song, "Too Dumb for New York City, Too Ugly for LA."

I've always liked Chicago. The Upper Midwest feels almost Canadian, and, for better or worse, the place felt like home, a working-class town, the younger, rough-edged sibling of New York City. Plus I knew that, despite its boring insistence on being ordinary, Chicago was one of the most cheerfully corrupt places on earth. Any place with a guy like Al Capone in its history had to have an interesting dark side. I doubled down on the search, renting an apartment in one of Capone's speakeasies so I'd have a place to stay on my extended visits.

At the time, nightlife in Chicago meant taverns, biker bars, and small music clubs. Underneath the crusty "fuck New York" attitude, I knew there was a hunger for excitement, a longing for a triumphant return to the days when the city was known for its Jazz Age glitter. The creative community had their faces pressed up against the shop window, looking on as people went wild in other cities, other venues. As far as I could tell there was not a single Chicago nightclub that charged a cover for entry. People in this city were going out to drink, not to dance.

My job, as I saw it, was to wake the sleeping giant.

I found the ideal shrieking alarm clock on the northern outskirts of downtown, in the River North neighborhood. The former Chicago Historical Society Building suited my purposes perfectly, a rock pile to outdo all other rock piles. The stone edifice had been built in 1892, at the height of the Gilded Age, just prior to the opening of the world's fair featured in the book *The Devil in the White City*. I thought it would be outlandish to situate a nightclub in a grandiose historic building such as that, an irreverent flair akin to opening in a deconsecrated church in New York. I knew the nose-thumbing, in-your-face quality of the move would serve as a great publicity hook.

The enormous building featured a forty-thousand-square-foot interior, which was plenty of room to indulge my wildest ideas. As with New York Limelight, the Historical Society Building had been originally designed for public assembly, so I wouldn't have trouble with zoning or fire regulations. *Playboy* magazine had once planned to use the place as a venue for one of its clubs, but the deal had fallen through. Even though the long-abandoned interior of the building proved musty, dusty, and crusty, it was structurally sound and nowhere the wreck that the former Church of the Holy Communion had been.

As soon as I walked into the place, I began to visualize how to make a great nightclub out of it. It cost me $3.5 million to buy the place and realize that vision. Just like New York, Chicago has a great creative community, and I hired local on top of bringing in veteran staffers I knew and trusted. After months of renovation and fine-tuning, I felt the anticipation rising in the town's club-going population. The night we opened, the last day of July, 1985, three thousand people stood in line. The publicity splash from New York Limelight had washed up on Lake Michigan's far shores. Three thousand!

Chicago Limelight gave the city a shot of the exotic. The entrance led to a grand stairway and a corridor lined with immense glass cases—used in the past, I imagined, to display historical artifacts such as Abraham Lincoln's stovepipe hat. We put performers in those glass cases: a Goth girl, a leather boy, body-painted models, elaborately costumed members of the "Family Plan" theater group. Essentially the entry hall served as a kind of human zoo, featuring anything my team and I could dream up, and the displays were constantly changed and refreshed, just like K. P.'s art installations in Atlanta. Patrons had to brave the gauntlet of these strange, alluring figures before they could even get into the club proper.

In the Dome Room, a cavernous central space, we installed a rotating selection of art and photography displays. There was also a Cube Room, measuring a perfect forty-by-forty-by-forty, where murals were replaced every three months by guest luminaries like Mark Kostabi. The vibe was eclectic and sophisticated. Chicago ate it up. Scenes of raucous decadence played out against the club's artsy backdrop. Club-goers in Chicago seemed to act out with a sense of grim determination, as opposed to the confident, cool-blooded voguing that was going on in New York.

Andy Warhol made it to Chicago for our opening, which lent the new Limelight the stamp of approval from the start. The local scenesters were impressed. Andy showed up in his signature antifashion outfit, straight out of the L. L. Bean catalog, as well as eyeglasses with pale translucent frames and what had to be the most frightening fright wig in his whole collection. He appeared to be a visitor from another planet.

"Oh, I like Chicago," he murmured, a mild-mannered statement on the whole affair. He always reminded me of Peter Sellers as Chauncey Gardiner in the movie *Being There*, whose banal, idiot-savant pronouncements such as "I like to watch" were interpreted as samples of deep wisdom.

If anyone would have asked me during this frenetic expansion push, I would have claimed that I was just a simple family man. That's how I saw myself. Yes, I might have spent less time with my three daughters than I had previously, and I mostly left Adrienne behind in New York while I worked furiously to make the new club a success, but, hey, I was busy. I still marked each kid's birthday with a trip to Disney World, still supported their educations with entry into the best schools in Manhattan, and remained on fairly good terms with my ex, Jen and Mandy's mother.

Hot off the opening, Chicago Limelight was going strong, drawing crowds of thousands per night. The performance art, dancing, atmosphere, and opportunity for release were enough to keep the club full and consistent. Things got an even more fiery boost that fall, when Tina Turner presided over a massive party that brought out the town's royalty. A local TV reporter, Oprah Winfrey, covered the action. Chicago Limelight started to become a recognized stopover for visiting celebrities, and we hosted people like Frank Zappa, Duran Duran, Kevin Bacon, local porn queen Seka, and the band Chicago.

The mirror doesn't lie, but the person looking into it might. A family man? Who was I kidding? In reality, my home life was slipping away from me. I wasn't starstruck, exactly, and didn't really give a damn about celebrities, but I was seduced by the undeniable exhilaration of putting together another smash success. Seeing that line in front of one of my clubs was like a drug, and I had become addicted to it.

"What shall it profit a man," the Book of Matthew asks, "if he shall gain the whole world, and lose his own soul?" To that famous biblical question, I might have provided a nonbiblical response. Looking around at the life I had built, I felt that, after all, at least such a man has the whole world.

Chicago might have been my new baby, but New York Limelight remained my true love. After a week in the Midwest, I slipped back into Manhattan as into a warm bath. Sixth Avenue was my street, and the former church on the corner of Twentieth and Sixth was the house that Peter built. And my family was in the city—both families, in fact: Adrienne and the girls, and Brian MacGuigan and the motley crew at Limelight. New York City was the place where I didn't have to choose between them.

Of course I had to go and upset the applecart. I spent a year running the New York and Chicago Limelights before ambition once again took hold of me. I couldn't help myself. I wanted more, wanted to outdo myself. The next frontier, I reasoned, was to expand internationally. I decided I would open a Limelight in London. Manhattan was home, but I had seen too many of my friends fall to AIDS, and nightlife in the city had a death-haunted feeling to it.

Developing a rotating schedule for myself, I spent a week in Chicago making sure the club was running smoothly, a week in London scouting locations, and two weeks in New York with my family, while alternately overseeing the club. It was a punishing itinerary, representing a measure of my ambition but also the streak of congenital restlessness that ran through my soul.

I didn't really have a great sense of how to be an engaged father. I'd fly into New York believing I was playing the part of Successful Dad perfectly, just by putting in an appearance. Then I'd jet off again to monitor my other ventures, returning home on the rebound exhausted and spent, barely able to marvel at the upscale lifestyle I provided for my family. Adrienne ran the household with an almost unlimited budget.

The kids attended elite Manhattan schools. Around this time Madonna was assuring everyone that we were living in a material world, and in that sense, my daughters thrived as material girls.

I told myself that the Gatien residence in New York was at least different from the one I'd grown up in, with my father figure who came home every night and sat silently, present but miles away. I myself was often literally miles away, and where was the harm? To me, that was just the job description: make the money, give the most of your time and the best of your creativity to your career, and while at home, stay pretty much out of the way so your wife can handle things on the domestic front. The logic wasn't sound, but it was deeply ingrained in my personality.

I acted as though I were on a mission. Blow up NYC. Demolish Chicago. Conquer the UK. I was too consumed to ask myself what could possibly be enough. What would finally satisfy me? Moon Base Limelight in the Sea of Tranquility?

It turned out that in London, as in New York City, fairy-tale castles weren't that hard to find, provided you had the right real-estate agent— or "estate agent," as they called them over there. Soon enough my search for a venue zeroed in on a former church in the heart of Covent Garden, on the far eastern edges of London's West End. I hoped history would repeat itself and what had worked so well in New York would work in London, too.

For the first century or so, the 1888 Welsh Chapel had served as a haven for the kind of stuffy English snobs that I'd known in my youth. All too happy to tweak the nose of the British Establishment, I took the building over, purchasing it outright, shelling out a million pounds during a period in the market when the pound and the dollar were trading virtually even.

On August 2, 1986, London Limelight opened its doors. Yes, indeed, I had gotten the opening-night dance down, step by step: identify an enchanted palace; find talented artists to create an alluring, surprising environment; make sure Andy Warhol is on hand to give his blessing; and voilà!—lines of eager patrons that snaked around the block. Jodie Foster and Rod Stewart showed up for our debut bash, along with members of the bands Wham! and Spandau Ballet. Boy George practically moved in. Rocker Bob Geldof's bachelor party, thrown just a few weeks after we opened, really cemented the club's reputation. Geldof was hotter than a pistol from mounting the Band Aid benefit and the Live Aid concert. It seemed that all of London showed up to fête the soon-to-be-groom.

Now I had three Limelights in operation, with the Chicago franchise six time zones away from the London one. Though it wasn't quite the case of the sun never setting on my empire, I found it comforting that at any given time of the day, someone, somewhere, was likely dancing in one of my clubs.

But alongside that thought was the frustration of not really knowing what was happening in venues where I didn't have an actual day-to-day presence. I could visit the Limelights in Chicago or London, get the entry numbers, and check the bar receipts, but that didn't give me a total picture. What was the mood on the dance floor? Were people having a good time? Were they staying until the end of the night or just dropping in and moving on?

I once was told that Nathan Handwerker, founder of the iconic Coney Island hot dog stand, used to visit his place at odd hours wearing a disguise, just so he could see what staffers were up to when he wasn't around. I've heard of other bosses who employ similar strategies. All business owners, and especially those of us in the hospitality industry, are control freaks—or they should be if they want their ventures to flourish. A boss needs to project an all-seeing, all-knowing aura, almost to the point of becoming Orwell's Big Brother.

Delegating authority is a sound and very necessary management practice. None of my clubs would have existed at all if I had to run them solo. But nothing beats daily, nightly, hands-on involvement. I saw my function as the ghost in the machine. Staffers had to know that at any moment I might suddenly magically appear, in a poof of black smoke and a clatter of cloven hooves. Well, in Chicago and London, the control freak in me freaked out. I could never be sure if the clubs were being run right or if the staff were merely putting on a show whenever I came by.

As I said, New York City felt more and more like home to me. In the mid-'80s, nightlife—life itself, really—had darkened and flattened out because of the AIDS crisis. Only a few years later, at the dawn of the '90s, the panic had lessened somewhat. By then everyone knew that no one contracted HIV from casual social interactions at nightclubs, and that the disease was commuted through behaviors like sharing needles or having unprotected sex.

At New York Limelight, I could feel the pulse of nightlife begin to quicken again. The former mix of queer and straight started to return in full force. It was as if the ship had been hit by a giant tsunami, almost got swamped, but now held a steady course.

My ambition didn't begin and end with the nightlife, and owning clubs often sent me on random trajectories that I never would have embarked upon otherwise. My first foray into theater and film production, for example, happened because of Limelight, almost by mistake. Chazz Palminteri worked security at the New York club for five years in the mid-'80s. I liked the guy a lot. He was smart, fast talking, and good looking, an ultimate tough urban kid who at times served as my personal trainer. We got to know each other pretty well. He could be lethally funny and was always a great storyteller, especially with tales of his upbringing in the Belmont neighborhood of the Bronx.

As with a healthy percentage of other employees on Limelight's payroll, Chazz had another life as a starving actor. Because he worked

My mother's extended family in 1945. My mother, Lilianne Henri, is second from left in the back row.

My jubilant, warmhearted grandmother Francine Sanguin Henri, one of my favorite people in the world.

My parents, Bernard and Lilianne Gatien, on their honeymoon in New York, March 1945.

The Gatien family on a camping trip to Meacham Lake in the Adirondack Park, New York, where we almost froze to death.

Here I am as a budding entrepreneur at the Pant Loft in 1971, with a couple of my first employees.

The timeless Grace Jones rocks Miami Limelight, 1978. (Photo © Tina Paul, 1978)

Miles of chrome and neon in the late '70s at Atlanta Limelight. (Photo © Guy D'Alema)

Auditioning a cougar in my office at Atlanta Limelight for the opening night role the infamous panther would ultimately earn.

Andy Warhol cohosts the opening night party at Atlanta Limelight. His seal of approval would be invaluable. (Photo © Guy D'Alema)

Queer evangelical Reverend Russ McGraw dancing with anti-gay-rights activist Anita Bryant at Atlanta Limelight, June 1982. The shot seen around the world. (Photo © Guy D'Alema)

Billy Idol, Perri Lister, and guest, with house photographer "Miss Chickie," in New York Limelight's VIP room, 1987. (Ron Galella, Ltd./Ron Galella Collection via Getty Images)

Madonna in the chapel at New York Limelight for the Amadeus *premiere after-party, September 12, 1984. (Patrick McMullan/ Getty Images)*

Mick Jagger and Jerry Hall at Nile Rodgers's birthday party, September 19, 1984, New York Limelight. (Ron Galella, Ltd./Ron Galella Collection via Getty Images)

Jack Nicholson and Anjelica Huston inside the chapel at New York Limelight. (Patrick McMullan/Getty Images)

Nightlife queen Dianne Brill and Sting enjoying William Burroughs's birthday party at New York Limelight. (Patrick McMullan/Getty Images)

Superstar artist David Hockney and a Speedo-clad swimmer at New York Limelight for the book party celebrating his new monograph. (Patrick McMullan/Getty Images)

Tina Turner letting loose at the Limelight after two nights of concerts in Chicago, 1985. (Fred Jewell/AP/Shutterstock)

Rap royalty Snoop Dogg at Tunnel, 1994. (Photo © Steve Eichner)

Big Candy and Mona, two of the women from our incredible security teams, at Tunnel.

A regular night at Tunnel, with the growing crowd awaiting entry on Twenty-Seventh Street, 1993. (Photo © Steve Eichner)

Selection of club flyers by Gregory Homs—one of the most talented designers who helped create the buzz for our nightly parties. (Courtesy Gregory Homs)

(Courtesy Gregory Homs)

(Courtesy Gregory Homs)

A Palladium club-goer uses the pay phone in the room designed by artist Kenny Scharf, 1985. (LGI Stock/ Corbis/VCG via Getty Images)

Father and daughter. I'm standing with Jen Gatien at the opening-night party for Club USA, 1992. (Photo © Tina Paul, 1992)

PETER GATIEN
& THIERRY MUGLER
INVITE YOU TO THE GRAND OPENING OF
USA
218 WEST 47TH STREET AT BROADWAY
THURSDAY 17 DECEMBER 11PM
ENTRANCE BY INVITATION ONLY
212/979-0292

The invitation to the grand opening of Club USA, presented with Thierry Mugler. (Courtesy Gregory Homs)

N ‖‖‖‖ 218W47 ‖‖‖ 8696103 ‖ Y

(Courtesy Gregory Homs)

The legendary Tupac Shakur at Club USA, 1994. (Photo © Steve Eichner)

Main dance floor with mezzanine slide at Club USA, 1992. (Photo © Tina Paul, 1992)

Left: Club flyer by Gregory Homs. (Courtesy Gregory Homs) Below: Club patrons in our "Ball Room" at Tunnel, 1994. (Photo © Steve Eichner)

An early adaptation of a foam party—a feature that got a lot of play in the '90s—New York Limelight, 1995. (Photo © Steve Eichner)

Balloons and money drop at Club USA. I'll always remember New York like this—one big, thrilling, raucous celebration. What an amazing ride. (Photo © Steve Eichner)

for me and got paid well, he never actually went without food, but he was an actor who auditioned constantly and couldn't seem to catch a break. Following the path of many misguided souls before him, Chazz decided it would be easier to starve for roles in sunny California than in snowy New York.

"Wish me luck, Peter," he said one afternoon in the late 1980s. "I'm moving to LA. I've got the names of a few agents and I'm going to give it my best shot."

Chazz had once been fired as a doorman at a nightclub for failing to recognize the uber-agent Swifty Lazar when he showed up for entry. That incident didn't engender a lot of optimism. I refrained from pointing out the odds against making it in Hollywood. We gave Chazz a raucous bon-voyage party at Limelight. I got news of him every once in a while, most of it secondhand and not a lot of it good.

"The guy's out there living on tuna fish and peanut butter," Barry Rhoerson, an assistant manager and one of Chazz's friends, reported. "We've got to get him back here! Tell him we still have a job for him!"

"He's a big boy," I said, trying to stay out of it. Chazz had this little dramatic piece, an autobiographical one-man show he had been developing forever, which he called *The Bronx Play*. He was always talking about it, and he wanted to get it produced in LA.

Chazz called one day with a proposition. "Peter, I know you've always wanted to produce theater."

I had to think. Had I really always wanted to produce theater? Did I ever mention that to Chazz? I didn't think so, but I let it pass.

"I've got this great play," he went on. "You know Dan Lauria, the guy from *The Wonder Years*?"

I didn't know Lauria or, for that matter, the TV show *The Wonder Years*. I figured that information wouldn't stop Chazz, so I remained noncommittal.

"Dan Lauria will go halves on producing my play, and I figured you for the other half. Can you send me six thousand dollars?"

I hemmed and hawed a little but eventually said I would back the play. As I said, I liked the guy, and six thousand was not a huge amount for me at the time. I figured Chazz needed the help. I certainly didn't expect a return.

Two weeks later, I got another call. "The play's really terrific, and we want to keep it up and running," Chazz told me. "Can you send me another six thousand?"

In for a penny, in for a pound, I figured. Two weeks passed, another call, another six. This went on five times in total, until I had $30,000 invested in a play I had never seen.

"You should go out there," Barry Rhoerson told me. He had gone to LA and seen a performance of the retitled *A Bronx Tale*. "It's actually pretty good."

Amid my constant trips to London and Chicago, I managed to fit in a flight to the West Coast. I was a little surprised to discover that what Chazz had worked up was, in fact, really very good. I agreed to produce the play off Broadway back in New York. When Robert De Niro saw that production, he loved the play enough to secure an option for a film version. With De Niro on board as star and director, Universal offered to back the movie, and I received a screen credit as executive producer. It was a massive, wholly unexpected thrill.

In the process of realizing a dream only Chazz knew I'd had, I gained entry into the moviemaking business in Hollywood, an industry that was, at the time, riding a crest of sexiness and prestige. I took meetings with the heads of five major Hollywood studios. But as the late, great screenwriter William Goldman said about Hollywood (and which may very well apply to the world as a whole), "Nobody knows anything." That seemed to hold true at the studios. If anyone knew a surefire way to identify a blockbuster, all anyone would make would be blockbusters, one after another.

A Bronx Tale, when it finally made it to the screen, was a hit that kept on giving. I did all right with it. We got a million and a half dollars up front from Universal, out of which I recouped my investment in the play, by that time totaling $400,000. Chazz took $200,000 of the Universal money as an acting fee, and we split the rest. Without my participation, the property went on to see success in legit theater and, more recently, as a Broadway musical.

All told, I must have taken in three or four hundred thousand in pure profit from *A Bronx Tale*. This should serve as a lesson to one and all: if anyone approaches you asking for money to invest in a play . . . run the other way, because stories like *A Bronx Tale* are one in a million. For me, the whole enterprise represented only a side hustle to my real gig of seeking out the next venue, the next splash, the next big thing.

CHAPTER EIGHT

King of Clubs

By the early 1990s, I felt myself caught once again in the familiar position of being both successful and restless at the same time. New York Limelight had become an iconic symbol of the whole era, with a worldwide reputation for sexual energy and flamboyant outrageousness.

But at times I felt as faded as Bilbo after too much of the ring. I missed out on the day-to-day experiences of my family. I had long realized that my personal relationships were in trouble. There was no way I could just blow in for two weeks a month and not represent simply an interruption of the normal routine. Settling down and repairing the damage was always something I intended to do eventually, but the right time never seemed to come around.

So I decided to draw in my claws, so to speak, concentrate all my energies in one city, if not on a single club. I wanted to have a home base. To be honest, I wasn't sure I really knew how to exist anymore in just one place, not to be always lusting after a new horizon. But New York was the place I loved, and even though I had never really left, I wanted to come back.

I sold the London Limelight. The million pounds I'd bought it for just a few years earlier turned into three million because of the escalating value of London real estate, and the exchange rate favored me, so my profit ballooned even more. In place of operating a far-flung, multi-time-zone empire, I sank those profits into creating additional venues in Manhattan, where I could spend more time with my kids and at the same time be able to keep a closer watch on day-to-day club operations.

Part of the decision was based in economics. In those days, to ask people to work in Manhattan for anything less than a thousand dollars a week didn't make financial sense. In one of the most expensive urban areas in the world, my staff had to earn rent money and be able to show up looking sharp. They needed to make their nut; they needed a thousand-dollar base income every week, and in turn that meant I needed the kind of cash flow that could keep everyone afloat.

In the eyes of the outside world, New York Limelight was the wonder of the nightclub world, an Energizer Bunny that just kept going and going even in the darkest days of the AIDS epidemic. I could have closed all the other Limelights, stood behind that single club, and still retained my standing among the most successful nightlife entrepreneurs in the world. But as usual, I was restless.

In the dim pre-internet past, the wooden-faced showbiz impresario Ed Sullivan had one of the most popular television shows on the planet, a Sunday-night variety program that featured singers, comics, dancers—and novelty acts. Among the performers there were often plate spinners, usually from Uzbekistan or some other place where circus acts are born. Their routine consisted of balancing a collection of swirling dinner plates atop a series of long poles. The pace was mad and manic, since the spinners had to keep every plate going even as they moved on to start others. Check YouTube, children, to see this ancient form of entertainment, still as wack, corny, and diverting as it was a half century ago.

The early 1990s were my plate-spinning years, my crazed, exciting, impossibly lucrative years. Money rained down. I bit off more than I could chew, then choked it all down anyway. I sold not only the London but the Chicago Limelight, too, at a profit, aiming to focus all my energies on New York City. But I never slowed down—in fact, I pushed the pedal down all the harder.

My clubs weren't just clubs, they were megaclubs. In the space of nine fast-and-furious months in 1992, I opened Club USA in Times Square, took over the lease of the fading Palladium on Fourteenth Street, and revived Tunnel on the West Side. All the while, Limelight in Chelsea was still packing them in.

In all, the four clubs represented over a quarter million square feet of prime Manhattan real estate—251,000 square feet, to be exact. Their official capacities totaled 18,000 party-till-you-drop club-goers, though because of exits and entries and crowd turnover, we often went well beyond the rated capacity. For example, Palladium was rated for a 6,500-person occupancy, but we once did 9,200 entries on a single night, a record for my career as a club owner.

We crunched the numbers once, years ago, and estimated that twenty million people have passed through the doors of my clubs at one time or another. To analyze that figure another way, a full one-quarter of the New York–New Jersey–Connecticut tristate population in the twenty-one-to-forty age demographic had been patrons of mine at least once.

My clubs might not have been Sunday schools, but they weren't drug dens, either. They mirrored their home turf: fathomless, fabulous, and flawed New York City. There never was a time, and there probably never will be again, when a single person controlled such a large percentage of New York nightlife.

Of the three new acquisitions, Palladium came to me first, in spring 1992. The place had opened with a huge media splash on May 14, 1985. Studio 54's Ian Schrager and Steve Rubell took over the old Academy of Music, located on a stretch of Fourteenth Street that enjoyed a celebrated nightlife history. During the Gilded Age, there were so many entertainment venues jammed into the neighborhood that it was referred to as "the Rialto."

Rubell and Schrager hired Japanese architect Arata Isozaki, who transformed the building into an art-and-architecture fairyland. Keith Haring did an enormous mural that loomed over the dance floor, Kenny Scharf decorated a phone booth and a bathroom, Jean-Michel Basquiat contributed a piece for the VIP room, and Francesco Clemente painted ceiling frescoes.

Seven years after the opening, the art remained in place but much of the glory had faded away. Riding a lambada craze gripping the nation, Palladium had turned into something of a salsa club. Rubell and Schrager moved on. Rubell had been diagnosed with AIDS, the disease that would kill him. He and Ian Schrager opened the Morgans, the first of their boutique hotels that revolutionized the business. The original club twins exited the nightlife scene.

I took over Palladium, with the place's then-current leaseholders giving me a sweetheart deal. I was obligated to pay the venue's rent only for the first month and the thirteenth month, about $100,000 in total, an amount that was more than canceled out by the $10 million sound systems and lighting arrays I inherited, not to mention the art. In essence, I paid zero key money and tripled the nightclub square footage I controlled.

Walking through the club on an inspection tour prior to signing the contract, I could feel the specter of the glory days still haunting the premises. Some of the features that seemed revolutionary in 1985 appeared campy and outdated, like the gigantic bank of TV monitors that overlooked the dance floor. But the sprawling place still offered superb possibilities, and it was especially great as a venue for live music. After refurbishing, we were able to attract Prince, Jay-Z, and A Tribe Called Quest, first-class acts that rocked the Palladium's epic, hallowed stage.

Then Ian Schrager brought me to Arthur G. Cohen, a real-estate mogul so big that for any deal in New York, the joke question would always be, "So what percentage did Arthur have?" Cohen had a theater available on Forty-Seventh Street, Minsky's, formerly an infamous burlesque house. In 1992 Times Square had yet to become sanitized, and it wasn't the magnet for tourists that it is today. Taking the old theater over and christening the place Club USA, I tried to stay true to the building's history and surroundings when we underwent an $8 million redo. I offered club-goers an extravagant adult playground accented by S/M touches, graffiti tags, and futuristic *Blade Runner* tableaus of urban decay.

The concept spoofed Manhattan in the Reagan '80s, everything larger than life, with huge signs and billboards throughout the venue, including a memorable automated one for Hoover vacuum cleaners. Fashion superstar Thierry Mugler created the top-floor VIP room, and the eminent Jean-Paul Gaultier did the furniture. Eric Goode and Serge Becker, the geniuses behind Area, consulted on the overall club concept. Preoccupied as I was running Tunnel and Limelight, I told them to go ahead and go nuts with the new venue. "Just be sure it's fun" was my only direction, and the two really came through.

One mezzanine wall was stocked with twenty-five-cent peep-show booths running old porn loops. A splashy modular graphic that I could change at will loomed over the dance floor, and a lounge on the lower level featured retro shag-carpeting décor. But the element that really stood out was the tubular, 120-foot amusement-park-style slide that delivered people from the mezzanine to the dance floor. We had an attendant stationed up top, handing out squares of burlap fabric to smooth the journey downward.

With Club USA under renovation and Palladium up and running, I remained hungry for more. On a late-fall afternoon in 1992, with a chilly wind coming in off the Hudson River, I found myself in front of a century-old redbrick industrial warehouse facing the docks

on Manhattan's Far West Side. The neighborhood felt almost creep-
ily empty. The old produce and meat markets that had once thrived
on what was then called the Lower West Side had moved elsewhere.
Nothing else had come in to take their place.

The warehouse on the Hudson was about as close to Moon Base
Limelight as I could find. The depopulated, postapocalyptic feel of the
neighborhood actually appealed to me. I'd come to realize that I wasn't
running ice-cream parlors, where success depended largely on foot traffic. I operated huge venues—destination clubs that patrons would go
out of their way to visit.

Outsiders flocking in always put pressure on the full-time residents.
With my other clubs I had been dealing with community boards on
a weekly, sometimes daily, basis, fielding concerns about noise, litter,
and the normal and unavoidable disruptions that always happen when
a couple of thousand visitors rub up against the locals. Along the barren
wasteland of Twelfth Avenue in those days, there was nobody around
to offend.

Brian MacGuigan and I had been through a lot together since he
began as my systems guy at the first Limelight. He understood everything there was to know about the physical plant of a nightclub, from
floor plans, lighting arrays, and sound systems to plumbing and electrical infrastructure. I relied on him heavily as a coworker and a friend.
Usually "genius" describes people in the scientific or artistic realms, but
Brian was a genius of brick and mortar and nuts and bolts. There was
no way I would vet a new club without him.

As he and I stood outside in the cold, Brian said, "I don't think
there's a single residential building within a five-block radius." He spoke
as if that were a positive state of affairs, and both of us were almost
dizzy with the thought. No one had to tell us about the headaches we
could avoid, or how much simpler operating a nightclub would be in
the vacuum of a sparsely populated neighborhood. Smoothing feathers
in Times Square and on Fourteenth Street, the respective sites of Club

USA and Palladium, had been taking up a considerable amount of my time.

The real-estate agent, Alex Picken, unlocked the front door of the building. He made a grand motion with his arm like a restaurant maître d' showing diners to their table. From the street-level entrance, the floor opened to a huge space with sprawling rectangular dimensions.

As with a lot of people in the real-estate biz, Alex liked to chatter. "This place is the old Central Stores Building of the Terminal Warehouse Company," he told Brian and me. "Built in 1890. They called it 'the Barn' and used it as a receiving dock that had freight trains pulled up and parked right inside here, so the teamsters and stevedores and whatnot could load and unload the stuff straight from the boxcars."

He gestured across the cavernous space. "You can still see the steel rails down there, embedded in the floor."

I barely heard what Alex was saying. I had been in the club business long enough to learn how to size up a space, understand the possibilities, and visualize what it could become. Central Stores reminded me not of a railroad station but of an airport hangar, as if you could fly down and park a little speed racer inside. I stood there at the threshold, gauging sight lines and crowd flow, imagining new floor plans, summoning up design ideas. Sparks were shooting out of the top of my head. I looked over to Brian and Brian looked back at me, an almost imperceptible nod passing between us.

We proceeded deeper into the rectangular main room.

"Built like a brick outhouse," Alex was saying. "Steel-girder super-structure, totally overengineered all around, the way they used to build things, like why use a two-by-four when an eight-by-eight beam will do, you know? This place has very good bones."

The room we had stepped into was long and narrow, with a vaulted ceiling that had a few blackened patches—from century-old locomotive smoke, I guessed. Empty and gloomy as the atmosphere was, the place had an Aladdin's-cave vibe.

"Hey, boss," Brian said softly, flicking his eyes toward the makeshift barrier where the tunnel-like space dead-ended.

"The previous tenants closed that part off," said Alex.

In 1986, just a couple of years after New York Limelight opened, the Central Stores Building had debuted as a club called Tunnel. Rudolf Piper helped open the club, with the longtime operator of Danceteria signing on to transform the rail warehouse into a destination dance hall. Rudolf, coming out of the music underground of Germany, looked like a silver-haired hipster and was very popular with the downtown crowd.

Tunnel had done well in its first year or so, but then it fell off a cliff. Slowly the owners started to shift the atmosphere toward salsa, and the club tumbled further downhill. Rudolf departed the scene in 1988. By the time we took that first walk-through, the place had been shuttered for four years.

My spider-sense tingling, I peeked behind the barrier at the end of the room. The vault extended farther, making the already large room potentially enormous. It really was a train tunnel, and I imagined seeing light at the end of it.

"Is there more?" I asked, not quite believing what I was seeing.

"Oh, yeah," Alex said. The original lease represented only a quarter of the building's available square footage. There were basement rooms, a mezzanine, the old washroom where the rail laborers used to clean up after work, and a half dozen other smaller spaces. As Alex Picken led Brian and me through the building, I realized where the original owners had gone wrong. They hadn't thought through the possibilities. Large as the space was, their nightclub had wound up being too small.

This space had the potential to dwarf all my other venues. I could do things in a larger club that I couldn't do in a smaller one— radical, cutting-edge things. The old rail warehouse inspired me to dream big. I imagined art installations, live concerts, elaborate themed events. Where the former owners leased less than a quarter of the available space, I would take over three-quarters, a full 85,000 square feet.

To my mind, there's a clear difference running a club with 3,500 entries a night as opposed to 1,000, but it's a question of creativity, not money. The trick is filling a large space night after night. You need a few more staffers, of course, but the overhead for the infrastructure remained pretty much the same. Tunnel was humongous. I'd just have to figure out how to attract enough patrons.

A large-capacity nightclub was an extremely rare phenomenon, tough to pull off, tougher still to maintain. But the megaclub was my sweet spot. Gross receipts can be incredible at a big club, but more than the money, I was accustomed to hosting parties with large crowds. Nothing could beat that. Looking over the balcony at Limelight, and seeing the floor below crammed with wild-ass dancers, gave me a physical thrill like no other. I kept coming back to the feeling, wanting to duplicate it, a junkie mainlining a packed nightclub.

With the light dimming outside on that cold afternoon, Brian and I took a last look back as we left the Central Stores Building.

"Lot of work," I said.

He shrugged. That kind of work was what we did. Big projects, big rewards.

I nodded, still peering back into the dim recesses of the vaulted space. "All right," I murmured, speaking to myself as much as to Brian and Alex. "Let's get started, shall we?"

"Sure thing," Brian said.

"OK!" Alex jumped in. "All right!" I think he actually rubbed his hands together at the prospect of making the sale.

The Tunnel was mine to do what I could with it.

CHAPTER NINE

A Half-Pipe on the Dance Floor

In 1992, when I took over the lease for the Central Stores Building, we hit the ground running. The job of developing Tunnel animated my whole staff. Everyone had a new toy to play with. The three hundred or so employees in my company were all acting like Keith Richards right after he went to that place in Switzerland to have his blood purified. We had a fresh infusion of life.

From the start, I was wary about siphoning off any patrons from my other three clubs, of which Limelight was the closest. I wanted to double my fun, not have two venues in the same area that split the action between them. Somehow, Tunnel had to have a distinctive vibe and draw a different crowd than Limelight. I knew there were plenty of warm bodies to go around in the local nightlife market. On any given weekend, a half million people spilled out onto the bricks in Manhattan, pleasure-seekers looking for a place to set their hair on fire.

Tunnel featured a much rawer physical environment than my other clubs, industrial and steampunk where Limelight was Gothic and ornate. Good bones or not, the Tunnel property basically needed a top-to-bottom redo. When the joint had closed four years previously, the premises had been left vulnerable to scavengers. Everything and anything that could be pried up and ripped off had vanished—furnishings, appliances, even the knobs on some of the doors. There was no sound system, no lighting array, no serviceable AC.

The original liquor license for the premises was long gone, too, so I couldn't make a simple transfer from the past owner. We'd have to jump through the multiple bureaucratic hoops dreamed up by some sadist in the state liquor authority. But I had been to that rodeo more than once, and I already had a support structure of lawyers, fixers, and blade runners in place. For any move I wanted to make in New York City, from securing building permits and certificates of occupancy, to obtaining an array of licenses and collecting sales taxes, I needed to hire a person called an "expediter" to untangle the almost-surreal amounts of red tape. Franz Kafka would have understood.

I had to keep Limelight going while creating an entirely new club six blocks to the west. A typical day meant dealing with dozens of niggling details—to use the old phrase, it was like getting nibbled to death by ducks. In this case the quackers were contractors, building inspectors, police officials in the local Tenth Precinct, plus those aforementioned sadists of the liquor-control board, as well as any other random bureaucrats who considered it enjoyable to employ a little authority over a hapless businessman just trying to get a nightclub up and running.

At Tunnel, I knew the effect I was aiming for. My Disney obsession had only matured over the years. When I took my girls on visits to the company's theme parks, I was always impressed with how efficiently the places were run. The attention to detail staggered me. Disney World might do thirty thousand visitors in a single day, yet everything went along smooth as silk. All the physical details of the operation, like garbage removal and supply delivery, were kept carefully out of sight. The audience, I knew well, just wants to see the marionettes, not the strings, and definitely not the puppeteers.

I strived for the same kind of smoothness in all my clubs. At Tunnel, it was going to have to happen on an even larger scale. I enlisted designers Eric Goode and Serge Becker to help, with artist Kenny Scharf providing some flourishes, too. I concentrated on flow, the idea that any single club-goer would be able to maneuver through the immense space without ever hitting a wall and having to turn around. I broke up the main room with a bar running directly down the center, seventy feet long and twelve wide, a double-sided battleship accessible both port and starboard. At one end of the bar I installed a raised platform for one of the club's five DJ booths, positioned for excellent sightlines to the dance floor. Then, at the far end of the room, we created an installation that I had envisioned during that very first walk-through of the place.

"How about a half-pipe?" I asked my staffers at our initial design meeting during the reconstruction process.

I knew how eye-rollingly insane the idea would sound, but I'd always been mesmerized by the pendulum rhythm of boarders as they rose and fell on the curving sides of skate-park half-pipes. It was hard to keep your eyes off them, like watching one of those drinking-bird toys, where you glance over at the damned thing and wake up ten minutes later still gawking. I imagined the lazy arc of skaters as a backdrop to the dance floor. Everywhere anyone looked at Tunnel, I wanted something to attract the eye.

"We have the room for it, don't we?"

Because the people who came to my clubs were mostly younger, I always felt I had to bounce ideas off staffers who fit the twenty-one-to-thirty-five club-going demographic. I needed that age-appropriate reality check. To their credit, Brian MacGuigan and the rest of the crew didn't shout me down. In fact, they actually got psyched for the in-club half-pipe proposal.

On the second floor, which was half the size of the main room, we installed another one of my brainstorm innovations, a coed bathroom. In the warehouse's old washroom, the lockers of the former rail workers still lined one wall. I created an elaborate space with its own bar and its own sound system, so no one would ever have to leave the party to heed the call of nature at Tunnel.

We put a ton of work in on the bathroom space, but we also left it as raw as we could, retaining the lockers and other industrial fixtures. Two bartenders worked back to back at the room's circular bar, which did a surprisingly brisk business. I once saw a handmade sign posted above a urinal in a dive bar: "We don't sell beer, we recycle it." Substitute "champagne" and you'd approximate the fluid situation in the upstairs facilities at Tunnel.

"That coed bathroom was beautiful and nasty at the same time," Ramona Diaz once told me. Ramona worked security, and she was one of my favorites among the Tunnel staffers. That word *nasty* was actually a compliment, and the facility quickly took on a reputation of its own, infamous as a space where male-female fault lines were erased and the genders mingled freely. We were ahead of the times, and the media loved it. The phrase "unisex bathroom" was always mentioned in the press coverage of the club, as if the concept was the most titillating thing in the world.

In reality, people adapted easily. There were both stalls and urinals, and the bathroom attendants didn't worry too much if people mixed and matched. For such a simple, easily implemented idea, the innovation turned to PR gold, shocking the puritans to the soles of their silver-buckled shoes, while allowing our patrons to believe they were on some cutting edge of social engineering.

While I spent so much time trying to keep a handle on operating four clubs at the same time, I was losing ground at home. My relationship with my second wife, Adrienne, suffered. We moved several times, never really settling, living in Tribeca for a year, then in a two-bedroom apartment at Sixty-Seventh Street and Columbus Avenue for two years, and finally taking a place on Central Park West.

When our marriage went south, so did I, taking residence in a suite at the Mayflower Hotel, near Central Park and within easy reach of all my clubs. Living at a hotel reminded me of my childhood days of watching *Have Gun—Will Travel,* a popular TV western that starred Richard Boone as a gunfighter for hire who called himself Paladin. I remember not being able to get over the fact that Paladin lived in a hotel, a lifestyle that appeared unimaginably exotic to my young eyes.

My daughter Jen, old enough then to get around the city on her own, moved into the two-bedroom, three-bath Mayflower suite with me. I felt confident that providing Jen with a credit card and access to room service represented a perfectly fine style of parenting. She spent the day at the suite and elsewhere—mostly with Adrienne, who looked after her, but she was an adventurous, independent kid. I thought that everything was being taken care of on the Jen front. I still had not gotten it through my thick skull that a child needed a dad's actual presence to feel whole.

A kid loose in Manhattan grows up fast. One night at the Palladium, I spotted Jen dancing onstage with Mark Wahlberg, a.k.a. Marky Mark. She was only seventeen at the time and still in high school. The sight of my dear daughter paired off with a well-known celebrity bad boy stung me, bringing up all the contradictions inherent in being a nightclub impresario who was also a father seeking to love and protect his kids.

Did I really want my daughter participating in the high-velocity world I knew so intimately? The situation reminded me that my life choices had consequences in the real world, but at the moment I wasn't prepared to deal with them. I took no action to retrieve my daughter or split the young couple up, hoping against hope those consequences would not somehow work to implode the family. My twin roles of club owner and parent continued to clash, haunting me increasingly as Jen, Mandy, and Hunter grew into young adulthood.

The club-going population of New York City—and probably every other metropolis in the world—swells on Friday and Saturday nights, then drops by half on the other nights of the week. Tunnel was so large it didn't make much sense to keep it open beyond those golden Friday and Saturday sweet spots, and at first that's all we did.

Opening three more New York clubs allowed me to promote my dedicated Limelight staff to better positions, which was good for morale. Almost all promotions at all the clubs came from within the workforce. I'd make a former bar boy at Limelight an assistant manager at Tunnel, say, or boost an assistant manager at Palladium to a manager position at Club USA.

When Jen turned eighteen, I brought her on board as a part-time employee at Tunnel. She was fresh out of high school and eager to work, so I hired her as a "list girl," checking in complimentary entries at the door. I neglected to pay my daughter a salary, since at the time I was supporting her liberally, gold Amex card and all. Actually putting her on the payroll, I thought, would have been like robbing Peter to pay Paul.

She worked the door Fridays and Saturdays, nights when Tunnel hosted glam, fashion-oriented crowds. The job of the club's list girls was to sort through two groups of entries: people who got in for free and others who were granted reduced admission. We compiled comps from dozens of sources, fielding suggestions from scenesters, celebrities, fashionistas, promoters, media, nightlife regulars, anyone who brought weight, had pull, or deserved to be treated with extra respect.

"Leakage" is how the hospitality industry refers to the myriad ways profits can be skimmed off by employees. A classic example would be the bartender who rings up short sales at the till, charging ten dollars for a cocktail and then reporting an eight-dollar sale. At other times a twenty-dollar bill would take a mysterious detour on its way to the cash register, when a staffer would drop it on the floor and then pick up the skim later, unobserved.

As with a top-level gambling casino, we had a whole hierarchy of controls in place to prevent leakage. Bar managers watched the servers, busboys, and barbacks; assistant managers watched the bar managers; managers watched the assistant managers; and I kept watch on them all. We lacked only a Vegas-style "eye in the sky." As every club operator, tavern keeper, and hotelier knows, and as everyone in a cash business understands, an owner can never wholly eradicate the practice of skimming. I could only try to limit the damage.

Leakage might occur at the door when a list girl accepted a twenty-dollar gratuity to let in a dozen customers. Those kinds of bribes were actually pretty rare. List girls would more often usher in a whole gaggle of their friends for free. I liked having Jen on the door because, intentionally or not, the boss's daughter served to keep the other staffers honest.

I also found it enjoyable to witness my oldest child at work. She was a sophisticated presence, a hip Manhattanite by way of small-town Ontario, pretty and fashion conscious and bright. But like the boxer who steers his kid away from a life in the ring, I worried about the wisdom of introducing her to the mad scramble of the city's nightlife. The image of her dancing with Marky Mark onstage at Palladium a year before remained fresh in my mind.

The idea that I was bringing her along too quickly tormented me. Even though I spent a lot of time at Tunnel, I could afford only occasional glimpses of her at work, mostly in passing. She usually looked happy, chatting with customers with a wide, genuine smile lighting up her face, a sight that soothed my worries somewhat.

Those first months after opening Tunnel, I felt energized and relatively fulfilled, but soon enough those feelings started to wane. I got antsy, once again looking for fresh adventure. For a brief period in 1992–93, I was juggling four venues at once: Tunnel, Limelight, Club USA, and Palladium. Wasn't that enough? What the hell more did I want? What kind of action could I have possibly been missing?

CHAPTER TEN

How Tunnel Reinvented Hip-Hop

"What are we doing here?" I would often ask my staffers. Most of them knew the routine well enough to answer back, sometimes comically and in unison.

"We're trying to create culture."

I thought of a club as a stone dropped into a pool, the ripples spreading out to stir the water everywhere. Limelight was one of those tossed stones, with theme parties such as Rock-N-Roll Church, Disco 2000, and a gay night called Arena, each bringing together vibrant communities, each sending out waves of cultural energy.

Tunnel might have jumped on Friday and Saturday nights, but the rest of the week it was dark or given over to private parties. I wanted more for the place. I saw it as a parent might see a kid who wasn't living up to their potential, hadn't discovered a true purpose. As the westside venue underwent its yearlong shakedown cruise, an unlikely pair approached me, an energetic party promoter named Jessica Rosenblum and a Bronx-born DJ who went by Funkmaster Flex. They were looking for a place to throw a weekly party.

There's an old song called "White Boy Lost in the Blues," and the promotional career of Jessica Rosenblum made me think of her fondly as a white girl lost in hip-hop. A blonde Barnard graduate who fell in love with rap music, dove in deep, and never came up for air, Jessica got her start in nightlife as a door person at Nell's, a small, trendy club that was the exclusive celeb hangout and hipster haven on Fourteenth Street.

In the early 1990s there was still widespread social resistance to rap music. Radio, in particular, remained deeply segregated. The reason, I believed, was racism, pure and simple. I could hear a white artist like Malcolm McLaren do his pale novelty riff, "Buffalo Gals," on pop radio, but never any cutting-edge stuff by NWA. No one in the executive ranks seemed to understand how popular hip-hop was with the young demographic, not only African Americans but Latinos, Asians, and Jersey white boys.

Out of pure ambition and excess enthusiasm, Jessica transformed herself into a hip-hop ambassador, hosting parties and promoting the careers of multiple young rappers. I knew Jessica was an effective party promoter because she'd done great events for me at my other clubs. She had a grip on both sides of the rap scene—the Street and the Industry, artists and music companies. There were unsigned, underground rappers in her Rolodex as well as record-label executives.

Jessica ran a well-known party series called Mecca, using events to promote the acts she managed. But good security was hard to come by, so Meccas often lasted no more than a few weeks in any one venue. The first parties would be hip and fun, but then the events would start to feel dangerous and fall apart. Mecca moved from one small club to another: Supper Club, Grand, and Arena. Jessica even tried out stuffy, high-end venues such as Tavern on the Green.

One of the rap acts she managed was DJ Funkmaster Flex. I took to him immediately when Jessica brought him around for a meeting at my Tunnel office. She might have been brash and ambitious, qualities absolutely necessary for the business she was in, but Flex acted as her low-key foil, laid back, measured, and a lot easier to work with. He demonstrated a clear-eyed understanding of running a business, how the devil was always in the details.

The two of them came to me proposing that they host Mecca events at Tunnel. Of course, I was willing to listen to any experienced promoter who might attract new patrons to my clubs. I had always been drawn to rap, from back when the music was just emerging as a commercial genre with Afrika Bambaataa, the Sugarhill Gang, and Grandmaster Flash.

"We're looking for a fifty-fifty split of the door," Jessica proposed at that first meeting. "Mecca is a very well-established event now, and it would be good for you, Peter, an excellent way to bring paying customers into the club on Sunday night, say, when you're otherwise dark. It's a win-win."

In negotiations, when someone suggested how much it would be to my immense benefit for me to make a deal with them, Marlon Brando's well-known question from *The Godfather* always came to mind: "Why do I deserve this . . . generosity?"

We settled on a seventy-thirty split of the door receipts, in the club's favor. Plus I would reap all the profits from liquor and coat check. Even so, I had my doubts. I had little experience with a hip-hop crowd and thus couldn't project what type of bar receipts I'd be getting. I had a general notion that it'd be smart to beef up security, given the recent history of hip-hop events and the difficulty Jessica had encountered securing a regular venue. Just a year before, nine people had died in a stampede of bodies during the infamous Heavy D AIDS benefit at Harlem's City College.

As I feared, Mecca at Tunnel didn't succeed. I hosted the event eight times over the course of three months before realizing that the seventy-thirty split Jessica and I had settled on was causing problems. Our arrangement meant that it was in Jessica's best interest to push through as many entries as possible, ushering in the hordes without understanding that curating a crowd was just as important as increasing quantity. To make her nut, Jessica needed patrons—the more the better.

Because of the come-one-come-all door policy, on the Mecca nights the gender ratio skewed heavily male, an atmosphere that was at best surly, at worst explosive, and, in the end, unmanageable. More males meant more fights and less fun. So Mecca and Tunnel parted company. As far as I was concerned, it had been a failed experiment. Jessica, never one to be stymied, gathered up her bundle of energy and went elsewhere.

A few weeks later, Flex showed up at my office. As I said, I'd liked the guy from the first. He was less splashy than Jessica, but more easygoing. Staying on top in the fast-changing world of hip-hop takes guts, smarts, and good instincts, and Flex remains on the scene today as one of the leading DJs on Hot 97. The man has always had an uncanny ability to spot trends and break new artists. As they say in the music game, he's got some of the best ears in the business.

"I thought what you did for us at Tunnel was great," he told me when he came to me on his own. "I wonder if there's any way that you and I could make it work."

"Well, we can't move forward the way it was," I said. "We would have to be in total control of the door." I wanted to play the long game with any party I offered, creating safe, secure, very chill nights, in contrast to Mecca's chaotic powder kegs.

"Yeah, yeah, for sure, for sure," Flex agreed. "You do the club, I do the jams, and that's it."

"What we need to do is find a way to keep everyone safe," I said. "We have to be able to maintain the heat without ever boiling over."

The atmosphere at Mecca tended toward the mean and dangerous, which is a certain kind of draw for people who enjoy living on the edge. Violence has the power to render an underground scene legit, creating excitement and controversy. Making the atmosphere overly controlled ran the risk of turning the party bland and vanilla. But realistically, any event that smacked of disorder and violence could never be maintained over a long run.

I ran my clubs with a built-in paradox. People dearly want to believe they're taking a walk on the wild side, while deep down they prefer to stay on solid ground. I needed to keep the scent of risk alive, the idea that on any given night anything could happen, but underneath that, I had to have a rock-solid sense of security and well-being.

A lot of high rollers come into the nightlife business not looking ahead to what happens beyond the first big scores. Party planners were hustlers, trying to make a living in a not-terribly-honest profession. They might have initially made huge numbers and considered themselves a success. Two months later they were wondering where all the partygoers went. Meanwhile I wound up having to clean up the mess they left behind. But just as I did, Flex sought to build something that lasted beyond a few nights.

I kept thinking about how the limited number of Mecca shows we hosted saw massive pushback from the local precinct house. Police are a pretty cynical lot, and New York's Finest, as much as I respect them, push cynicism to the extremes. On the Mecca nights, I heard the word "animals" spit out too many times by too many cops. I felt a reflexive anger toward that mentality, though because my mother did not raise fools, I always kept my reaction carefully under wraps. But the racist blowback against hip-hop always brought to mind the prejudice I saw growing up as a Catholic French Canadian.

The people turning out for hip-hop-themed parties at nightclubs were New Yorkers like anyone else. They deserved the same opportunity to bust loose and party down. Pursuit of happiness is a guaranteed constitutional right, and it isn't supposed to be dependent on the music you like or the color of your skin.

As far as violence went, I remained a relative babe in the woods. On the streets of my childhood, fights were usually conducted with fists, not knives and especially not handguns. Over the years, and with all the public blood that's being shed, it's become clear to me how deeply embedded gun violence is in the culture of the States, and how violence stains the American soul. As the '60s civil-rights firebrand H. Rap Brown said, "Violence is as American as cherry pie."

For all my years living in the city, I still wasn't really aware of that period's incredible unrest in the Bronx, or Queens, or uptown. Like most clueless white people, I thought I had a general idea. I read the newspapers and heard reports filtering in from the front lines. But I didn't have a boots-on-the-ground understanding of what was going on.

If I had possessed a true understanding of the extreme situations those outer-borough communities were facing every day and night, I might have hesitated in resurrecting hip-hop parties at Tunnel. Because it was bad. From the late '80s up to and beyond the time Flex and I sat down together to strategize, the Bronx had the highest murder rate in the country. Forget LA's Compton or Chicago's South Side—in the projects of the Bronx, Queens, and Harlem, the bullets flew and young people died with a depressing regularity.

Castle Hill, Soundview, and Mitchel Houses in the Bronx; Woodside, Edgemere, and the Redfern Houses in Queens; the Polo Grounds Towers and Harlem River Houses in Manhattan—places caught in a crushing vise between gangs and drug violence on the one side and police brutality on the other. Brooklyn had its share of violence, too. Cheap crack cocaine and official neglect was the lethal combination that worked to transform any neighborhood into a battleground. It was a tragedy going on out of sight and out of mind of most Manhattanites.

Bad neighborhood. Don't go there. Drugs. Gangs. Murder. Such was the refrain the privileged sounded to their children. But the kids from neighborhoods under the gun didn't have a choice of environment. They created powerful, dynamic rap, the soundtrack of their lives. They listened to it, danced to it, traded mixtapes of it. They'd heard about the

Tunnel parties through word of mouth, and they were the ones Flex and I were trying to provide a safe space to let loose.

I trusted Flex to know the music. What I didn't know was how to feature it in my club on a consistent basis. I had seen so many venues follow a predictable trajectory: there'd be a big splash when a club opened, followed by a gradual but inevitable decline, with downtown trendsetters yielding to the bridge-and-tunnel crowd from the outer boroughs and Jersey, then maybe a Latino period, then closed doors and lights out. That was how it had happened with the original Tunnel, and I had witnessed a similar pattern all over downtown.

Club promoters had tried catering to hip-hop in the early 1980s, when I first opened New York Limelight. But the drug violence that engulfed communities during the middle of the decade scared most promoters off. Even in the early 1990s, crack was still a malevolent force on the streets. Any incident with weapons, any reputation for serious violence could kill a club faster than a lost liquor license.

"We have to find a way to keep people safe," I told Flex. "At Mecca we were taking blades away from kids all night long."

"You've got to understand. Those people are getting out of the club at two or three a.m., riding the subways because they can't afford a livery cab. They have to make it back to their own front doors in one piece. Of course they're going to be carrying something to protect themselves."

"So what do we do? I can't have blood spilled on the dance floor."

He leaned forward. "It's simple," he said. "We take their shit off them before they get inside. You ever been to Rikers, Peter?" he asked.

New York City's correctional facility on Rikers Island was a notorious hellhole, a familiar second home for anyone unfortunate enough to be caught by the police while being black in the city.

Flex answered his own question. "Nah, I know you ain't ever been to Rikers, because you ain't got the complexion for correction."

He was right. Compared to him, I was a north-country bumpkin. Flex detailed the elaborate searches that visitors to the jail had to endure in order to visit their loved ones. Metal detectors, strip searches, body-cavity searches—the correctional officers at Rikers were infamous for their heavy-handed and sometimes illegal thoroughness. Meanwhile, contraband such as weapons, cell phones, and drugs somehow still got through to the inmates.

"We do it like that," Flex said. "Like Rikers, only better."

"Look, I can't put people through a fucking proctology exam just to get into my club. Nobody would stand for it. Word would get out."

"You ain't getting me," Flex shot back. "A lot of folks don't have a place to hang out without fearing for their lives. They always have to be looking over their shoulders, worried some asshole will go off on them. You provide a super-chill place, a safe zone, with all the usual bullshit totally cooled out. You take care of that, and if I'm bringing the sounds, I promise you they'll put up with anything just to get through the door."

We had a long series of talks. I wanted in, but only if we could do it right. Mecca at Tunnel had gone wrong. But rap was a sort of pressure valve for communities that had a heavy weight pressed down on them. It was the next big wave in culture. I knew pop music would eventually embrace hip-hop, and no amount of bigotry or small-mindedness could stop it from happening. Italian greasers who'd attack any black kid who dared to walk through their neighborhoods were cranking Run-DMC, NWA, and Public Enemy on their car stereos. Like jazz and rock 'n' roll before it, hip-hop busted down social barriers. It was just that powerful.

With Flex and other staffers brainstorming, we made a fundamental decision regarding Tunnel's Sunday-night door policy. One way to keep things chill on the dance floor was to maintain the gender ratio at a sixty-forty mix in favor of young women. I had toyed with the idea of separate entry lines for women and men in other clubs. The strategy might have appeared sexist, but it seemed the only method to keep the crowd from becoming overwhelmingly male. In some old-style school buildings you can still see doorways labeled "Boys" and "Girls," built for those gender-segregated times, which amounted to a similar strategy.

For the Sunday-night hip-hop parties at Tunnel, I put in place two separate entry lines, one for men and one for women. The new door policy flowed not so much from sexism as from realism. From long experience I understood the difference in the atmosphere of a club with majority testosterone or majority estrogen, and I could glance at a dance floor and make a good estimate of the gender ratio just from the vibe. Seventy-thirty, with males in the majority, was a recipe for testosterone-fueled aggression. Sixty-forty in the other direction made for a much healthier, much smoother, much sexier experience.

I always remember the tense exchange in the movie *Marathon Man* between Laurence Olivier's Nazi and his torture victim, played by Dustin Hoffman. "Is it safe?" Olivier demands over and over again, asking about a lost cache of diamonds. On Sunday nights, while I monitored the atmosphere of Tunnel, the question echoed in my mind.

Is it safe?

CHAPTER ELEVEN

Hypnotize

Keeping things chill would turn out to be the key that made Tunnel Sundays the phenomenon they became. I understood the reality of the street only in an abstract sense. I was a lower-middle-class kid from Canada, after all. In the 1950s, the Ontario version of a Saturday-night-special handgun might be a cricket bat, say, or a broken beer bottle. That was the extent of it.

For Tunnel Sundays, I needed security people with hard-core experience. My pool of applicants expanded once word got around in the community of New York bouncers, bodyguards, and security muscle that there was work to be had at a newly reopened nightclub on Manhattan's wild West Side. Hiring man-mountain Sterling Cox as Tunnel head of security was a vital first step to our success. Sterling knew the Street, and also was familiar with practically everyone in the business.

Ramona Diaz had come to me via the illicit underground circuit of bare-knuckle boxing matches, a real-world version of the fictional *Fight Club* that existed in gyms, basements, and back lots all over New York City. Mona had transitioned from fights to bodyguard duty and then to security at China Club, before finally landing at Palladium. With the

gender-separate door policy at Tunnel, I needed female security personnel to perform searches on female customers.

Mona was the perfect hire. She used to bring her infant daughter,
Nicole, to work with her, a situation not uncommon with my staffers.
"Club babies," we used to call them. Nicole would sleep in reception
while her mama performed her duties at the door, twenty feet away.

Nobody got over on Mona. Most Sunday nights she took her place
at the entrance to Tunnel in a trio of kick-ass females, including two
more streetwise women, Diamond and Big Candy. The three had an
easy camaraderie and a no-nonsense approach to security that I came to
admire. They understood that deflecting aggression rather than answer-
ing it in kind represented a fundamental secret of the job. In security,
attitude is everything.

Mona and the others clearly enjoyed their work. When the male
supermodel Tyson Beckford came into the club, Mona performed an
extra-thorough search on him. She went at it as if the public face of
Ralph Lauren Polo was in reality a well-known terrorist. She wasn't
about to let the guy off easy. Stopping just short of a cavity search,
Mona then passed him on to Big Candy and then Diamond for similar
treatment.

"We used to handle the shit out of him," Mona recalled, laughing.
To Beckford's credit, he took the elaborate procedure with a grin.

Customers vocally objected to getting searched all the time, especially celebrities. Puffy would come in and curtly inform door security
that this time he would not submit to getting patted down.

"I'm not getting searched," he would say, the words *Do you know
who I am?* at the tip of his tongue.

"Yes, you are getting searched," Mona would say, and something
about her simple declaration convinced Puffy it would be futile to resist.

"We knew Puff was always going to be a jerk," recalled Lee Coles,
one of my top security guys. "He usually had a beef with someone. It
was always something."

Everyone knew damned well who Puffy was, who Method and Redman were, or Jermaine Dupri or Lil' Kim, but every single person who came through the door on Tunnel Sundays was getting searched without exception. If you violated the security rules in some minor way, you were banned from the club for a week or two. It was the only strategy we had to keep the place safe. Even then, the strict search policy failed to discourage some people from presenting themselves at the door "walking heavy."

"Biggie used to come all the time with a gun on him, a little over-and-under derringer," remembered Lee Coles. "We must have taken that fucking thing away from him a dozen times."

The informal policy was to confiscate and keep blades, saps, and Mace, but to secure firearms and return them to their owners when the night was over. There were four or five empty beer cases on the floor in the search area, and by the end of the night, they would be cluttered with random weaponry.

"To this day I still have some of the knives," Lee Coles told me recently.

Some of the Second Amendment enthusiasts who came into Tunnel walking heavy were high-profile names.

"This your nine, 'Pac?" Coles asked Tupac Shakur one night, after extracting a 9 mm handgun from the small of the volatile rapper's back. "Take it back to your ride, brother, because you ain't bringing it inside." The rap star had a particularly thorny reputation among my security corps.

"It was funny with him," Coles remembered, "because if 'Pac came in alone he'd be a pussycat, but if he was with a posse, man, we had to watch out—he'd always act like a real asshole."

Lee Coles and the other door personnel understood that security involved more than weapon searches at the door. It extended to the whole area around the club, especially to the line of patrons waiting to get in. The line for Tunnel Sundays became legendary. It ran from the door at Twenty-Seventh Street and the West Side Highway, around the corner toward Eleventh Avenue and, most weeks, well beyond.

Across Twenty-Seventh stood the enormous Starrett-Lehigh warehouse, a place just like Central Stores, where trains could be pulled up right inside. The block formed an urban canyon of sorts—a convection oven in the summer, a howling wind corridor in the winter with gusts blowing in directly off the Hudson River.

The wait on the line was usually two hours. The slow progress along Twenty-Seventh from Eleventh to Twelfth was often compared to the journey from East Berlin to West during the Cold War. Our version of the Grenztruppen der DDR, the notorious East German border guards, was the NYPD. We worked with the local precinct to close the street and erect curbside barricades. Cops used to post themselves at the door of the club or thread their way along the line, actually carrying mug shots with them, trying to ID bad guys.

"That line would start at two o'clock in the afternoon," Mona remembered. "Girls would pee themselves during the wait all the time. They'd arrive at the door all stinky and I'd say to them, 'Damn, girl, why'd you not just find somewhere to go?' And they'd say, 'What? I ain't losing my place.' Some of them, Tunnel Sundays was their whole life."

There were dozens of recognized hiding places for weapons in the area. Coles knew them all. He didn't look overpoweringly big or muscular, but he was one of the toughest mothers I've ever encountered in all my years. He could handle anything. He often went undercover in the Tunnel's main room, checking for drug transactions, displays of weaponry, altercations in the making. Most people instinctively got out of his way. We used to call him Moses, because he parted the Red Sea.

Monitoring Lee Coles's progress from afar, I'd marvel at his abilities to chill out unruly patrons.

"You wish to speak to the manager, sir?" he'd say, the soul of patience. "Well, OK, that's strike one right there. Keep on with your shit and we're going to put you to sleep." Sooner or later the trouble-makers, many of whom Coles knew from growing up, would get the message.

But sometimes his message went ignored. Whenever anyone stepped too far out of bounds, especially if they went so far as assaulting a staffer or another club-goer, I'd be the one who ultimately made the decision.

"Get 'em out!" Lee Coles would call. If the incident was particularly severe, he'd add one fateful word. "Headfirst!"

In those instances, their "head opened the door," as Lee Coles dryly phrased it. Mona had a slightly different take. To her, the ejected customers resembled a well-known cartoon character. "They were like Coyote in a *Road Runner* cartoon, you know? They'd fly straight out and then hang in the air for a little while."

The security corps at Tunnel Sundays formed a tight, mutually supportive community. I always liked to hire older men and women, people with families and steady home lives, who didn't feel they had anything to prove. After a few months the staffers began handling recruitment themselves, and the whole arrangement virtually ran on its own. Many times Big Candy, Lee Coles, or others would hear of prospects and know their actual release dates from Rikers Island. They would be out there at the bus to greet them and offer them jobs.

"You're the one they call Tank?" they'd ask, and later that night the big guy would be on the job at one of my clubs.

The people working security ate takeout together, joked with each other, had each other's backs. I was struck by the fact that the Mona–Big Candy–Diamond trio would keep tampons, deodorants, and other such products on hand at the door.

"Girl, you smell funky—I'm not going to let you in the club like that!" I once overheard Mona saying to a woman she was searching, sending her to the bathroom with a blast of perfume.

My security people often used to get tipped for escorting patrons to their cars at the end of the night. Other times they'd act as guardian angels for the talent. Busta Rhymes was a regular. He led a totally chaotic life outside the club. Lee Coles would treat him to a meal and give him rides home, week after week. Coles was also good at handling talent more volatile than Busta. It happened more often than you'd think that an artist would attack a fan. He took it as part of his job to defend the crowd from the rappers.

Many of my security personnel carried weapons outside the club, most of them unlicensed. What I didn't realize at the time was that some of them were armed inside the club or at the door as well. Mona kept a .38 in a shoulder holster and a smaller-caliber pistol in her boot. I guess what I didn't know didn't wind up hurting me.

Tunnel Sundays represented a sensational collision between Street and Industry. Record company A&R people were drawn to the nights like bees to honey. One of our regular patrons was a street-educated, South Bronx–born scrapper, Chris Lighty. He became a recognized fixture at Tunnel. Lighty was a take-charge kind of guy, a *presence*, a force to be reckoned with in pretty much any situation, no matter how extreme. His don't-fuck-with-me nature came hard won, from a childhood growing up in the Bronx River Houses.

When I met him in the early '90s, when he was in his midtwenties, Chris was already making moves in the music business. He'd founded a company called Violator, named after a street gang he'd been involved in during his youth. He displayed an instinctive business sense that was similar to Flex's. The cliché had him educated in the school of hard knocks, but Lighty always put it a different way: "I gained my MBA in hell." His "streets to the suites" saga would become the stuff of legend, and his self-made journey got a big boost at Tunnel.

Chris Lighty often took a place among the personnel at the door. He knew the troublemakers, because, like Lee Coles, he had a personal history with many of them. Chris looked kind of baby-faced, and he was ace at keeping his attitude neutral, not aggravating a situation by going all aggro himself. As a manager of young talent, he always boasted about his inside status at Tunnel Sundays. He put many of his protégés, including 50 Cent, onstage at the club.

The force propelling hip-hop into the mainstream was gangsta rap, the irresistible G-funk beats coming out of the West Coast hip-hop community in the late '80s, beginning with NWA and especially the genius of its vanguard superstar, Dr. Dre. There's a lot of debating the point, a lot of East-West rivalry, but the truth is that, in my club, gangsta rap was what finally bridged the underground-mainstream gap. A lot of bourgeois people cowering in their gated housing developments hated and feared the music. And if they didn't hate and fear it, they failed to understand it.

White-boy Canadian that I was, I still heard the essential truth of rap right from the beginning. In the early 1980s, I saw how the Limelight dance floor convulsed when George Clinton's "Atomic Dog" came on the sound system; it was one of the first songs we ever played at the New York club opening. People *howled*. It was music-fueled ecstasy.

"To rock the Tunnel," DJ Flex said, "you just can't play it like any other club. It's all about the people in that room, who are some of the most aggressive, most hip people on the planet. They saw artists like Jay-Z, Busta Rhymes, DMX, and Biggie grow from being in the club with them to being on the stage and then on MTV and beyond."

I counted on associates such as Flex to keep me current, but I was also constantly reading, listening, absorbing what was happening in the culture. I dipped into dozens of magazines a month—at one time I counted over two hundred of the slicks lying around the house: news mags, fashion mags, music mags, top sellers like *Vogue* and *Vanity Fair*, alternative publications like *SoHo Weekly News*, *PAPER*, *Details*, and

HX. Anything, everything, all the way down to random underground zines that were no more than a few xeroxed sheets stapled together. By the time a trend hit the pages of *Time* magazine or the *New York Times*, I knew it was already on its way out.

I understood one of the core truths of popular culture: if parents hate a type of music, it's almost a guarantee their children will like it. Parents *hated* gangsta rap with a vengeance. They didn't hear the pulse of life in it, but instead registered violence, threats, insecurity. It was designed to upset people, to rub their noses in uncomfortable realities. Brutal and muscular, this brand of hip-hop simply would not be denied.

"Rap music is funny," Ice Cube once said. "But if it's not funny, if you don't get the joke, then it's scary."

I'm not sure if I really got the joke or not, but I definitely connected to the sound. Mainstream radio boycotted rap, with only a few exceptions. Tunnel, a solitary nightclub on the west side of Manhattan, became a conduit for what eventually rose to become the most dominant cultural trend of the day. Flex, Jessica, Chris Lighty, and I, a whole crew of us, approached the massive dam holding hip-hop back, took a few hammers and picks, and put a crack in it. The explosive force of what poured through was the Tunnel Sunday-night phenomenon.

It was hip-hop's coming-out party.

The seventy-foot bar running down the center of the main room served as Tunnel's central artery, delivering the buzz that kept the party going. It split the space in two, with the dance floor at one end and the stairs down from the entrance at the other. I kept a dozen bartenders working both sides, and made sure a few of them were big enough to double as bouncers.

No one had ever heard of bottle service back then. But when real money began to flood into the hip-hop community, nobody flush with new cash was going to be satisfied with just a single snifter of cognac or a few fingers of Jack Daniel's. Everyone was trying to be top dog, and they wanted the whole world to see them succeed.

Patrons began ordering bottles of high-end French champagne—Moët, Cristal, and Dom, no glass necessary, thank you very much. The traffic got so fast and furious that the bar would run out and we'd have to raid Palladium or Limelight for resupply. Servers used to load a half dozen bottles into the plastic tubs of busboys and distribute champagne that way. It was lucky no one wanted glasses, because we wouldn't have had enough to go around.

Plowing through a raucous club crowd while gripping the neck of your very own bottle of Cristal represented conspicuous consumption at its finest. Customers would keep the empty bottles in front of them on the bar so everyone could witness the impressive number they had purchased. One night I watched as Sean Combs and Jermaine Dupri competed not in a battle rap but in a bottle rap, seeing who could line up more dead soldiers, one side of the bar against the other.

In the beginning, at least, Sean Combs was king of Tunnel Sundays, back when he was still known as Puff Daddy. Combs was a gifted rapper—try listening to "Can't Nobody Hold Me Down" without it going through your head for the rest of the day—but he started out as a promoter and manager. Puffy's real genius lay in recognizing talent in others, putting together scenes, creating energy. He's one of hip-hop's most brilliant entrepreneurs, and in the early 1990s, when Tunnel Sundays were ramping up, he was just beginning to hit his stride.

Puffy's joint, Bad Boy Records, brought along a relatively unknown and unproven Brooklyn nineteen-year-old named Christopher Wallace, helping to transform him into the Notorious B.I.G., a.k.a. Biggie Smalls. The gifted rapper pretty much single-handedly broke the dominance of West Coast hip-hop and pushed East Coast rap back to the forefront. Like a stand-up comic trying out his routines at a comedy club, Biggie developed raps live onstage on Sunday nights, including many cuts from his breakout 1994 release, *Ready to Die*. Week after week at Tunnel, I heard him work out a smoother, more fluid style. It was like watching Picasso paint or Michael Jackson choreograph.

Biggie was our guy, a creation of Tunnel Sundays as well as of the streets of Brooklyn. Dark and violent as his lyrics could be as he chronicled his upbringing in Bedford-Stuyvesant, Biggie appeared as a gentle teddy-bear presence at Tunnel. In the beginning, there was no VIP space on Sundays. The artists mingled with the crowd. Biggie wasn't that huge a name before *Ready to Die* dropped. But insiders knew, and since so much of the Sunday-night crowd consisted of insiders (or people who thought they were), he was lionized, always getting a lot of love from well-wishers. Being mentored by Puffy helped.

Another Tunnel regular who was cut out of the Svengali Puffy mold, Jermaine Dupri, came in fresh off his success managing Kris Kross. The boys, Chris "Mac Daddy" Kelly and Chris "Daddy Mac" Smith, were still underage and couldn't make the club scene. Dupri basked in the success of "Jump," the blockbuster Kris Kross debut single that spent weeks atop the charts.

Jermaine Dupri and Puffy represented only one of the many rivalries on the club floor, face-offs between boroughs, between crews, between followers of various artists. But the excitement everyone felt just being at Tunnel kept the atmosphere from boiling over. The clubbers were young and alive, the scene was fresh and new, and that made Sunday nights a be-there-or-be-gone phenomenon. No one had ever pulled off weekly hip-hop parties that attracted three or four thousand people a night. The promise I extended to them—that Tunnel would be safe and secure—made the nights into a rolling, one-of-a-kind party.

Most importantly, the safety measures allowed women to feel comfortable. While female rappers like Missy Elliott and Lil' Kim made the scene onstage, the real lady action went down in the audience. Women came outfitted and coiffed to an incredible degree, not satisfied with being dressed to the nines but, like Spinal Tap's amp, dialing it up to eleven. The nail-lacquer artistry on display deserved a fashion spread of its own.

Tunnel allowed women in free before eleven p.m., so the crowd was definitely estrogen heavy when the first wave of paying customers hit. The numbers wouldn't even out until well after midnight, so the men had a kids-in-a-candy-store look in their eyes when they finally made it through the line, got searched, and entered the main room. The DJs would play mostly R&B for the ladies until the clock struck twelve, and when Flex dropped the first hip-hop groove, the dance floor seemed to explode.

Street plus Industry equaled a raised roof. Record-label execs and power brokers—some of them, like Chris Lighty, already in positions of power, but a lot of them not yet launched—made everyone in the club feel like someone was about to be discovered. Tunnel Sundays developed into a womb that gave birth to careers, recording contracts, chart-topping hits.

The list of label execs who saw their careers rise after frequenting Tunnel Sundays is stone-cold impressive: New York–born Lyor Cohen, brought into Def Jam under Russell Simmons, later became head of Warner Music Group and is presently global head of music for YouTube; Cohen's protégé Julie Greenwald is now chair and COO of Atlantic Records; Todd Moscowitz rose to CEO of Warner Records, and Kevin Liles also became an exec at Warner. Joie Manda worked as a promoter before becoming VP of Interscope Records. They were all consistent presences at the Tunnel hip-hop parties, contributing to an intoxicating sense of possibility among the young and unsigned.

So the artists made a lot of great music on Tunnel Sundays, and the music industry spun off a lot of business. But juicing careers was never the main reason for the parties. *Creating culture*—those were the bywords I used to tell the troops at all my clubs, as a way of rallying them to the collective cause. Ever since I'd first started in the night-life business, that had always been my goal. I never wanted simply to go through the motions of running a nightclub. I wanted something bigger, grander. My definition of culture was a communal form of creativity, like crowdsourced art.

A few of my staffers might have remained skeptical about my grandiose ideas. *Tell the truth, Peter*—I could see the judgment in their eyes. *You are in the business of making money.* A cynic takes the least influential aspect of anything and declares it the most important. I'll tell you right now that money was never the real motivating force for me, not compared to stirring the pot of popular culture. Tunnel Sundays might have been lucrative, but more importantly, they turned out to be revolutionary.

Without experiencing it, it's hard to grasp how the main room would become so densely crowded that at times no one could move. You had to shoulder your way through a great wall of flesh, VIPs and young fans crammed in together, sharing the moment. Jay-Z might be up onstage, rapping about the very place where we all were standing.

Me and my operation runnin' New York night scene
With one eye closed like Peter Gatien

The week after Biggie Smalls died at the tender age of twenty-four, Flex cued up "Hypnotize," and I watched as three thousand people in the club chanted along or silently wept. That night of mourning deepened the bonds of the community, getting beyond neighborhood rivalries or the East-Coast-vs.-West-Coast rap wars. The heartrending scene epitomized Tunnel Sundays for me. By design or by accident, we had managed to generate a real sense of kinship, an impression that everyone present was part of something great.

CHAPTER TWELVE

Plate Spinning

Tunnel admittedly took a lot of my attention, but I had three other megaclubs to run. I was forced to compartmentalize, breaking the business into easily accomplished tasks. For all the ink that has been previously spilled about the club world, an essential fact has been missed: Limelight, Palladium, Tunnel, and Club USA were each very different clubs on different nights of the week. A fashion-oriented party and a Goth night attracted totally different crowds, and I had to supply different music, different personnel, different environments, even different lighting to suit each clientele.

A sample weekly lineup at Limelight during the classic years, for example, included Rock-N-Roll Church on Sunday, Communion (Goth) Night on Tuesday, Disco 2000 on Wednesday, high-end fashion with DJ Jeff Mills on Thursday, and Techno on Friday; Saturdays were mixed, and Mondays were dark. Limelight wasn't a single club, as outside commentators usually portray it. It was six or seven different clubs that happened to share the same venue. Only on Monday did Limelight remain dark, since we had to have at least one day for maintenance and repair, to recover from the wear and tear of some eighteen thousand patrons passing through on the other six nights.

On my nightly rounds I might first check in at Club USA for Bump, a gay-night party, with three thousand people packed into the venue. Afterward, I would head downtown to Palladium, where Nathan Lane was hosting a Broadway benefit, then jump westward to Tunnel, where Mary J. Blige performed, before finishing up the night with heavy metal at the Rock-N-Roll Church at Limelight, which played host to bands like Guns N' Roses and Pearl Jam.

Between the four clubs, I was doing multiple separate theme nights, which sometimes made for a total of twenty-seven individual parties in a week. It was a crazy, exhilarating, punishing schedule. In the space of a few hours I was able to traverse an incredible variety of New York cultural scenes and become immersed in them all. It was a wonder I didn't get whiplash. I had to employ three drivers—two full time and an extra one on weekends—just so I could make my rounds effectively. I routinely put in fourteen-hour workdays.

In that pre-internet world, nightclubs served as our Facebook, our Instagram, our Snapchat. If people wanted to discover new music, new fashion, new trends, they had to go to the clubs. No one could get a sense of the pulse by sitting at home staring at a screen. Record-label execs came out to hear which cuts got people up on their feet and dancing. Designers such as Alexander McQueen and Marc Jacobs likewise hit the nightlife world to scope out what trendsetters were wearing.

I'd see things on my dance floors that would show up a year or two later in suburban shopping malls. Lady Gaga's outrageous style was born at my clubs. Voyeurism, S/M, glam, Goth, androgyny, the cult of the supermodel, hip-hop style, gay chic, outré chic, kiddy chic, retro chic, body modification, and antifashion fashion were all trends that grew out of the nightlife underground. I had to create environments where each of these radically different styles could fit in and thrive.

As the operator of a thousand-employee organization, I always had fires to put out somewhere. I scrambled to deal with a clause in Pearl Jam's contract rider while at the same time advising the drag queen Lady

Bunny on whether a pink or turquoise gown suited her skin tone better. I refereed spats between employees, monitored security arrangements, passed judgment on the success of this or that DJ.

Matching the right music to the right crowd could make or break a party. In the early days of Limelight, I recall agonizing over paying Moby the grand sum of $300 for a night on the turntables. Now, of course, superstar DJs knock down hundreds of thousands of dollars per appearance, and Calvin Harris recently topped the *Forbes* list of highest-paid DJs with yearly earnings of $48.5 million. Moby himself became a leading artist in his own right, with millions of records sold. He and I laughed recently as we reminisced about the lowball Limelight fee.

"I did feel that three hundred dollars was a lot of money at the time," Moby said.

When prima-donna DJ Junior Vasquez's beloved Jack Russell terrier, Oscar, went missing and Junior was much too upset to show up for his weekly Palladium gig, I reached out to *New York Post* gossip columnist Cindy Adams. She ran an item on the missing-pet situation. Voilà—Oscar was found and the show went on.

A typical day in the life started at eleven a.m., when I arrived in the office (at Tunnel or Limelight) to deal with various duties, most of them involving staying on top of bookkeeping. I'd go through payroll, maintenance, readouts from the night before that listed cashier receipts from the door, bar, and coat check. Then I'd meet with the beverage managers to check on inventory.

At noon, promoters would begin to arrive, and the day would start to take on a speed-chess kind of atmosphere. I'd dash between my different offices, where there would often be two or three parties to plan for each upcoming night. This meant approving the budgets, checking out the invitation designs, and taking care of technical requirements such as sound and lighting arrays. I had to examine the contract riders for musicians slated to appear, which dictated that a certain kind of slippers had to be supplied from a specific luxury boutique, perhaps, or that two dozen white candles must be present but not smell of gardenia—all sorts of "no brown M&M's!"–style demands.

I paid bills, oversaw supply contracts, made sure all the city permits and certificates of occupancy remained current. With fees controlled by some obscure actuarial calculus, liability insurance would cost $500,000 one year, then get lowered to $200,000 the next. Dealing with heating or air conditioning, addressing wear and tear on the premises, freshening club décor, getting four venues ready for their ten o'clock openings— it all demanded my attention. As I said, the real nuts-and-bolts work of operating a club always went on during the daylight hours.

From seven to nine each evening I tried to make it home for a stretch, hoping to remind my children that their father was a real living, breathing, physical presence. Family life required a whole different style of juggling. I had to head back to the clubs for the shank of the evening, playing the boss again from nine p.m. to four a.m. Patrons could party all night and never catch a glimpse of me. I usually made only occasional forays to the door to survey the crowd out front waiting "on line," as they say in New York (in the rest of the country, of course, it's "in line").

The reason I was known for rarely being out front at my clubs was that I needed to be in my office doing business, planning future events, figuring out what was needed where and when. Keeping all the plates spinning and all the spot fires doused took up the bulk of my time. I stopped only a few times a night to take a breath, watching from a balcony or mezzanine as thousands of people cut loose.

Then there were what Jack Kerouac referred to as "urgencies false and otherwise," events and circumstances nobody could possibly anticipate. For reasons known only to him, Tupac Shakur once appeared outside Palladium and began to shoot up the club's marquee. We had to get the mercurial rap star bundled off and away from the scene before the cops showed. That incident happened around the same time that Johnny Depp came into Club USA to research his role for *Donnie*

Brasco, bringing along a crew of street guys who were helping him get in character. True to form, his mob people and my security personnel got into a brawl over entry into the VIP room.

At Limelight, we once put up what the *New York Times* labeled "the oddest double bill of 1990 or 1991." Cab Calloway opened the 1990 New Year's Eve celebration at Limelight, and the other act on the bill that night, performance artist Laurie Anderson, was slightly abashed at having to follow the outrageous Hi-De-Ho Man onstage. "What they have in common," stated the *Times*, "is that they both look spiffy in white suits."

Prince often came out to my clubs, and His Purple Majesty fell head over platform heels for a bartender by the name of Raven who worked for me. Depending on the night, she would be assigned to any one of my four clubs. When the Purple One arrived at Limelight looking for her, we'd have to immediately send a car to Palladium, Tunnel, or wherever she was, to bring Raven back.

Then there was the time a young male club-goer, probably seeking some kind of boasting rights, approached Mike Tyson in Tunnel's main room, took a beer out of the heavyweight champ's hand, and deliberately slopped the liquid all over the man's shoes. The outrageous move instantly snapped my security people into high alert, and nearby spectators froze, expecting a fight. But luckily, Tyson laughed his high-pitched giggle and strolled away. My staff and I had to be on our toes, ready to deal with whatever the night brought us, and no two nights were exactly the same.

A few of those nights beg to be erased from memory. There was a bathroom off the hallway near the Limelight VIP room with a sliding glass door, and as I passed by one night, a hand reached out and a voice called, "Have a paper square, mate?" I went to the supply closet and returned with a roll of toilet paper, handing it in to my longtime idol Mick Jagger, sitting regally unembarrassed atop the porcelain throne.

Nightclubs in New York City usually have the staying power of rainbows. It's hard to believe, but the classic Rubell-and-Schrager Studio 54 scene endured only from spring 1977 until the infamous IRS raid on December 14, 1978—twenty months total. Danceteria, the World, and Area all survived for limited periods. I managed to put together a run that lasted for eighteen years.

For the better part of two decades, at least, my party never ended. Truth be told, I have to believe that if it weren't for a certain New York City mayor and his wrecking-ball policies, my clubs would still be up and running. We would continually transform them as we always did, evolving our approach to fit the times and the trends, but they would still be packing them in.

I thought I was immune. I believed the dark side of nightlife would never touch me. And for a long time, it didn't. All around me, the culture of illicit drugs took a toll, on the young and foolish, on the rich and famous, on nearly every human society in the world. But from the point when I began refusing shots at the Aardvark, through Limelights in Miami—where I had to ask what was happening the first time I saw a patron snort cocaine—and Atlanta, all the way up to the expansions into Chicago and London, I could have served as a poster boy for abstinence.

It wasn't a case of never once touching a drug, but I didn't dive into it with the fervor and recklessness I witnessed all around me. I just never really developed the taste, and I steered clear of a habit. I saw the best minds of my generation embrace illicit substances as a lifestyle. Marijuana in the sixties became cocaine in the seventies became you-name-it in the eighties. Methamphetamine, Ecstasy, Special K, Rohypnol, psychedelic mushrooms, GHB, heroin—and drug cocktails featuring a mix of these and other ingredients—all showed up with increasing frequency in the clubs.

None of it touched me much. As a club owner, I understood two contradictory truths. For legal and practical reasons, I could not allow substance abuse to occur in any venue I owned. At the same time, there was simply no possible way to prevent a pill, a dosed slip of paper, or a tiny packet of powder from coming into a club. I could have my customers searched until the cows came home and I would still fall short.

I wasn't about to strip-search patrons or bring in drug-sniffing German shepherds, because I had to maintain some sort of balance between the buzz and the buzzkill. The government, the entity that in its wisdom passes laws against use of illicit drugs, also controls a sprawling system of prisons and jails. Strip searches, body-cavity searches, and, yes, drug-sniffing German shepherds are among the anti-smuggling measures in place, and yet substance abuse in those very jails is notoriously common. If John Q. Law can't keep his own house in order, how could I be expected to?

We did the best we could. We were as clean as nightclubs could be. Lee Coles and others in my security detail went undercover among club-goers, confronting and tossing out anyone openly dealing or buying drugs. We confiscated whole pharmacies of substances during searches at the door. But to claim a zero-tolerance policy would have been a joke, though I never felt that my clubs were more drug-drenched than Wall Street or Hollywood.

So the darkness lapped at my shores, and I wielded brooms, shovels, and buckets in a constant but not totally effective effort to sweep it back and keep it out. What I didn't expect was exactly what happened—the darkness seeped its way into my own life.

I can't pinpoint the precise time when recreational use started to degenerate into a drug habit that affected my family. I enjoyed good wine but usually stayed clear of hard liquor, and I always dabbled in the recreational stuff—a hit or two of acid, a joint here, a rail or two of coke there. But in the mid-1980s, the stress of running four clubs broke down my defenses. The pressure began to feel murderous. I'd tried freebase cocaine, found a relief valve, and began resorting to it with increasing frequency.

I maintained at least a façade of being in control. I carefully constructed a firewall between my substance abuse and my personal and professional lives. I did drugs discreetly, off club premises and out of sight of colleagues and family. When the strain of plate spinning got to be too much for me to bear, I rented a hotel room, stocked up on the Bolivian marching powder, and binged.

My drug sprees lasted for a day or two, and occurred about four or five times a year. I imported party girls and went completely off the rails. In my mind I made bullshit justifications, telling myself that I couldn't afford the time off to relax with a Barbados vacation or a trip to the French Riviera. A thousand-dollar-a-night suite in Manhattan was my only option. I used to strip off my clothes and then insist everyone else get naked, too. We never descended into group sex, but the scene turned pretty raucous and decadent.

My schedule was hectic enough that my wife never questioned my disappearing for days at a time. I could keep the wild time-outs a secret from my family, though inevitably the truth came out in a nightmarish way. My daughter Jen was just a teenager when she arrived unannounced at the hotel where I was holed up, knocking at the door. I panicked. I knew I couldn't have Jen catch me at the best of my worst, wrecked and disheveled.

"Now's not a good time," I shouted through the closed door.

I could only imagine her greeting me, peering over my half-naked shoulder toward the other unclothed occupants of the suite. The door remained shut, the symbolic barrier between us in place. I retreated farther into the suite where I couldn't hear my daughter's pleas. I didn't physically curl up into a fetal position, and I never became so ashamed that I called a halt to what I was doing. I simply fired up the base pipe and hopped aboard the oblivion express once again. On the morning after, I staggered out of bed, rinsed my sinuses out with saline, and reported for duty at my clubs.

My family life was on the edge of imploding, and I was too selfish to realize it. I didn't want to reckon with the mess I had made. I wanted only to look forward, to stay on the razor-sharp blade of the cutting edge.

The same year I opened New York Limelight, 1983, the longtime bureaucrat attorney Rudolph Giuliani jumped from one federal job to another, from associate attorney general of the US in Washington, DC, to US attorney for the Southern District of New York. Brooklyn-born Giuliani was a creature of Ronald Reagan, who as president made both appointments.

Rudy had started out as a political idealist, working for Bobby Kennedy's doomed presidential campaign in the 1960s and voting for George McGovern in the 1972 presidential race. But eventually he came out of the closet as a craven opportunist, switching his voter registration to Republican a month after Reagan took office.

The newly minted Reagan man came from a famously corrupt family. Rudy's bartender father was convicted of felony assault and robbery and did a stretch in Sing Sing prison, literally "up the river" from New York City. The elder Giuliani's brother-in-law was a gambler and loan shark heavily involved in organized crime who, when in need of muscle, often employed his father-in-law, Rudy's dad, the bartender-felon.

During the years when I was wandering around the globe opening up nightclubs, Giuliani was a very busy federal prosecutor in Manhattan, picking off four of the top five Mafia family bosses in the city. He missed nabbing one because before he got his chance, underboss John Gotti had the Gambino family godfather, Paul Castellano, murdered in front of Sparks Steak House, a few blocks away from Grand Central.

The crusading Giuliani was following the path to power of another New York gangbuster, Thomas Dewey—whose rise from the Brooklyn prosecutor's office in the thirties, to busting racketeers, and finally to the New York governor's mansion, was a perfect mirror career. Like Rudy, Dewey failed in his repeated attempts at the White House.

You have to wonder what Freud would have to say about Giuliani, a mobster's son who made his bones going after mobsters. Or maybe Nietzsche is a better reference: "He who fights monsters should be careful, lest he becomes a monster." Because that's what Rudy would develop into: a monster who easily buried his father and his father's brother-in-law in the scope of his corruption. Steal a little and they toss you into a cell at Sing Sing. Steal a lot and the president hires you as his attorney. With his wet mouth, hunched-over posture, and large, blocky head, Giuliani eventually turned into a cartoon character, or a fever dream out of a David Lynch movie.

But back when Rudy was making his first power moves as a US district attorney in New York, I didn't pay much attention. I didn't think it mattered who the hell occupied the federal prosecutor's chair, or, for that matter, who was in the mayor's office or in the White House. Because I dealt with numerous neighborhood community boards, I was somewhat involved in local, street-level politics, but that was about it.

Donald Trump repeatedly showed up for parties and events at my clubs, and I always judged him as something of a clown. Because of my near-monopoly grip on the New York megaclub scene, the *Times* labeled me "the Donald Trump of the night"—a label I didn't relish. But the comparison indicated that I was becoming establishment, at least as much as a nightlife entrepreneur could become part of the establishment.

I was too busy to pay much mind to what I was called. I'd branched out from clubs. I'd started *Project X*, a nightlife magazine. And in the wake of our success with *A Bronx Tale*, Dan Lauria and I formed a production company. We developed off-Broadway plays and also worked on feature films, including *Faithful*, a 1996 comedy directed by Paul Mazursky and starring Cher and Ryan O'Neal. Lauria and I branched out, and suddenly I had multiple film and theater production projects in development.

Such endeavors represented a place to park all those vast mountains of nightclub cash flowing into my coffers. There's a scene in Martin Scorsese's *Casino* that takes place in the back rooms of Las Vegas, where the money piles up almost faster than it can be counted. That wasn't exactly my situation, but the feeling was similar. During that period, 98 percent of my business was cash. No one laid a credit card on a bar tab back then. My weekly gross averaged a million-two. On weeks with holidays or three-day weekends, I took in double that amount.

I had to have eight cash-counting machines to tally it all. Monday mornings, the machines would be going full blast, totaling the weekend income from each of my four clubs—$300,000 from Limelight, $300,000 from Palladium, equal amounts or more from my other two clubs. It took hours to count it all.

In case of altercations, I always had security cameras installed at the front door of every club, but I never allowed them inside. I wanted to provide a sense of sanctuaries, away from the prying eyes of the outside world. Most of the people who worked for me were honest, but, as in any cash business, and especially while running a bar, the basic assumption is that there are those who will steal.

So while we never had an "eye in the sky," I had to put systems in place to keep from being robbed blind. But we got jacked anyway, two times for over $100,000 each. The first time, I went down to the Tenth Precinct and filled out a report.

"We'll check if there's video," the duty sergeant told me. I never heard from them. The second time we got jacked, I didn't bother with a report. There were also several attempted robberies, botched by thieves who seemed to go out of their way to demonstrate the stupidity of the criminal class. The atmosphere around the clubs was such that I took out kidnapping insurance for myself and my family.

Is the glass half-empty or half-full? Did I have one eye closed, as Hova had said, or, as I like to think, one eye wide open? Whichever way you want to see it, something had to give during those fast and furious plate-spinning years. Some piece of pottery had to crash to the floor.

Predictably, what I lost was any semblance of a home life. The estrangement between Adrienne and me really began during the time I had Limelights in Chicago, London, and New York, while I was racking up the frequent-flyer miles trying to keep track of my far-flung empire. I recognized that my marriage was beyond saving. Adrienne and I had been living apart and finally legally separated in 1991.

Soon after that, I met Alessandra Koe, who worked the door at New York Limelight. We began dating, and Alessandra rose in the ranks of the company hierarchy. She demonstrated such tough-minded expertise that when the time came, I handed over the management reins of Palladium to her with perfect confidence. In 1993, we had a beautiful son together, Xander.

I remember a summer day in 1995, when Alessandra and I were coming out of one of my favorite haunts, Daniel Boulud's flagship restaurant, Daniel. We strolled along Fifth Avenue toward our townhouse. Ever since Xander was born, my "lost weekend" binges had become a thing of the past. I felt healthy and more balanced than I'd ever been before. The sun was out and there was a slight breeze cooling us down. I had an incredible woman by my side.

As we walked I began to think of a book I had read when I was young, a rags-to-riches story that centered on the glamorous world of Fifth Avenue. The title was lost to me, but the majority of what I'd read back then fell squarely into the enticing realm of trash fiction, so it was probably something from Jackie Collins or Jacqueline Susann. When I pored through those pages, the New York depicted in the novel had seemed like something from another planet. Yet there I was, part of the scene myself, with a home in the same neighborhood as Jackie O., eating at a world-class restaurant and feeling as though I belonged.

Against all expectations, I had reached a certain level of social respectability, of a kind not often accorded to nightclub owners. Disney, my squeaky-clean obsession, had asked me to develop a nightclub in a just-purchased Times Square property. Almost simultaneously, the committee handling the 1996 Atlanta Summer Olympics proposed that I design and operate its "Club Olympic" hospitality pavilion for athletes. Then CNN did a segment on me for its *Pinnacle* series, focusing on people at the tops of their fields. I was right up there alongside future billionaire mayor Michael Bloomberg, the Public Theater's Joe Papp, and fashion icon Karl Lagerfeld.

Disney, CNN, and the Olympics. I couldn't have asked for a better stamp of approval from society as a whole. The straight world, the Establishment, the people who lived their lives in the daylight had embraced me. An advertising campaign used to ask people at the peaks of their careers what they would do next, and I had the answer on the tip of my tongue: "I'm going to Disney World!"

I started playing a more active role in my family. We did, in fact, hit Disney World fairly often. In addition to a 10,000-square-foot Upper East Side townhouse, we had a weekend place in the Hamptons and a vacation home in Canada. I started to collect a fleet of luxury cars, indulging the kid who used to boast about his uncle's Lincoln Continental. I had a Ferrari convertible, a pair of BMW 7 Series sedans, a Mercedes SL600, and a Lexus SUV at my disposal. My daughters were attending either private school or elite colleges: Jennifer at Columbia University, Amanda at USC, and Hunter in elementary grades at Trinity School. As a family or as a couple, we always traveled in first-class luxury.

I've done really well, I remember thinking that sunlit afternoon. *Could my life get any better?*

When the gods hear a line like that from the lips of a mortal, the Greek concept of hubris kicks in. I was blissfully unaware that a series of unconnected events was coming together just then, ready to shatter my life in ways I could hardly imagine. I look back at the head-in-the-clouds dreamer on that Fifth Avenue stroll and almost feel sorry for him. I had no idea about the tidal wave of trouble that would soon crash down on me.

PART TWO: BUSTED IN BROOKLYN

CHAPTER THIRTEEN

The Three Fates

After failing the first time to defeat David Dinkins in a mayoral election, Rudy Giuliani tried again and won, assuming office on the first day of 1994. His campaign slogan might as well have been *This city's going down the tubes*, and that theme played to the middle-class frustration with panhandlers, public urination, and other petty urban grievances. Giuliani portrayed himself as the tough-on-crime crusader who was going to bring the city to heel.

He kept his own sordid background under wraps. His family ties to mobsters were never mentioned. Giuliani embraced the "broken windows" philosophy of policing, which held that if cops cracked down on quality-of-life concerns like graffiti, turnstile-hopping, and vandalism, the overall crime rate would go down. In practice, the strategy meant stop-and-frisk harassment of anyone with dark skin.

"There are no small crimes," Giuliani stated. A sentiment he conveniently eschews as a lawyer for the president. Rudy brought the mindset of a professional prosecutor to the office of the mayor, demonstrating little understanding of the political nuances of the job.

In truth, the crime rate had already been going down under his predecessor, David Dinkins. Rudy ranted away regardless, employing law-and-order rhetoric against the lowest levels of society. He singled out so-called "squeegee men," the panhandlers who waylaid cars at intersections and used a rubber squeegee tool to clean the windshields and then demanded money of the unsuspecting drivers.

Around this time, the mayor's mom was quoted as saying, "He's definitely not a conservative Republican." Helen Giuliani went on to explain, "He thinks he is, but he isn't. He still feels very sorry for the poor."

In his relentless war against panhandlers, street sex workers, and the homeless, Rudy displayed no sorrow for the poor at all. When cops looked into the squeegee beggars, they discovered there were actually only about seventy-five of them in a city of over seven million. Still, Rudy had made them into his favorite whipping boys, and, miracle of miracles, the cops were able to target them and eliminate the phenomenon within a couple of months.

"We found out they were a pretty small union," Giuliani's deputy mayor, Peter Powers, joked to the press.

The victory over the squeegee scourge represented a clear triumph for the new mayor. Here was a man who could get things done.

I hadn't given two shits about Giuliani back when he was a US prosecutor, and I still didn't give a damn when he became mayor. I believed that particular road ran both ways: I would have been shocked to learn he cared anything about me. I operated a multimillion-dollar, aboveboard business, and my taxes filled the coffers of the city to the tune of thousands of dollars a week.

As an upstanding member of the community, I considered my position to be fairly secure. I was protected by the rule of law, due process, and the principle of fair play. There had always been a bit of back and forth between government authorities and purveyors of entertainment. But any mayor of New York City surely had to recognize that nightlife was an essential element of the town's reign as a globally renowned cultural mecca. He wasn't exactly mayor of Podunk.

The quick demise of the squeegee men meant the mayor had to find another menace to set up and knock down. "Paper tiger" is the term for a created enemy that can be made to look threatening but is actually not, and guys like Giuliani always, always need an enemy to exploit. In summer 1995, when he had been in the mayor's office for a year and a half, Giuliani needed a new paper tiger. He looked around and spotted a certain eye-patch-wearing club owner who stood prominently atop the city's nightlife scene.

That year, a pair of cowboy DEA agents named Robert Gagne and Matthew Germanowski busted an Israeli smuggling ring that worked out of JFK airport. The Israelis specialized in MDMA, also known as Ecstasy, X, E, or molly. A fancy-ass form of amphetamine, MDMA had actually been around since the "speed kills" warnings of the sixties. Back in the winter of 1985, the first raves took place amid the raging night-club scene on the Mediterranean island of Ibiza. From there, MDMA emerged from its long hibernation and quickly spread to the European rave scene. Soon enough, the drug hit New York City.

I grasped the fact that E was becoming more and more common. Simply from the perspective of a club owner, I wasn't very enthusiastic about Ecstasy. People on E tended to drink far less, so bar receipts suffered. But during the last half of the '80s and the first half of the '90s, Ecstasy became as American as apple pie. It was showing up everywhere—at concerts, on college campuses, during music festivals.

As a public menace, E was definitely a Drug Plague Lite. Crack cocaine had crippled the ghettos in the '80s. Heroin had people nodding out in doorways. Ecstasy was a much friendlier substance, nicknamed the Love Drug, with users searching the world desperately looking for someone to embrace. Early experimenters in the psychiatric community wanted to name the drug Empathy. When researchers gave MDMA to octopuses, the animals reached out for a hug, attempting to accomplish an eight-armed embrace.

Personally, I had cleaned up my act, but I wasn't sober, just not overindulging the way I had been. Off premises and in private, I tried a tab of E myself, simply because I wanted to know what the fuss was about. To me, it didn't feel all that different from a hit of speed.

"It's like the opposite of paranoia," gushed a friend who will not be named, my E connection and a great fan of the drug. "When you're rolling, you don't feel like everyone's out to get you. You feel like everyone is out to help you.

"Ecstasy's just the best high in the world for dancing."

They might not have been drinking as much, but those E-kids sure were out on the floor for extended periods of time. At Limelight I watched as a grinning, upbeat mood took hold, midway between a marathon dance contest and a love-in. Leave it to the buzzkill geniuses at the Drug Enforcement Administration to declare war against the love drug. In the mid-'80s, a US senator from Texas, Lloyd Bentsen, pushed hard for the DEA to classify Ecstasy as a dangerous Schedule I drug. That category included heroin, LSD, and marijuana, substances that are subject to the most severe restrictions by the government.

The Schedule I listing went on the books, but ten years later, there had yet to be a major Ecstasy bust by the Feds. Agents Gagne and Germanowski were out to change that. During a street buy, they stumbled upon a pair of luckless smugglers from Tel Aviv named Israel Hazut and Michel Elbaz. When the DEA agents brought a case against the two, the dealers turned talkative. Ecstasy was all the rage, they told the agents, who were only vaguely aware of a drug that had already made extensive inroads on their turf.

New York State had not yet bothered to make Ecstasy illegal. But the federal government, not the state, was the DEA's master, and there was E, classed as dangerous right alongside heroin. To a hammer, everything looks like a nail. To a DEA agent, everything looks like an opportunity for a drug bust.

Like a lot of people, I was disgusted with the War on Drugs. The whole business seemed like a disaster, criminalizing large sectors of the populace, filling the jails with nonviolent offenders, costing a fortune while producing only uneven results. If it wasn't even illegal in New York State, I wasn't worrying about it. In my experience, cocaine was what the police were looking to bust.

But there was also a dark undertow swirling in certain sectors of the club scene. Coke wasn't enough. Ecstasy wasn't enough. People began mixing drug cocktails like mad scientists. Frankenstein combinations like crystal meth, Ecstasy, and psychedelic mushrooms, or Rohypnol—the "date-rape drug"—went into the mix. PCP or angel dust could trigger deathlike trances for the enjoyment of users. Ketamine, an animal tranquilizer with a lot of different names—Special K, Kitty, K-Way—was Ecstasy's evil twin. Users disappeared down a "K-hole," a strange, out-of-body state of disassociation and induced oblivion. The drug of choice was *more*.

The mid-'90s was the era of the club kids, a group of young sybarites who gloried in *épater la bourgeoisie*, tweaking the noses of the uptight middle class. They dressed in outrageous outfits, getting costumed up as if they were headed for a psychedelic carnival, and then went to one of my clubs.

Shirtless and shaved clean of body hair, wearing fishnet stockings and a pair of patent-leather bunny ears, a club-goer might top off his look with a dental insert giving him enormous front teeth. Teased hair; an overtight nurse's uniform; a dozen pair of nested, multicolored eyeglass frames; a prop syringe the size of a baseball bat; and suddenly an ordinary, mild-looking twentysomething transformed into a phlebotomist from hell.

On and on came the cavalcade, with mad accessorizing as pumped up and surreal as the outfits—diaper pins, top hats, leather masks, enormous headpieces. The club kids loved to hate the straight world, and the straight world returned the favor, gazing upon the bizarre assembly with disgusted fascination.

All told, there were only about a couple hundred club kids. Writer Amy Virshup gave them their name in a *New York* magazine cover story, essentially creating a scene by codifying it. After that came a storm of media interest. In old-time circus sideshows, the "geeks" indulged in all sorts of outrageous antics—biting the head off a live chicken was a favorite—designed to freak out the locals. The club kids served the same function. Club kids were perfect daytime-talk-show fodder; their appearances lent the whole phenomenon national visibility.

Host Joan Rivers: "Do you ever walk down the street and see someone with a pierced nose, or blue hair, and you wonder, *What does their mother think?* Or *Why do they do that?* Or *What does that person do for a living?* Well, today, right here on *The Joan Rivers Show*, you are going to meet people who go out of their way to dress to get attention, people whose very existence says, *Look at me! Look at me! Look at me!*"

I like outrageousness. I like people who are different, who cross a line. So purely on a personal basis, I enjoyed the club kids. I knew a lot of them from the club, and I looked upon their antics with a fond eye. I had been employing people just like them since my Atlanta days, as catalysts who inspired others. Clara the Carefree Chicken, a club kid at Limelight who dressed every night in a ratty yellow poultry costume, was an employee of mine. I even rigged up a swing apparatus so the big bird could swoop over the dance floor. I wasn't about to throw a wet blanket over free artistic expression like that.

Purely from a business standpoint, I appreciated the club kids even more. They represented an essential piece of my puzzle. We usually comped them at the door, but they brought in loads of other customers who were eager to gawk at the geeks. I was in the business of getting paying customers into my clubs, and anyone who helped me in that effort got my respect. But just as geek acts were only a part of the action at an old-time circus sideshow, club kids were just one element of the whole nightlife scene.

They brought a lot of attention to themselves, and they brought a lot of attention to me. They also talked a lot about drug use. I don't know which part of their act most offended the sensibilities of middle America. Was it the gender-bending costumes? The fact that none of them ever got out of bed before the middle of the afternoon? Or was it the constant chatter about molly and Special K and cocaine?

All those behaviors rolled up into one outlandish package, but only the last one, the drug taking, was illegal. As such, it was a practice that the straight world could do something about. *Go ahead, tweak the noses of the bourgeoisie, but don't act surprised if you get tweaked right back, twice as hard.*

Around the time club kids were becoming media darlings, actively promoting E as not only an essential ingredient of their lifestyle but the greatest thing since sliced bread, the government started to use another, more ominous term to describe MDMA. It wasn't the Love Drug after all. No, in the hearing rooms and legislative language of Congress, and in the minds of DEA agents such as Gagne and Germanowski, it became "the Club Drug."

The Greeks had the idea of the three Fates, a trio who rule over what happens to mankind. One Fate spins out the thread of our lives, another measures, and a third snips. The three old hags definitely had their hand in what happened that summer of '95. A JFK Ecstasy bust by a couple of rogue DEA agents was only the first act.

Next up was a counterfeit arrest out in the suburban wilds of New Jersey. Nineteen-year-old Sean Bradley passed some bad bills at the Woodbridge Center shopping mall and got caught doing it. The whole thing should have ended there, but in order to cut a plea deal,

Bradley reached out to the DEA and eventually found himself talking to Germanowski and Gagne.

"In all the New York clubs," Bradley breathlessly told the agents, "the kids are wild for Ecstasy."

"Oh, yeah?" Germanowski responded, forty-two years old and not exactly hip to the scene. "What clubs?"

"Oh, you know, Studio 54, Limelight, Nell's, Palladium, CBGB, all of them."

Some of the places Bradley mentioned were already defunct. It didn't matter. The DEA agents were bloodhounds that had been given a scent. They were off and howling. Caught up in paramilitary fervor, they labeled their squad "Delta 35" and allied themselves with Rudy Giuliani's wide-ranging crackdown on disturbers of the public peace.

"I can get you into all the clubs," Bradley told the agents. The gullible duo signed him on as a confidential informant. Bradley realized he would have to take the agents in hand if they were going to fit in with the nightlife crowd. He actually brought Gagne and Germanowski clothes shopping and performed something of a makeover on them, just so they could get past the door.

The results were mixed. Gagne dressed in drag. Germanowski dyed his hair platinum, wore a dog collar, and had his partner lead him around the club on a leash—living the dream of some secret fantasy, no doubt.

I saw the two when they showed up at Tunnel, a couple of strange stiffs standing among the rest of the hopefuls. They stood out. I've seen my share of freaks over the years, but something about these two rang false. The one I would come to know as Gagne had hooded eyes and a thick Cro-Magnon forehead. Waiting for hours in the pathetic crowd that always collected in a U-shape around the door personnel, begging for entry, they were allowed in only at the tail end of the night. When they got involved in a shoving match outside one of the VIP rooms, they were tossed from the club.

The third element in my downward-spiral trifecta came when a teenager named Nicholas Mariniello hanged himself at his family home in New Jersey. The kid had been at Limelight the night before. The coroner's report ruled he died from suicide by self-asphyxiation. Although no physical evidence of drug use was found, Mariniello's father embarked upon a grief-stricken crusade, looking for someone to blame. His focus settled on drug use at Limelight and, eventually, on me.

I sympathized with the father. I can't imagine the pain of losing a child, and I don't know how I would have acted in his position. But the well-connected Mariniello family had contacts in the offices of New Jersey governor Thomas Kean, who picked up the phone and called across the river to Mayor Rudy Giuliani.

Robert Silbering, the special narcotics prosecutor for New York City, laid out the situation in a surprisingly candid statement to the press:

> We knew there could be drug use in Madison Square Garden and Yankee Stadium, but they're not going to come in and shut those places down. Peter Gatien was a marked man, and one way or another he was going down. He was the big fish, and if you could get him, it would send a message to the other club owners.

An Ecstasy bust in Queens. A counterfeit arrest in New Jersey. An eighteen-year-old's suicide in New Jersey. These events occurred within a few months of each other, and I remained blissfully unaware of all three.

That August my wife threw a birthday party for my forty-fourth, a bash that featured many, many cases of Dom Pérignon champagne. A gaggle of kids—not club kids, but real, actual children—toddled around underfoot. Employees from the clubs crowded in among friends, family, and business associates. Daniel Boulud, my favorite chef, created the feast.

The night seemed like a righteous reimagining of my parents' holiday parties in Cornwall, but I should have known something would go wrong. I should have glanced up into the sky above the party, where I would have seen a vision of a balding Republican mayor peering down at me through some sort of Wicked Witch of the West crystal ball. Writer H. L. Mencken's classic definition of puritanism suited Rudy Giuliani to a T: "The haunting fear that someone, somewhere, may be happy."

Well, I was one of those happy someones. Like the old anti-substance-abuse slogan had it, I didn't need drugs, I was high on my life.

The first shot in the war of the straight world against New York nightlife came on Saturday, September 30, 1995. September was something of a dark month that year: the state of New York reinstated the death penalty, the *New York Times* published the Unabomber's manifesto, and the serial-killer film *Se7en* was in theaters. But all anyone talked about was the OJ trial.

I have this crystalline memory of the week before the closure, the calm before the storm. We were doing close to thirty different theme-night parties then, but Mondays, the only day the clubs were dark, gave me a chance to catch my breath, reassess our progress, tweak our approach. Usually something needed correcting, or something had been trashed the week before. But I remember walking in that Monday floating on a pink cloud of satisfaction.

The previous week had gone pretty much perfectly. We'd maximized the number of entries every night, even on the traditionally slower ones, like Tuesday. Normally we would tinker on Mondays when the clubs were dark, change out the DJ lineup, maybe, create a new theme, bring in different promoters. That Monday we didn't need to change a thing. For the first time in my life as a club owner, I thought I had everything figured out.

The following Friday we were closed down.

That night, undercover cops fanned out through Limelight, look-ing for sales of illicit drugs. The actual raid hit at closing time, five a.m., on the first of October. A squad of uniformed officers moved in and joined their plainclothes cohorts. The cops ordered the music shut down. They herded all the patrons into the lobby and then out onto the street. There, they ushered them into an impromptu lineup. I remember seeing my former customers huddling in the cold night air.

The legal justification for the raid involved an old city statute. The so-called nuisance-abatement law had never been employed to shut down a nightclub before. It was originally designed for use against brothels. Directed by Giuliani, the City Hall brain trust had come up with the new strategy, put into play by Silbering, the special narcotics prosecutor.

I made for an easy target. *Look for a guy wearing an eye patch.*

We had 3,500 people in the club that night. For all the high-profile brass, plainclothes, and uniformed personnel involved in the operation, the cops made only three arrests, all on misdemeanor weed charges. One of my busboys got swept up in the net when he was pestered over and over by an undercover who said he was looking for a high. Annoyed, the busboy finally gave the guy a single joint of his own, and paid for the act of charity by getting popped.

I myself wasn't busted, but it was as if Limelight itself had been. Silbering had a paper sticker slapped across the front door that was like an eviction notice:

BUSINESS CLOSED BY ORDER OF THE NEW YORK CITY COMMISSIONER OF POLICE. EFFECTIVE DATE: 09/30/95. TO LICENSEE/ OWNER OF ESTABLISHMENT: Under Public Safety Threat/Summary Closure, the Police Commissioner has issued an order requiring the immediate cessation of all

business activities at, and the closure of this establishment. The Police Commissioner has determined that this
establishment presents a public safety threat due to an
offense occurring at this establishment during the establishment's operating hours, involving the licensee/owner,
or its employees, agents or patrons, or otherwise involving circumstances having a connection to the operation
of this establishment. The Police Commissioner has
determined that continued operation of this establishment presents a danger to the public and has ordered its
Summary Closure.

The notice wasn't signed by Rudy Giuliani, but the sticker had his
fingerprints all over it. He held a press conference crowing about the
closing. Mr. Mayor had found a replacement for his squeegee-man bug-
aboo. The bloodhounds Gagne and Germanowski had put their noses
to the ground on the trail of Ecstasy. Their informant Sean Bradley, the
luckless counterfeiter, had spun his tales of nightlife decadence. The
suicide death of young Nicholas Mariniello was cited in the aftermath
as a reason for the raid.

I never made a single cent off a drug sale, ever. In my business life,
the sole sacred, overriding principle was always protecting my liquor
license. Without that, I had nothing. There didn't seem to be any due
process. The judicial hearings that led to the closing were all ex parte,
meaning I didn't have the chance to plead my case. *Bang*, I was shut
down, and the court action to get reopened could take weeks.

Silbering confronted me amid the chaos of the raid. "I've got to ask,
Peter, were you involved?"

I picked up a bottle of Perrier that rested on top of a nearby bar.
"You see this, Bob? I can buy one of these for a dollar and sell it here
for seven dollars. Now why in God's name would I jeopardize a sweet
arrangement like that to get into selling pills?"

That night, I overheard a phrase that would come to symbolize the Giuliani administration's rancid view of nightclubs, one I would hear repeated again and again in the coming months. "This place is like a drug supermarket," the *New York Daily News* quoted an undercover cop on the Limelight raid. "You find everything in there: pills, marijuana and cocaine. You name it, they have it."

A "drug supermarket." A ridiculous concept, especially when the raid had actually turned up only a paltry amount of weed. But police, prosecutors, and the media fastened upon the term, as though Limelight operated some sort of illicit Duane Reade. "Drug supermarket" became a convenient catchphrase, a two-word package tied up in a neat bow and used to sway public opinion. A Big Lie was born and took on a life of its own.

Don't fight it, my lawyers advised me, *settle.* I was a little stunned by the turn of events. In over twenty years of club owning, nothing like this had ever happened to me. I had no playbook. The attorneys counseled me to take the hit meekly, to avoid making trouble. I agreed to post a large bond and had to close the club for five days.

The silver lining, which took me a while to identify, was that the incident opened up a dialogue with city authorities. In the atmosphere of hysteria that surrounded the raid, the cops offered soothing assurances.

"Our goal is not to close the Limelight forever," police spokesperson Robert Messner told the *Times.* "It's a feature of New York City and it is a positive thing for a community to have nightlife. What we want is to change it from a place that has rampant drug use to one that has no active drug life."

All right, I thought. *I mean, good luck with that.* In 1990s America, and especially in nighttime Manhattan, a place with "no active drug life" sounded like a pipe dream. No such location existed—not City Hall, not Rikers Island, not St. Patrick's Cathedral. It lived in the fantasies of conservative puritan Nazis, maybe, but nowhere else. Still, I liked

the sound of "it is a positive thing for a community to have nightlife."
Amen, brother.

The term of the original indictment was six months. Under the
terms of the settlement agreement, I met once a month with representatives from Manhattan Narcotics, the same arm of the NYPD that
had shut me down. We still had something of an adversarial relationship, but at least we were talking. Face-to-face, I had to believe that
Silbering and his crew would realize I didn't have horns growing out
of my head, that I was being tasked with an impossible job, and that I
would continue to demonstrate goodwill in an effort to comply with
the city's demands.

The settlement also dictated that I hire a security consulting firm. I
chose Kroll Associates, a leader in the field. Now I had security monitoring my security. I could furnish Silbering and Manhattan Narcotics
with glowing reports from Kroll, which indicated that I was actually
doing an effective job at drug interdiction in my club. I eventually hired
Kroll for all my venues, a hefty undertaking at $10,000 each per week,
but one that might keep my other clubs safe from similar treatment.

I had taken a first shot across my bow. I duly reefed in my sails,
steered my vessel into port for a temporary refitting, and hired on more
crew. But I was determined to captain on. I didn't think there was anything else I could do.

CHAPTER FOURTEEN

When the Whip Comes Down

After the weeklong padlocking of Limelight in fall 1995, I somehow fooled myself into thinking the raid and its aftermath represented the end of government harassment. I was making a good-faith effort to work with city authorities. I kept hearing rumors about a large-scale investigation into my affairs, but New York City is rampant with rumors, especially in nightlife.

One aspect of running a multimillion-dollar company involved palling around with the powers that be by attending fundraisers and benefits that seemed to dot the social calendar with the regularity of religious holidays. It's called the "rubber-chicken circuit," for the inedible food customarily served. Usually my in-house legal counselor and all-around superconnected New York advisor, Susan Wagner, encouraged me to attend. Susan had worked in the Koch administration and had a lot of credibility, to the extent that I considered her my conscience and usually did whatever she told me to do.

I always hated the whole black-tie merry-go-round of events at the Waldorf, Cipriani, the Rainbow Room, and other upscale outposts of the business and social elite. But Susan convinced me that attendance at those dinners was obligatory, a way of claiming my place in the power structure of the city. I would skip them at my own risk.

Among the soirées I attended that winter was a prestige fundraiser for the Republican Party in the Waldorf Astoria's big banquet hall. The featured guest was Mayor Rudolph Giuliani, and the celebrity attendee was Donald Trump. I got herded into the receiving line as soon as we entered the hall, suddenly finding myself face-to-face with Rudy, who reached out to shake my hand before realizing who I was.

By that time, I had a fully formed distaste for the man. Not long before that dinner, an AIDS group that had criticized him had suddenly lost city funding. When it was below zero outside and the homeless shelters were packed, the mayor routinely sent cops in at three a.m., rousting everyone and checking for outstanding warrants. Ever the prosecutor, Rudy hounded newsstand operators, buskers, and street artists in a relentless campaign to make New York City a more boring place to live. He had a habit of issuing authoritarian directives like some military dictator, then seeing his moves get knocked down in court.

That night at the Republican benefit, Giuliani grabbed my hand for an automatic receiving-line shake.

"Mr. Mayor," I mumbled.

As he recognized me, a stricken expression crossed his face. He briefly looked panicked, then dropped my hand like a hot poker. Recoiling, the man muttered something I didn't catch, an oath or a curse. I'll never forget the look Rudy Giuliani gave me, a mix of fear and loathing that stunned me.

The incident chilled me, but not enough to prevent me from going about my business. I had enterprises to run that employed over a thousand people. Juggling four clubs—three when Club USA closed in 1995 after the building landlord went bankrupt—meant that I was too busy to care what the mayor of New York thought of me. I had events to organize, a million details to attend to, staffers to supervise, cajole, and encourage.

In the wake of the Limelight raid, my security personnel expanded. I never wanted cut-and-buff gym rats, the kind that were often jacked up on steroids. The job was not to win fights but to prevent them. I favored the more difficult-to-find people with military experience in black ops, or ex-cons who were well equipped to deal with outbreaks of violence. My team of Secret Service–level professionals could have provided security for the pope or the president.

I also continued to employ my usual army of managers, technicians, hostesses, graphic artists, cashiers, bartenders, door people, and maintenance crews. Professionals I took on included lawyers, insurance advisors, community liaisons, corporate event bookers, and specialists in government relations. On a nightly basis I dealt with cops, crooked or otherwise, and less often with city inspectors, community board members, and petty officials.

Tunnel had five different sound systems, and sound technicians had to make sure they were all running properly. I hired one lighting tech whose sole job was to go around to all the clubs and change the gels on the lights for the evening's theme parties—bright, fun-filled pastels for gay nights, darker and more brooding tones for Goth and rock 'n' roll, fire-engine red for hip-hop.

The '80s and '90s represented the era of the party promoter in nightclubs, and some of my time back then was spent managing a corps of people who were not quite employees, and not quite freelancers. I had never really had to deal with promoters before I entered the New York City market. I'd publicized my clubs in Atlanta and Florida via word of mouth or, rarely, in Miami, through radio advertising.

Even in New York, using planners wasn't a universal practice. The Sunday-night hip-hop parties at Tunnel, for example, never required promotion. Word in the neighborhood was all I needed. "You are now about to witness the strength of street knowledge," as Dr. Dre rapped. And even though DJ Flex is often credited with "creating" Tunnel Sundays, it wasn't the DJ or promoter who made events happen, it was the entire organization behind the promoter. No single person can do anything in nightlife without a strong organization.

Party planners were mostly small-time operators whose main skill was putting together lists of viable contacts, and whose value was their ability to attract customers to my clubs. They mostly were young, avid club-goers themselves, working to support their nightlife habits. In the pre-AIDS glory days of the early '80s, a promoter might deliver eight hundred to twelve hundred entries, but that level of success faded quickly. By the '90s, a good party planner could bring fifty or a hundred people into a club, and a great one might attract four or five hundred.

Gradually I began to engage several planners for each night we were open. They had different constituencies, so four or five promoters together might be able to guarantee a thousand or so paying patrons—not a negligible number.

For each club I owned, I blocked out future dates on massive whiteboards installed on the walls of my offices. Planning went on weeks, sometimes months, ahead of time. Surrounded by my scrawled-over whiteboards charting what dates were coming up, I would assemble party planners for busy, chaotic, sometimes raucous afternoon meetings where we hashed out the details.

The planners were specialists; certain promoters handled themed parties that catered to the queer community, for example, while other promoters focused on rock nights. Party planners were forever promising me the moon, swearing they could deliver crowds, hordes, whole armies. I didn't pay any attention to anyone's assurances, but simply checked the door lists at the end of the night. If they guaranteed me hundreds and delivered a dozen, they were out.

I employed three in-house art directors, each with a staff of five, to work on the nightly transformation of each club. I also hired an incredibly talented artist named Gregory Homs to create advertising and invitations for the different parties at all of my clubs. Well known for his album covers and movie campaigns, he took on the challenge of coming up with multiple designs every week. Gregory was inclined to emphasize the outré aspects of nightlife. I recall him saying at the time that "a culture is defined by its taboos," a philosophy I shared. That attitude showed in his work.

Postcard-size club invites became a symbol of the era as surely as Monica Lewinsky's blue dress. It's almost a quaint concept, in an internet age, to recall a time when an actual paper-and-ink object represented a way for people to connect. The invites—which granted free or reduced-price admission—served as nightlife currency.

I worked with dozens of planners in the course of setting up parties and events at my clubs, juggling twenty or thirty theme nights a week. The most a planner could expect to knock down was a few hundred dollars a night. The attraction wasn't money but prestige, influence, camaraderie, the warm-and-fuzzy feeling of being an insider. Those clubs were a place where kids who felt alone, who felt like outsiders, could find each other, and the feeling of belonging is a powerful thing.

The only notorious party planner ever, the one who played a part in the fall of my nightlife empire, was an Indiana-born live wire who was about to turn thirty in spring 1996. Michael Alig started as a busboy at Danceteria and become a ringmaster of the club kids, promoting a Wednesday-night theme party at Limelight called Disco 2000.

I originally signed Michael on because he'd attended Manhattan's Fashion Institute of Technology, and FIT served as a locus for the young, hip, and creative. FIT students salted the Limelight crowd with a bit of flamboyance and color. I liked Alig well enough, but most of the time he was like a gnat buzzing around my head, asking for favors, claiming my attention. He was born to push people's buttons, and he shared that characteristic with a lot of people on the club scene.

On the night of March 17, 1996, Alig and his roommate, Robert "Freeze" Riggs, murdered another club kid, Andre "Angel" Melendez. (Angel had long been eighty-sixed from my clubs.) Days later, they then dismembered Andre's body and disposed of it, ineptly, in the Hudson River.

The murder and its ghastly aftermath didn't come to light until about eight months later, when the police started investigating in earnest and local outlets picked up the story. Alig had apparently started the rumors among the club kids that he and Freeze had killed Angel. He told so many stories no one could keep them straight, and one month later, in December 1996, Alig and Freeze were busted.

Not a single element of the crime took place anywhere near Limelight. But rumors swirled, as rumors will. That I employed Angel to supply my clubs with drugs (nope). That he was killed in Limelight's basement (of course not). That I ordered the hit (no, no, no). The stories were wild, and eventually the incident came to symbolize the druggy decadence that supposedly infested New York's nightlife at the time.

How the straight world loves tales of druggy decadence! It's one of their favorite titillations. Articles were followed by books, memoirs, documentaries, and not one but two feature films—one of them starring Macaulay Culkin—that all exploited the Michael Alig story. The motive for the murder has been spun a number of different ways. Alig pleaded self-defense, but at other times he claimed it was premeditated. Others theorized Alig had been dope sick, or he was having a midlife crisis as a club kid approaching thirty, or he was a symbol of everything wrong with modern culture. You'd almost conclude from the way people talked that Alig was worthy of all the ink spilled about him, all the miles of celluloid. As far as I was concerned, he wasn't.

All right, I understand that every writer and filmmaker needs a hook upon which to hang their story, and homicide is an obvious choice. But the basic truth is Alig was a smart planner who promoted a theme night at one of my clubs. He was also one of the most prominent club kids of the era, serving as one of the ambassadors to that specific cultural moment, appearing everywhere from Joan Rivers's talk show to the cover of *New York* magazine.

Business-wise, I knew that Alig could bring a couple hundred warm bodies into a club, consistently, and his flashy publicity efforts helped popularize the nightlife scene. But Alig never acted alone. He succeeded at Limelight only because he was a cog in a well-oiled machine—managers, designers, sound techs, security people, cashiers, bartenders, community-relations attorneys, the cleaning staff, a whole host of people working to make sure the Wednesday-night Disco 2000 parties went smoothly.

My personal relationship with Michael Alig—not Michael the overhyped symbol, but Michael the person—was that I wanted to be a good boss. I wanted my employees to enjoy work. I wanted to create a caring environment. In all my clubs we did our best to accommodate childcare, medical appointments, and court dates. I handed out loans or advances when necessary. That was the ethos that had gotten me into backing *A Bronx Tale*. Sometimes generosity worked out for me. I was never quite sure where the line between being compassionate and being an enabler fell, and I carried more than one addict on my payroll long past the time I should have.

Alig was a favored employee. I found him interesting. He threw good parties. When his drug use started to interfere with his basic humanity—not to mention his hygiene—I presented him with a simple choice, one that I have posed to more than a few employees.

"Either get into rehab or I am going to have to cut you loose."

"I'll go, yeah, yeah, I'll go, right away. Today. Tomorrow at the very latest."

But to the best of my knowledge, he never did. So I fired him.

His mother, Elke, came into my office soon after to plead his case. "Please don't fire Michael, please. You're all he's got."

In the period after I let him go and after Angel's killing, Alig picked up a couple of new employers: Agents Gagne and Germanowski of the DEA. As rumors spread about Alig's crime, the Feds allegedly offered him a way out of his legal difficulties. *Give us the dirt. Agree to testify against Peter Gatien.* They took the killer club kid under their protection, offering him lenience on the murder charge that was sure to come his way. The government had discovered a crown jewel in the ragtag informants they'd found to build a case against me. Alig took his place alongside Sean Bradley, the failed counterfeiter from New Jersey.

Also enlisted around that time was Sean Kirkham—Sean number two in the DEA roll call of sources. Kirkham had grown up in Canada, and that's about all I can say with confidence about him, since at different times in his life he put forth several different origin stories.

Kirkham showed up in New York City in 1990, and a couple of years later we gave him a gig at Club USA. He worked as an usher for ten days before he either dropped out or was let go—the history is hazy. I don't recall meeting him, though he claimed that he came to know both Alig and me through his job at Club USA. Kirkham then decamped to Miami and somehow managed to hire on as an informant for the Feds. The guy careened from one scam to another, at one point stealing an address book and selling celebrity phone numbers to party promoters, at another point bilking victims he found on the web, always portraying himself as a supersuccessful, nonsociopathic good guy.

He returned to New York City at the end of 1995 and fell in with Gagne and Germanowski, reaching out to them when he heard about Limelight's closure. He described his methods during this period in a documentary film, *Limelight*.

> I'd been an informant for almost six years at that point in my life. I'd worked with countless agencies and hundreds of agents. Without question it's physically impossible to prevent people like me from closing down your place of

business. All it takes is a simple call to a drug dealer to come to your place of occupation. I'd have to make a drug purchase, and under the nuisance-abatement laws, your business will be closed.

Human society is mostly a collection of human beings who have their psyches in good working order, going about their days and ways filled with good will and honest expectations. Meanwhile, there are a select few sociopaths who all seem to have a vital piece missing. How else to explain corporate raiders, tribal warlords, corrupt politicians, scammers—and amoral loose cannons like Sean Kirkham?

After the Limelight raid in fall 1995, and despite the rumors of a government initiative against me, I spent months in a sort of cloud-cuckoo-land, desperately wanting to believe I was in the clear. Robert Morgenthau, the Manhattan district attorney and Robert Silbering's boss, subpoenaed my business records in a sales-tax investigation—but, publicly, at least, that seemed to be the extent of my legal problems.

Behind the scenes, though, at the US Attorney's Office for the Eastern District of New York, prosecutors prepared to indict me on drug charges, secretly conducting interviews with sources, getting all their ducks in a row. And a trio of odd ducks they were: Alig, Bradley, and Kirkham, criminal informants for hire.

That spring, the government case against me took a hit when police busted Bradley for selling drugs at a New Jersey shopping mall. US Attorney Michele Adelman went ballistic.

"You know what an embarrassment you are?" she allegedly screamed at Bradley, visiting the hapless kid in jail. "I gave you a 5K letter [a type of official memo recommending leniency for a cooperating witness], and now I'm going to look like an asshole!"

That little glitch in the prosecution's best-laid plans failed to slow the government steamroller. Shortly after the arrest of their prize informant,

US Attorney Zachary Carter's office issued a felony indictment against me for conspiring to distribute Ecstasy.

When I answered the front door at five thirty that morning, hair tousled from sleep, wearing only a T-shirt and my pajama pants, a whole platoon of DEA agents confronted me, guns drawn. Gagne and Germanowski were nowhere to be seen. I felt like I was caught in a bizarre scene out of the Wild West. Alessandra and Xander were home and I feared that they might get harmed in the chaos.

"Are there weapons on the premises?" agents kept barking, guns still out, ignoring my repeated replies of *No, no, no.*

I couldn't understand what was going on. A random idea that made no sense occurred to my sluggish, newly awakened brain, that maybe a drag queen working one of my theme nights had gotten into trouble. The lead agent on the raid, Jay Flaherty, hustled me upstairs to dress.

My mind fumbled to keep up with the cascade of events, all the while wondering, *Is this really happening?* The sidearms of the government agents and their DEA windbreakers informed me that *Yes, indeed, it's going down right now.* And I still couldn't believe it. The cuffs went on and I *still* didn't believe it.

"Don't worry," Agent Flaherty told Alessandra as he led me out. "Peter will be home for dinner."

He lied. In fact, I wouldn't have dinner at home with the wife for quite some time. Flaherty had me whisked away, first to the DEA's Manhattan headquarters for processing, then to the Metropolitan Detention Center (MDC) near Red Hook, Brooklyn. I had been arrested at six a.m. and wasn't processed until midnight.

I had never been in jail before. The MDC struck me as a scene from a bad movie. When I walked onto the cell block, a chorus of catcalls greeted me along with the other newbies. For the sake of keeping the peace, the whole place was racially segregated. The dorms had separate rows of cots for African Americans, Anglos, Asians, and Latinos. There was even a zone known as "heroin corner" devoted to junkies.

For reasons I'll never understand, the corrections officer—the CO, and don't call them "guards" if you value your well-being—led me to the area that was reserved for Italian wise guys, a fifth-floor dorm, quiet as a church.

"Who's this punk?" growled an inmate, in a way that made me think I didn't want to ask too much about his business.

"Yeah, buddy, you want to take care of this one," the CO responded. "He's going to be on the front page of the *Daily News* tomorrow."

He was right. My arrest landed me not only on the cover of the *News*, but on the front pages of the *Post*, *Newsday*, and the *New York Times* national section. I was jailhouse famous. When I awoke in lockup the next morning, one of my fellow inmates approached, speaking in a hushed tone.

"What do you want?" he muttered. "I can get you heroin, cocaine, weed, uppers, downers, anything you need."

No doubt if I had asked him for a hit of the infamous club drug, Ecstasy, the guy would have come through. I had been charged with conspiracy because I allegedly allowed drug use on premises I operated. In my smelly, crowded detention dorm, the clamor from other inmates providing a background roar, I wondered who in the government could be hauled into court for allowing drug use in its jails.

CHAPTER FIFTEEN

Trial by Fire

For years, I'd been running dead presidents through cash-counting machines, filling up one armored car after another, shoving shovelfuls of money into this or that bank account, leading the life of the reasonably well heeled. I wasn't rich by the standards of the Manhattan uberwealthy, but I was better off than most.

Getting slammed into the slammer narrows your life down to a pinprick. From the first moment I entered New York City's Metropolitan Detention Center, all my mental energy focused on a single overriding question.

How do I get out of here?

I was plagued with uncharitable thoughts about the MDC, infamous for being a real shithole. My review: zero stars. The food was lousy and there wasn't enough of it. My fellow guests were surly and the service staff unfriendly. The most surprising aspect of life inside was how hellishly loud the place was. It wasn't suited for quiet meditations on your sins.

How do I get out of here?

That question drummed in my brain and pretty much chased out all other thoughts. I'd take a break to curse Rudolph Giuliani once in a while, before jumping right back on track. *Get. Me. The. Hell. Out. Of. Here.*

Prosecutors convinced Magistrate Robert Levy to set my bail at $1.7 million. According to US Attorney Zachary Carter, as a Canadian citizen I could be considered a flight risk. Since their number-one goal was to keep me inside, the US Attorney's Office performed a full-frontal attack on my assets. I woke up to find my accounts locked tight and a lien placed on Limelight, a Sixth Avenue freeze-out that meant, even though I owned the building, I couldn't raise money mortgaging it. My corporate entities were given the bum-rush by Chemical Bank, where I had held accounts for over a decade. Suddenly I found myself rendered nearly penniless.

It's impossible to mount a defense if you're broke, and doubly so if you're incarcerated. The great majority of federal cases never go to trial. They plea out. In order to prepare the ground for negotiation, prosecutors need their targets inside, desperate, chock-full of fear and loathing. They figure that way, prisoners will be more open to compromise. In my case, the Feds felt that if I was out on the bricks, going on my merry way after making bail, I might somehow forget that the long arm of the law had my nuts firmly in its grip. The government prefers you vulnerable and out of your mind to make a deal.

The other poor souls who got swept up with me on the same day, mostly random club-goers, all got unsecured bail. They were released on their own recognizance, just by putting their signature on a form. Meanwhile, the big fish, the tabloid poster boy, remained in durance vile. This despite the fact that I had deep ties to the community, sent my kids to school in New York, and owned property there.

The government treated my case as if I were a mob boss. I had originally believed that the main question in my mind—*How do I get out of here?*—had a one-word answer. *Bail.* When I found out I had been rendered broke, that question gave way to another, equally pressing one. *Where's all my money?*

There was a single glimpse of hope. The US Attorney's Office couldn't touch my holdings in Canada. Performing a financial fandango by transferring property up north to my brother Ray, then having him take out a mortgage, I managed to scrape together $750,000 in cash, still falling well short of the $1.7 million total.

My wife, Alessandra, tried to arrange my bond. My friends tried. It all took time. With mounting panic I watched day one slip into day two, day three, day four . . . Agent Flaherty had promised Alessandra I would be home for dinner. He didn't specify on which day.

I'm a proud man. I've made my own way in the world, always paying back whatever government aid I got in the way of small-business loans. Early business partnerships, minor as they were, never worked out. Now it killed me to have to go to my brothers with hand outstretched. My self-image as the supersuccessful one in the family crumbled. I had to ask Maurice, Ray, my ex-wife Sheila, and my mother to dip into their pockets so that I could be sprung from the MDC.

During the long wait, I had nothing to do but pay attention to what was going on around me. Through the jail grapevine I heard that a fellow inmate had been stabbed the first night I was there. I watched another inmate get beat up for the high crime of taking too long on a call to Nigeria. A constant scramble surrounded the bank of pay phones, and the victim had violated his allotted time.

Everywhere, people were spending their days bulking up. Instead of barbells they used two buckets of ice suspended on broomsticks. My interactions with my new cellies did not go well. One of them approached me, sporting biceps the size of howitzers. This guy looked as though he could snap me like a twig.

Without preamble he blurted out, "Hey, man, I lost my oyster in your motherfucking club."

Lost his oyster? I thought it was a euphemism, like losing your cherry. Whatever it meant, it sounded like a bad thing. Only later I found out that there was a kind of Rolex called an Oyster, very expensive, and the dude had gotten his stripped off him in the crush on the Tunnel dance floor. I was terrified that the confrontation might blow up, but then the guy just laughed the whole thing off. It took me hours to stop looking over my shoulder.

I spent two weeks marooned in MDC, dodging dangers both real and imagined. It seemed to take forever for friends on the outside to help me make bail. My fellow producer on *Bronx Tale*, Dan Lauria, bless him, pitched in right away.

"Anyone who helps the arts is a friend of mine," Dan explained to the press.

Lauria, Alessandra, my mother, Sheila, and my brothers all signed the bond. As did Sidney Levinson, a longtime tutor of Jen and Amanda's, a retired educator who had become one of the family. He appeared at my bail hearing to offer up his book-and-record collection as collateral, since he had no other property to pledge. I get choked up just thinking about it, and I believe Sid Levinson's selfless offer made a difference, since the magistrate saw him as a man of integrity.

By that time I had met with and hired an attorney, a fierce litigator named Ben Brafman, named in the press as "the man to have on speed-dial when you're in really big trouble." I had known Ben only socially before my own "really big trouble" began. The year I was arrested, 1996, *New York* magazine labeled Limelight the best nightclub in New York City and called Brafman the best criminal-defense lawyer. Like Clarence Darrow, he had made his bones defending mobsters. In my situation, I figured I needed to hire the best.

It turned out I was in perfect tabloid company. Around the time he signed on to defend me, Brafman was also representing accused murderer Daphne Abdela, a fifteen-year-old who was charged alongside her boyfriend, Christopher Vasquez, for allegedly gutting a victim in Central Park. The *Post* loved to use the tag of "Baby-Faced Butchers" for Daphne and Chris. I liked the fact that Ben was accustomed to defending clients who were being tried not just in court but in the press.

His wife, Lynda, nicknamed Ben "HP," for all the high-profile cases he handled. With my face splashed across every newspaper and TV news show, I was in his wheelhouse. During my initial meeting with him, in one of the supposedly soundproof lawyer-client conference rooms at Metro, it didn't take long to realize I had found my man. He convinced me of the one thing I absolutely required of my attorney: he believed I was innocent.

Ben told me he worked by invoking a somewhat subversive legal strategy. "My philosophy," he said, "is to take the theory of prosecution and demonstrate its weakness. If that can be done with the government's own evidence, it is successful. It's difficult for the government to challenge the strategy, because essentially it's theirs."

Turn the prosecution's case on its head. Hoist the government on its own petard. Again, as with the Limelight closure, the indictment had Rudy Giuliani's fingerprints all over it. It came out of a US attorney's office, just like the one he had spearheaded for six years. I wanted to see Rudy revealed as the con artist he was.

Brooklyn-born and raised in Queens, Ben Brafman proved to be a bare-knuckled scrapper in court. He had no Harvard Law pedigree, but he had done a stint in the Manhattan DA's office, then struck out on his own. When Rudy the racket-buster went after the New York Mafia families, Ben was on the other side, arguing cases for the defense. A poster hangs in his office bearing the label "Tough Guy."

That toughness was on full display during my bail negotiations, as Ben argued to get the bail reduced from $1.7 million to an even $1 million, arranged for the bond signatories to make their guarantees, then got the magistrate to release me on the promise of a check for the balance, to be delivered the next day.

On Wednesday, May 29, after fourteen nights inside, I walked out of MDC into the summer air of Red Hook, Brooklyn.

Then my real troubles began.

The New York journalist Jack Newfield and I should have been on the same side of the political fence. Newfield was a longtime *Village Voice* reporter who self-identified as a muckraker, making his name as a crusader for mostly lefty causes. But soon after my bust he began a vendetta against yours truly, and over the course of the next two years he wrote sixteen slanderous, ultrasensationalized columns on the subject of my evil days and ways.

In the overheated prose of Jack Newfield, my clubs were "satanic," with a "long history of illegal drug sales and violent assaults." I woke up every morning with a feeling of sick dread, knowing I would be demonized in the *Post* that day. I couldn't figure out what I had ever done to provoke such unrelenting nastiness.

Now, I had long been accustomed to attacks from right-wing puritans. The spectacle of public exhilaration on the dance floor of Limelight, Tunnel, or Palladium really bothered some people. I've encountered such attitudes all my life. In a lot of cultures the act of dancing itself is subject to all sorts of prohibitions. New York City's restrictive cabaret law had been used to hassle artists, taking down Billie Holiday, among others. Nightlife, my chosen realm of operations, had tended to trigger hysterical attacks from the "daylife" world.

Upright citizens always seemed on the verge of lighting up the torches, grabbing their pitchforks, and getting the mob together to snuff out the fun. I had assumed that some of the behavior was motivated by the hatred that adults harbored for the carefree ways of the young. Kids partying until four a.m.? Don't they have to *work*? And there were other more bigoted motivations for the hate, such as homophobia and, especially in the case of Tunnel, outright racism. I'd always been sure I was on the right side of the nightlife-vs.-daylife battles.

I never would have thought that Jack Newfield was a member of that priggish, conservative crew. He seemed to be something of an old-school liberal and had always been a loyalist to the cause of organized labor. In his columns he championed the fight against lead paint in public housing, targeted corrupt politicians, exposed predatory nursing homes, and fought the prosecution of a man who'd been wrongly convicted of murder. He seemed like a guy I might like to have a drink with.

But Newfield took a hard right turn on his way to liberal sainthood. His rants changed when he left the *Voice* and transferred to Rupert Murdoch's *New York Post*. The *Post* was not really a newspaper so much as a propaganda sheet for right-wing causes. "I read three newspapers and the *New York Post*," was a line I heard around town. The tabloid acted as a newsletter for Rudy Giuliani, and Newfield went to work on me as Rudy's hatchet man.

"The point is not to confuse objectivity with truth," Newfield wrote, justifying his deeply subjective approach to reporting, where opinion and fact mixed together.

Something else, something deep and dark and personal, motivated Newfield. He had a personal ax to grind. Rumor was that Newfield had some close personal experience with drug addiction. As in the case of Nicholas Mariniello's family, Newfield apparently felt the problem stemmed from another, outside evil—or so he wanted to believe.

Being trashed, lied about, and roasted in the media was incredibly frustrating. There was not a damned thing I could do about it. You can't win a war against anyone with a printing press. It's an unfair fight, and you're doomed to surrender. Unfortunately, in 1996, the internet was just a fledgling platform for chat rooms and AOL. It wasn't the great democratizing influence that it became just a few years later. I could have used a few young bloggers speaking up about my clubs and telling the truth about what went on behind our velvet ropes. As it was, the press was dominated by the old guard, and the old guard had decided to "clean up New York" at all costs.

At William S. Burroughs's Limelight birthday bash, the guest of honor made a few funny, choice remarks that included this pithy bit of wisdom: "An old drag queen once told me something and I've never been able to forget it. 'Bill,' she said, 'the world is divided into the Pricks and the Johnsons. Pricks always want to impose their views on you and control what you do. Johnsons mind their own business and leave you alone.'"

But Burroughs, in all his wisdom, forgot to mention that sometimes Pricks and Johnsons switch sides. Jack Newfield's move to the *Post*, where he was reduced to carrying water for Murdoch, was a classic case. The process by which a Johnson reverses course and becomes a Prick has since fascinated me. I'll never be able to understand it.

After my arrest, the *Post* sent undercover reporters into my clubs. They pronounced each "boring," without any evidence of illicit drug use. In a Newfield column published only a month later, he rebranded Limelight as a den of iniquity, with club-goers using hypodermic needles to shoot up in dark corners, a tableau that was titillating but false.

Most of the other press coverage I got after getting busted piled on the negativity. A select few of the downtown mags came to my defense, with a memorable line in *PAPER*: "Why don't you go ahead and crucify Peter Gatien while you're at it?" But in general, the media were eager to try me and judge me guilty.

Ben Brafman warned me that the defendant's chair was "the loneliest seat in the world." But having him sitting next to me made a measurable difference. He viewed his role of defense attorney as akin to rescuing a drowning man. "It's like I'm a great swimmer and I can pull you out of the water, no problem," he told me. "But there's also a tide we're both fighting against, made up of all the other factors that are added on top of what's happening in court. The tide can be a corrupt prosecution, say, or the portrayal of you in the media, and despite me being a great swimmer, that stuff can sweep you out to sea."

After he took my case, Ben Brafman signed on as the defense lawyer for Vincent Gigante, an organized-crime figure nicknamed "Vinny the Chin." Apparently a nightlife king and a baby-faced Central Park killer weren't enough for Brafman.

"Hey, Ben," I asked him, "is it really good for our team that you're defending someone like the Chin right now?"

"That's funny," Ben responded. "He said the same thing about you!" I like a lawyer with a sense of humor.

I knew that in the past I had cultivated a dangerous air. My eye patch helped to distinguish me from the crowd. The press referred to it as my "trademark" eye patch, as if I wore it for fashion, just an overage club kid playing dress-up. Because of that image, I served perfectly as a villain for Rudy Giuliani and a scapegoat for Jack Newfield. There I stood, or, rather, there I stood out, the face of New York nightlife, a convenient mark.

Yes, absolutely, there were drugs being consumed in my clubs. But there were drugs being consumed pretty much everywhere else in the known universe. Any claims—and there were many—that I employed "house dealers" to supply them to club-goers was fantasy, a macabre straight-world vision of what a downtown club was like.

The way I saw it, the authorities had presented me with an impossible task. I couldn't prevent a pill from coming into Limelight. I needed customers, and I wanted them to let loose and have a good time. Telling the difference between a happy transplant from the Midwest who thinks he's finally found an urban nightlife paradise, and a partier high on E, was a task my bouncers couldn't consistently perform, just as they couldn't be expected to distinguish between an inebriated woman simply exhausted from dancing and one plummeting down a K-hole.

It would have been ludicrous to label anyone involved in a New York City nightclub "innocent." I swam in the same waters as everyone else. In our society, recreational drug use was a fact of life. Ever since I learned my lesson at the Aardvark, I didn't drink, smoke weed, or do other drugs while I was on the job. As the Kipling poem had it, "If you can keep your head when all about you are losing theirs . . ." Amid the late-night wildness in my clubs, I was the designated driver.

But the nightlife profession in general and my eye-patch persona in particular did a great job of making me look guilty.

The wheels came off the prosecution's war wagon almost immediately. The team assigned to the case was headed up by a pair of assistant US attorneys, Michele Adelman and Eric Friedberg. That summer they spent a lot of time doing triage as their prize trio of informants—Sean Bradley, Michael Alig, and Sean Kirkham—began to implode.

Sean Bradley's arrest for dealing narcotics was the prosecution's most immediate concern. Finding himself in deeper and deeper trouble, Bradley wrote an incredible rambling, incriminating "Dear Judge" letter, detailing his experiences during his six-month stint as Gagne and Germanowski's confidential informant.

The agents supplied him with drugs, Sean stated in the letter, taught him how to mask his urine tests, and in fact encouraged him to continue to distribute Ecstasy. To keep Bradley's pipeline open, the DEA agents allegedly allowed a shipment of ten thousand hits of the drug to be imported from Amsterdam by Sean's girlfriend, Jessica Davis.

"While undercover," Bradley wrote, "Agents Gagne, as well as Agent Germonowski [sic], they used XTC, Agent Gagne smoked pot, and did Special K on more than one occasion."

Bradley whined about being repeatedly shorted on his "c.i. money," meaning the pay the government provides for confidential informants, which in Sean's case meant $750 or $1,000 at a time. He complained that Gagne posed rude questions to him about his go-go dancer girlfriend. "Has Jessica ever fucked another girl and you at the same time?" and "Does she take it in the ass?" Agent Gagne, stated Bradley, was "one of those stereotypical males who think they are very macho, and have to prove this by bragging about their sexual conquests." Such talk made Sean "feel so very uncomfortable," and "upsetted" him.

He seemed to have a better relationship with Germanowski, and there's a pathetic quality to certain sections of the letter. The kid makes it sound as though he got played.

> Now as far as Agent Gormonowski [sic] goes, I was so happy to have met him. We became friends, I don't mean just mere associates, I mean we were friends. He seemed really concerned about me, not just the case, but with me and my girlfriend . . . I would call Gee [Germanowski], talk to him, see how he was doing, always asking about his wife and son. He was like the older brother I never had . . . He took me to his house in Tinton Falls once, he even gave me his home phone number. He said he never did that with any other c.i., that it was against the rules. Gee once came to the bar that my girlfriend strips at to watch her dance . . . He also promised me that when the case was over, he would move me to a safe place, and I could start a new life with the reward money.

Sad, as Donald Trump would say. And a little chilling, too. Of course, it's against policy for DEA personnel to fraternize with CIs, not to mention provide drugs to them, do drugs with them, go on drug runs with them. Anything coming from Bradley had to be taken with not a grain but a whole pillar of salt. On the word of a whack job like this I was facing twenty years?

"Agent Germanowski and Gagne made it clear to me the government wanted Gation [sic] at all costs," Bradley wrote. "They bent rules. They broke rules." He quoted Agent Gagne: "If criminals lied, and cheated, sometimes the government had to do the same to get their targets."

Bradley claimed that the DEA agents assured him that as a payoff, as a pot of gold at the end of the rainbow, he would receive a percentage of all assets the government seized in the case. "Basically [Germanowski] promised me over a quarter of a million dollars."

A quarter of a million dollars was, apparently, the prize that kept Sean Bradley interested and in the game. For anyone that kind of money would serve as powerful motivation, but especially for a young kid with dollar signs in his eyes. The US government runs a lucrative racket by seizing the assets of the accused, and in the case of civil forfeiture, the subjects don't even have to be convicted in a court of law. There are stories from all over the country, but mostly in the South, that allege sheriff's departments arrest people simply because the cops are interested in confiscating a Lamborghini or Tesla.

Freezing my bank accounts was simply the government's first step. Next they hoovered up all the funds from those accounts, putting liens on every property, confiscating cars, just seizing any and all assets. Sean Bradley was apparently eagerly awaiting his cut of the blood money.

Bradley's "Dear Judge" letter prompted AUSA Adelman to come down on him like a ton of bricks. She also discovered that he had reached out to my attorney through one of my legal team's investigators, John Dembrowski. Bradley was charged with making a false statement to a DEA agent, and Adelman threatened to "bury him" if he continued to communicate with my defense team.

Gagne and Germanowski did all they could to shore up the government's tumbling house of cards. They visited Michael Alig. Even though Michael was under increasing suspicion over his involvement in Angel's murder—mostly because he was blabbing about it to "anyone who would listen"—the DEA agents offered all sorts of wild deals. Michael said later he was promised he would walk on the murder if he cooperated in the case against me.

Around the time that promise was being made, a cork-lined wooden crate washed up on a Staten Island beach, containing the remains of Andre "Angel" Melendez. The whole club scene had become convinced that Alig had been involved in the killing, and those who weren't were tipped over the edge by an article in the *Village Voice* that spelled out the details. Yet the DEA agents were so set on nailing me that they were allegedly willing to give Michael a pass on a gruesome murder.

Next to implode was Sean Kirkham, the last-recruited of the informants that the government pinned its hopes upon. Kirkham turned against his government handlers, alleging that, while he was running a gay escort service, AUSA Eric Friedberg called him up looking for sex. Kirkham said that while working for Friedberg, he himself became the prosecutor's boy toy. Playing both sides, he reached out to Ben Brafman and offered to sell the Fed's investigatory file in the case against me for $10,000. Ben immediately contacted the US Attorney's Office, a sting was set up, and the Feds busted their own informant.

After all that went down, and as I watched the case blowing up in their faces, I thought AUSAs Adelman and Friedberg would toss in the towel and admit defeat. I myself always try to listen when the universe seems to be telling me something. But the prosecutorial mind-set of "win at all costs" prevented Adelman and Friedberg from hearing the clear message being sent.

Instead, they followed the advice of the old street wisdom: "If at first you don't succeed, lower your standards." Employing a legal strategy that involved a "superseding indictment," the two AUSAs simply changed the rules of the game. They filed a reworked criminal complaint that did not depend on the testimony of Bradley, Alig, and Kirkham. Incredibly, Adelman and Friedberg would employ that tactic nine separate times before I finally faced them in court, filing one reworked criminal complaint after another. Even that situation didn't entirely settle my fears. I knew the government's problems were growing, but the prospect of twenty years in the slammer had a tendency to bring out the cynic in me.

Michele Adelman wasn't going to quit. The woman had a photo of me tacked up on the wall of her office, and I don't think it was because she liked my looks. It was a huge, blown-up poster, lacking only a bull's-eye pattern for target practice on a gun range. I was Michele's literal poster boy.

While waiting for trial on the conspiracy-to-distribute charge, I became very familiar with the many ways the government could fuck with me. Alessandra and I were indicted by sales-tax raps that would have swept up any merchant operating a cash business in New York.

I kept scrupulous books. I paid my taxes. But I also sometimes doled out payroll in cash. I dotted every *i* but occasionally failed to cross every *t*. *So sue me,* I'd think. But that's exactly what New York State did. Listing my wife on the charges was a cruel twist of the knife.

The sales-tax charge was followed by a barrage of permit denials, regulatory demands, and nitpicking violations of municipal ordinances. For example, Limelight carried a certificate of occupancy for four thousand people, a status carried forward from when the building had served as a house of worship. Lo and behold, that certificate was withdrawn, and a new one was filed that limited the club's occupancy to 375 people. At that rate, the staff would have outnumbered the customers.

On and on it went: fire inspections; building inspections; sanitation violations; police actions; citations for noise, loitering, unlawful assembly. Death by a thousand cuts. The government doesn't run out of money, and it doesn't run out of time. Meanwhile, waiting for my court date, I was running out of both.

Under the ongoing assault I managed to keep my clubs open, but barely. I was beginning to understand that I couldn't defend myself without money. I desperately needed cash flow to pay my legal fees, which were spiraling into the stratosphere.

I once made a stab at totaling it up into some sort of grand figure, representing what kind of fortune I would have needed to survive it all. I came up with a ballpark figure of $20 million. That's what it takes to keep the government off your back nowadays. Twenty million to pay the lawyers, the court costs, and the fines, and make up for lost revenue.

And I still had to show up in court to face Adelman, Friedberg, and company, trusting that my champion, Ben Brafman, would win the day.

CHAPTER SIXTEEN

Up Against the Wall

"The jury is here," Judge Frederic Block of the United States District Court, Eastern District of New York, announced. "I'm going to bring them into the courtroom now."

Those words kicked off the most excruciating, absurdist, belief-defying, panic-stricken four weeks of my life. I stood accused of conspiracy to distribute drugs. The US Attorney's Office had tossed in a RICO charge in the last of the seemingly endless "do-over" indictments they threw at me.

RICO (the Racketeer Influenced and Corrupt Organizations Act) is a law originally created to target Mafia dons. But increasingly it's being invoked against more ordinary joes, because it is devilishly difficult to defend against. Prosecutors love it. In RICO prosecutions, hearsay testimony is allowed, among other adjustments that stack the deck in favor of the government.

A few weeks before, after they had spelled out all the indictments, I'd had a single face-off with Agent Gagne. Tunnel had been under surveillance by Gagne and Germanowski, who had posted themselves in a warehouse across the street that housed Martha Stewart's business headquarters. Gagne and Germanowski supposedly witnessed me working in my office.

That day, Sean Bradley was along for the ride with his DEA handlers, and he later told the tale to Ben Brafman. According to Sean, a stakeout is screamingly boring. Sitting in a warehouse, watching a guy go over paperwork and take meetings with his staff, apparently lacked the exciting evildoing that the surveillance team had been hoping for. During the downtime, Gagne suddenly erupted in a laugh.

"Wouldn't it be funny if we saw Gatien taking a hit of coke right now?" he asked.

That fantasy of Gagne's went on to become the first line of the charging indictment, claiming the DEA agents had seen me remove a "one-hitter" from a drawer in my desk and inhale cocaine. There were several problems with this. Given where they were staked out and where my desk was, I wouldn't have been visible through my window, whether I was dancing naked, doing drugs, or howling at the moon. On top of that, my desk didn't have drawers. It was just a simple slab of glass.

Before the police showed up to shut down Tunnel that night, I'd read in the indictment the accusation of my coke use at work. By that time a club closure had become a regular occurrence, so I can't even recall the specific infraction. A noise complaint? Sidewalk crowding? I passed Gagne outside Limelight, stopping to confront him.

"You're Agent Gagne, right?" I asked.

He nodded, an odd, stricken expression crossing his face.

"Come on," I said, "let's air it out, right now, right here, man to man. You know as well as I do that you didn't see me snorting coke in my office—that'd be physically impossible."

He gave a shit-heel smirk. "Don't worry, it'll all come out in the wash."

"'Come out in the wash'? What does that mean? You upend my whole life, close my businesses, hassle my family, and that's the most you can say? 'It'll all come out in the wash'?"

Gagne just shrugged and walked away. I was disgusted and furious, but I had to keep a lid on my emotions. I was afraid any comment, any hostile move I made, might come back to me in court.

On Wednesday, January 14, 1998, my first day in front of a jury, I sat beside Ben Brafman and his defense team. If convicted on the charges, I faced a maximum prison sentence of twenty years. Unlike state convictions, where you're out on good behavior after a third of your stretch, on federal raps you're legally bound to serve at least 85 percent of your sentence. I was staring at a prison term that might have me incarcerated until I was sixty-three years old.

In his opening remarks, Ben Brafman told the jury bluntly that the prosecution was "asking you to end someone else's life."

That may sound like an exaggeration, since even if the prosecutors wished to strap me into the electric chair at Sing Sing, the conspiracy charges they ginned up against me weren't technically capital crimes. But I felt the full force of Ben's statement. Being convicted would end my life as I knew it—my life with my children and family, my life running a successful nightclub empire.

I was producing plays and feature films, developing plans for getting into the hotel business, planning for a future that would shepherd me into a life beyond nightclubs. All that would disappear with a long prison sentence. Directly behind me, in the gallery, Alessandra, Jen, and other members of my family sat, as they would for every single session.

That morning the prosecution and defense teams introduced themselves to the members of the jury, who numbered eighteen people, twelve jurors and six alternates. Looking middle-aged and middle-class, the jurors didn't have the opportunity to introduce themselves to us. Among them were a truck driver and a couple of housewives. None of them looked like they had seen the inside of a nightclub recently.

Boning up on advice for how to behave in court, I had read that the defendant should avoid staring at the jury. I had also read that I shouldn't avoid looking at them. Which piece of advice was right? I didn't know what to do.

Five people sat at the prosecution table: three assistant US attorneys—Eric Friedberg, Michele Adelman, and Lisa Fleischman—and two special agents of the Drug Enforcement Administration, Robert Gagne and Matt Germanowski. I was facing down the same pair of vultures who had been circling me for years, ever since they busted some Israeli smugglers who'd blurted out that Ecstasy was popular in "all the clubs."

And that quaking accused gent sitting beside Ben Brafman? That would be me. I have no hesitation in admitting that at that moment, as the proceedings opened, I was scared shitless. Pure, gut-wrenching terror.

I felt torn between two contradictory understandings. I believed that the government's legal action was a total charade, a total mutt of a case. I didn't even know what the hell I was doing in Brooklyn, since none of my clubs were located there. Ben told me he'd heard that the DEA had shopped the case across the river to the US Southern District of New York, which covers Manhattan. The US attorney in that office, Mary Jo White, didn't want any part of it.

So I should have been sitting pretty. How could I possibly be convicted when the government's case was trumped up, venue-shopped, relying on the testimony of thugs, addicts, dope dealers, rogue federal agents, and, in one instance, a convicted killer? The "flipped" witnesses were testifying in return for leniency on their felony crimes. In a just world, the judge would dismiss the charges, hold the government responsible for overreaching, and send us all home.

But a second, much darker understanding spurred my panic and woke me up in a cold sweat every morning. Through the year and a half that I waited for my case to come to trial, I gradually realized that the government *doesn't play fair*. In my case, at least, the US Attorney's

Office had embarked on a crusade to end my life, as Ben put it. The prosecutors were out for blood.

"You are in for a knock-down, drag-out slugfest in this case," Ben told the jury.

I tried to think of reasons why this might be so. The only answer I could come up with was that Rudy Giuliani was invested in this legal assault, and that it wouldn't stop until it landed me behind bars. There were plenty of other indications that the case possessed some mysterious urgency for the government, that I was being specially targeted. When Ben attended a proffer session, where the defense and prosecution get together to see if terms of a plea deal can be hammered out, the prosecutors treated him as though he had leprosy.

"I've been doing this for thirty-five years, and I've never had a proffer like that," Ben told me. "I can understand if prosecutors might characterize you as a piece of shit, since you're the defendant, and that's the way they justify themselves. But I'm an officer of the court, same as them. I know I don't lie and I don't cheat. They treated me at that meeting as if I, personally, was a piece of shit, simply for acting in your defense, and that's not OK. In fact, it's very far from being OK."

Just two days before we went to trial, I opened the *New York Times* during a break in the opening session of the court proceedings, and I ran across a tiny story headlined "Possible Trial Witness Dies." The text read:

> A woman who was considered a potential witness in the upcoming trial of the nightclub owner Peter Gatien was found dead Monday in a Queens apartment, the apparent victim of a drug overdose, the police said. No foul play was suspected. Cynthia Haataja, 22, was discovered by her roommate in a bed in their apartment at 1129 47th Avenue in Long Island City.

I knew Cynthia Haataja by the name of "Gitsie." She ran with the club kids who frequented the Wednesday-night Disco 2000 parties at Limelight. Pretty, with curly hair that was blonde when it wasn't dyed green, she once went on Phil Donahue's talk show with a few other members of Michael Alig's crew, putting herself on display to frighten and appall Mr. and Mrs. Front Porch America. I liked Gitsie and considered her one of the more sane aliens visiting us from Planet Club Kid.

DEA special agent Matt Germanowski had been bearing down on Gitsie for months, shaping her up to testify against me. Gagne and Germanowski were put on her scent by the cops from Manhattan's Tenth Precinct, who arrested her on the street with $40,000 worth of ketamine. The DEA agents told Gitsie they could make the drug bust go away in exchange for signing up as an informant in my trial.

But even when Gitsie agreed to testify, Germanowski wouldn't leave her alone. The middle-aged federal agent seemed obsessed with Gitsie, who was just twenty-two, saying how pretty and sexy she was.

"I love you," Germanowski told her repeatedly, badgering the woman to take a trip to Florida with him. Gitsie became frightened, confiding to her mother how extreme the situation was. She also reached out to my daughter Jen, pleading for help, saying she was afraid of the DEA agent and didn't know what to do.

"You've got to speak to a lawyer," Jen told her, and gave her a name to call. The attorney contacted the DEA and demanded that Agents Gagne and Germanowski cease all communication with his client.

Gagne and Germanowski must have had visions of Gitsie spilling details in court about their own crimes and misdemeanors, the multiple ways they skirted the law. Thoroughly spooked as Gitsie was, she could have blown Gagne and Germanowski out of the water. Repercussions from Gitsie's betrayal of the DEA were immediate. Undercover agents targeted Jen, attempting to build a case against my daughter for dealing drugs. There didn't seem to be a line that the agents wouldn't cross.

Brafman heard additional sordid tales of the two agents in a deposition he took from Alig. Michael claimed they smoked weed and did cocaine in front of him, ignored glaring evidence of drug use in his apartment, and once even took him with them to score dope. I didn't think Michael Alig would make for a particularly believable witness against government agents, but it turned out he was telling the truth. Ben subpoenaed cell-phone records that tracked the Feds to the apartment of Alig's drug dealer.

Their explanation was that Alig was their confidential informant, and he had crapped his pants while they were driving around with him. They stopped off at the dealer's house, Gagne and Germanowski solemnly explained, merely to let him get cleaned up.

When I faced such opponents, what did I have in my defense? I knew I was innocent, but that seemed a very small, fragile truth to pin my hopes on. I had always maintained my faith in the US Constitution. I didn't think America was a police state. But since my arrest, I had entered into a realm where up seemed to be down and the supposed good guys behaved like criminals.

The only thing that stood in the way of me getting crushed was Brafman. "If I didn't win this case," he told Alessandra later, "I was going to quit practicing law."

"Ladies and gentlemen," he told the jury, "in this case, you are going to see, I submit, government at its best and government at its worst." He continued:

> Government at its best is this: an open trial, in a public courtroom; no secrets, everything comes out, before people randomly selected—average New Yorkers who said they could be fair and impartial—with a trial being conducted before a fair and impartial judge. That's government at its best. That's democracy at its best. Anybody who thinks our system doesn't work, they are wrong.

Then Brafman went on to characterize the methods that the prosecution used to develop its case as "government at its worst." Strongarm tactics, multiple superseding indictments, plus use of ridiculously flawed informants like Sean Bradley, Sean Kirkham, and Michael Alig, all of them criminals themselves. God help the poor schmuck who finds himself in the crosshairs of a prosecution using tactics such as those.

CHAPTER SEVENTEEN

Chitty Chitty Bang Bang

The government took five weeks in 1998, from mid-January until mid-February, to present its case. I'd say about 10 percent of that time was devoted to my alleged transgressions. The rest was spent on enumerating, investigating, and deliberating about the crimes and trespasses that the witnesses testifying against me were either convicted of or charged with.

I had never experienced a criminal trial before. The proceedings would have been comical if there weren't such serious consequences. Everyone else, from Judge Block on down, seemed unruffled by what was, for me, a series of through-the-looking-glass moments. Time and time again, I was startled to hear the prosecution elicit testimony that placed its own witnesses, I thought, in an extremely bad light. As the trial progressed, Friedberg found himself having to prompt a particular government witness to tell the court how he had ripped off other drug dealers, how he had lied, how he had stolen, how he had assaulted people. He kept asking the witness if he had lied in specific instances and the witness kept confirming that he had.

Jesus Christ, I thought, *if this is the prosecution's case, I can't wait to hear the defense.* I kept glancing over at the jurors. But I couldn't read their expressions.

The prosecutor summed up that same witness's testimony:

> AUSA Friedberg: It was brought out on direct examination that from 1991 to 1995, there were a lot of situations that you lied in, isn't that correct?

> Witness: Yes.

> AUSA Friedberg: At the time it was brought out on cross-examination that you believed it was in your interest at that time to lie, isn't that right?

> Witness: Yes.

Ben Brafman characterized the government witnesses as "not worthy of belief." I kept looking over at Friedberg and Adelman to see if they were embarrassed, but they were like the Queen of Hearts in *Alice in Wonderland,* seemingly incapable of any thought beyond "Off with his head!"

The trio of informants who had been listed in the initial indictment, Michael Alig and the two Seans, Bradley and Kirkham, were long gone, deemed too compromised to testify. Gitsie couldn't testify because she was dead. Another witness, Brooke Humphries, was supposedly operating as a confidential informant for the DEA, but she was caught muling heroin between New York and Texas, and had to be crossed off the list.

Agents Gagne and Germanowski, proudly seated at the table alongside AUSAs Friedberg and Adelman, wound up not taking the stand. Gagne spent his time glaring at Ben Brafman, in such a constant, maniacal, and demented way that Ben privately expressed fears that the agent might somehow plant drugs on him or otherwise engineer his arrest. He had seen Gagne's and Germanowski's reckless disregard for the rule of law. He finally confronted Gagne outside court one day.

"What the fuck's your problem?" he demanded of the man. "I'm just here doing my job."

Instead of its star DEA agents, or its original informants, the government recruited other criminals who'd been busted and turned, hanging all its hopes on them. They also carefully tried to portray my alleged offenses in the most despicable light.

AUSA Friedberg: "This case is about Mr. Gatien essentially aiding and abetting and organizing people to essentially poison the youth of this city, at clubs, with drugs."

AUSA Adelman: "You might be shocked by the appearance of some of these club kids. You will even be more shocked by the huge amount of drugs that they distributed at Peter Gatien's nightclubs."

The prosecutors tricked up Exhibit 185, a poster-board presentation. It was modeled on the stereotypical diagrams of criminal hierarchies plastered on the walls of every television detective's office known to man. At the top was a shot of yours truly, with what I thought was a random collection of faces laid out below me.

The night of my arrest, when I'd been tossed into a holding cell with other people who had been picked up in the sweep, I couldn't figure out what we all had in common. As far as I could tell, they'd busted a few dozen drag queens, penny-ante hustlers, anonymous vagrants, and marginal hangers-on. Trying to solve the mystery of what brought us together, I asked a few of them.

"Hey, look, do you know me?" I asked.

"Nope," came their responses. Or "Nah, man, I don't know you, but I'm a friend of Steve, who works in your club."

The next time I saw them was when a few of their mug shots appeared on the prosecution's display board. I couldn't understand

Exhibit 185. Looking at the lineup, it seemed I was the godfather of a vast criminal enterprise. A couple of my alleged associates were busboys at my clubs, but other than that, I was at a loss.

The list of names and nicknames rattled off in court certainly sounded like a rogues' gallery: Paul the Baker. Junkie Jonathan. Gene the Rabbit. George E. The It Twins. Christopher Comp. Baby Joe. Desi Monster. Flyin' Brian. Frankie Bones. Anthony Acid. Lord Michael. Goldyloxx.

Friedberg and Adelman exposed details of my "hotel parties," drug binges that had occurred during the period covered by the indictment. They brought up four such instances over the course of five years. The prosecution used the parties as an element in the RICO conspiracy, theorizing that those multiday blasts were a way I rewarded drug dealers for their service, instead of a series of poor, hedonistic choices made by an addict who'd yet to seek help.

Ben Brafman objected:

> The hotel parties is the only testimony that will come before this jury linking Peter Gatien directly to the use of drugs and personally to the distribution of drugs. What [the prosecutors] have done, Your Honor, is [develop] a very weak theory that Mr. Gatien was a drug user and a drug distributor and that's why the jury should convict him.

Apart from trying to create a link between the people on the board and the RICO conspiracy, it seemed that the prosecutors' motive was simply to embarrass me in court. It worked. I had to face my wife and children after they heard details of my coke use, wild parties, and raucous behavior.

The blowouts had been extreme, I have to admit. I'd ordered mounds of food, towers of seafood, catered dishes, a lot of which were brought to the room and left untouched. Coke doesn't exactly make you ravenous, just full of extravagant thoughts. At the end of a two-or-three-day binge, inhaling and freebasing ounces of the stuff, I would inevitably enter into a state of paranoid delusion. I remember gazing out the window once from the luxury suite at Manhattan's Four Seasons Hotel, witnessing what I believed were armies of aliens, advancing through the streets and coming to get me.

I'd been totally out of control. My drug use had been one of the things that had cost me my previous marriage, and had shredded my relationships with my kids. Now I was suffering for it all over again. I endured my fifteen minutes of shame. No one enjoys having their worst moments trotted out in public, their most extreme, indefensible behaviors aired out. The picture painted wasn't pretty. My sins, which were exhaustively and accurately told, were placed in the limelight, so to speak.

Friedberg and Adelman seemed particularly intent on highlighting my extravagances, focusing on how much the hotel parties cost, for example, and how readily I put the charges on my Amex card. They took every opportunity to point out my wealth. They let the jury know that my credit-card bills were sometimes $50,000 or $60,000 a month. It was true. I used credit cards for business expenses, booking talent, everything. Running three megaclubs was expensive. Adelman routinely referred to me as a millionaire. My vacation home in Canada was characterized as a "mansion."

The move felt calculated. The jury of my peers likely did not have American Express cards, or if they did, the monthly charges were very different. The hotel parties, my income, my upscale lifestyle worked to alienate the middle-class men and women on the jury. *Look at this rich schmuck, he's out of control, he has to be guilty.* Watching it play out, I had to conclude that Adelman and the other prosecutors were trying to convict me on the basis of being a rich fuck, even though that particular charge wasn't technically listed on the indictment.

After all the talk and all the testimony, through all the back and forth between lawyers and prosecutors, a simple, glaring fact remained: *I was not in court accused of selling drugs, taking a cut of drug sales, or even doing drugs at luxury hotel blowouts.* The government's "drug supermarket" theory maintained that the availability of drugs at my clubs attracted customers, who paid entry fees, and, therefore, I had profited by conspiring to promote drug use.

The whole idea was offensive. I was the most successful nightlife entrepreneur at that time. I had gotten to that position not by encouraging drug use but by working my tail off to make sure that coming to my clubs was an outrageous, inspiring, and cutting-edge experience, as well as a smooth, pleasurable, trouble-free one. It was a tremendously difficult feat to pull off. A lot of people had tried, and no one had succeeded to the extent that I had, running top venues in a cutthroat business. Now all that work, all that expertise, all that creativity was being written off. My success, said the prosecutors, was due to lines of white powder and batches of little smiley-face pills.

Ben Brafman cleverly totaled the number of patrons who visited my four clubs over the years covered in the indictment, then also tallied the number of hits of Ecstasy mentioned in all the testimony presented.

> Brafman: We come up with 6,866,000 people—6,866,000 people went to Mr. Gatien's clubs during the period charged in the conspiracy . . . That is a lot of people, isn't it?

> Witness: A lot of people.

> Brafman: Lot of people to be using 40,000 pills over five and a half years?

Wielding a pocket calculator in front of the jury, Ben concluded that among the club-goers there had to be a lot of them—around 6,826,000, in fact—"who did not get Ecstasy." The *Times* labeled Ben's defense a "virtuoso performance." I'll take those numbers and apply them to anywhere else in New York City, from Madison Square Garden to City Hall, to Metropolitan Detention Center, and to the pedestrians on any block of Fifth Avenue.

The phrase "drug supermarket" continued to be used in court, and continued to piss me off. David Lee Roth had been moody and restless in the Limelight VIP room in April 1993. He liked to smoke weed, and was disappointed in being unable to make a connection at the club. He left to score, and an hour later he wound up getting busted in a drug sweep of Washington Square Park. The park was a real-life example of a drug supermarket, and it was under the city's control, not mine.

The government had eight hundred hours of wiretapped phone calls on audiotape—informants, party promoters, people who worked in nightlife. Not once, in all those tapes, was my name mentioned in any context. I finally understood Ben's plan of defense, using the government's own evidence to blow up the prosecution's case. Eight hundred hours of painstaking surveillance, he pointed out, that yielded exactly zip.

"Look," commented Judge Block as the trial drew to a close, "this is not one of the more uninteresting trials I have had in my young career so far."

I, for one, was riveted. Though I didn't feel any less frightened as I saw the case unfold, as far as I could tell it was a wheezing, clanking, smoke-belching machine, a Chitty Chitty Bang Bang contraption of sorts, but one that wouldn't fly. Somehow, the less competent the prosecutors seemed, the more dangerous they appeared. If they could bring a mess like this into court, I reasoned, they were capable of anything.

Ben Brafman was especially baffled that Agents Gagne and Germanowski, who had sat at the prosecutor's table for the whole trial, failed to take the stand. "Never, in all my years in court, have I ever seen an instance where the arresting officers didn't take the stand. It's just unheard of."

He came to me near the end of the excruciating trial, just before the government completed presenting its case, with a radical idea. "Peter, I'm thinking of resting without calling witnesses," he said. "I want to rest essentially without presenting our case to the jury."

"That's best?" I asked, not knowing what else to say. "Isn't it a risk?"

"There's a risk, and I've agonized over the decision. But we don't have to prove anything. The burden of proof is on them, on the government, and you sat in that court just like I did. They haven't come anywhere near to proving their case. The prosecution was a travesty. I've never seen worse. It's just . . . unbelievable. I point that out in my summation."

Over the previous year and half, we had worked hard at preparing our defense. We'd hired investigators to interview dozens of witnesses. We'd exposed the activities of the lead DEA agents in the case to the extent that the prosecution had been afraid for them to testify. All told, in investigator's expenses and attorney fees, I think I laid out close to $2 million developing our response to the government's case. Now Ben wanted to forget all that and essentially take a flier.

I couldn't process my thoughts. "If you think it's the way to go," I said weakly.

"You're the defendant, Peter, and if you tell me we ought to go in there and present our case, and have witnesses testify, I mean, if you strongly believe that . . ."

He trailed off. Then he said, "Let's think about it, come back to it, talk it over some more."

Consumed with Hunter S. Thompson levels of fear and loathing, I finally agreed we should let the government hang itself all on its own. Ben told me that he, too, spent a sleepless night before coming into court with that decision.

In the end, the prosecution's case, full of sound and fury, signified nothing. After five weeks of court proceedings that included sixteen days of hearing testimony, on the morning of February 9, the following exchange occurred:

Judge Block: Defendants rested?

Ben Brafman: Yes.

Judge Block: All parties rest. [To the jury] Ladies and gentlemen, the testimonial part, the evidentiary part of the trial has now been concluded.

Though I hadn't been a religious man since I was a child in Cornwall, had I been in the habit of praying, I would have taken the opportunity right about then. We were trusting the members of the jury to see the holes in the government's case, which we believed were big enough to drive a semi through.

But I couldn't read minds. I didn't know what the jury was thinking. What if they hated the picture of thousands of people dancing in a sweaty, exuberant mass, partying until the sun rose? What if they resented extravagance and addiction? What if they hated me?

CHAPTER EIGHTEEN

All Yesterday's Parties

On Wednesday, February 11, 1998, as darkness fell on a raw late afternoon, I stood in the Brooklyn courthouse waiting on the clerk of court to announce the jury's verdict.

Of all the things I've done, of all the situations I've found myself in, nothing was more life defining than that moment. Fate had reduced me to a cornered animal. Ben Brafman stood beside me, and Alessandra, Jen, and other loved ones were nearby, but they weren't the ones facing prison. Isolated, solitary, vulnerable, I felt the enormous power of the state bearing down on me.

"I understand you reached a verdict," Judge Frederic Block said to the jury foreperson.

I knew the statistics. The federal government wins 95 percent of its cases that go to trial.

"The clerk will take your decision," Judge Block said. The clerk stepped forward.

"Has the jury reached a unanimous verdict?" the clerk asked the foreperson.

"Yes," came the answer.

After a five-week trial, the jury had deliberated for all of three and a half hours. The legal experts I had read all agreed that fast verdicts are more likely to be guilty ones. I had also read that before the decision is announced, if jurors failed to meet the eyes of the accused, it was because they would be returning a verdict of *guilty*. Gazing over at the twelve-person jury, not one of them would look at me.

I took off my wristwatch and my rings, passing them back to my family. I wouldn't need them in prison. My heart hammered in my chest. Ben shook as he grabbed my hand. In a rush I thought of Cornwall, the Aardvark, the first Limelight nightclubs in Florida and Atlanta.

Andy Warhol popped into my head. In later years he'd tired of his famous line, "In the future, everyone will be famous for fifteen minutes," and had taken to riffing out variations, such as "In the future, every fifteen minutes someone will be famous." I felt as though the clock was running out on me.

"Racketeering Act One," intoned the court clerk. "Conspiracy to distribute MDMA, cocaine, and flunitrazepam—proven or not proven?"

"Not proven," said the jury foreperson.

"Racketeering Act Two, distribution of controlled substances, Future Shock parties, proved or not proved?"

"Not proven."

Racketeering charges are deemed proven or not proven, and all six came back exonerating me. Three conspiracy counts yielded *not guilty* verdicts for all of them.

Not proven. Not guilty.

The high from those verdicts surpassed any drug experience I've ever had in my life. I embraced Ben Brafman, tears streaming down both of our faces. Then I turned to Alessandra, climbed over the courtroom bench that separated us, and lifted her off the ground, trying to give her the strongest, most tender embrace she had ever experienced.

A wave of love passed over me, for my family, for Ben, for life itself. Jen raced out of the courtroom to a pay phone so she could spread the news to the rest of the family.

Nothing could have been sweeter. I thought I was home free. The weight had lifted. I had triumphed.

But the government, in its limited wisdom and unlimited power, wasn't through with me just yet.

"Why can't we get this guy?" wailed Rudy Giuliani.

Ben Brafman heard of the mayor's *cri de coeur* through the legal grapevine. Rudy was reacting not to my acquittal, but to our victories in a series of court cases that had followed in the wake of the federal trial. By slipping out from under the RICO conspiracy charges, I had only enraged the government, making it come after me all the more.

As intense as the federal trial had been, the shit that came afterward was nonstop. I got hit with a barrage of venue closures, one after another. Tunnel would get closed by this or that fugazi application of the nuisance-abatement laws, and it would stay dark for months while I awaited a court date. But every time I had a chance to appear before an actual judge, instead of before a city inspector or bureaucrat, I won the case. Over and over.

No wonder Rudy was frustrated. But so was I. After I beat one city agency in court, another one would step up to take its shot. In a stretch of fourteen months, Tunnel was closed for seven of them.

I had always retained my Canadian citizenship as a fail-safe. First out of concern for myself, and then for the well-being of my son, Xander. The US had a terrible tendency to get involved in wars, "police actions," and military interventions. I didn't want either of us drafted into another Vietnam. But keeping my passport opened me up for criticism in court.

"This man is nothing but a carpetbagger, with no feelings of patriotism toward the US," fumed one prosecutor.

The government action that finally brought me down came not from the Feds, not from New York City, but from New York State—the tax-evasion charges that had been wending their way through the courts for a long time. Paying some of my employees in cash was my crime, one that I shared with perhaps 99 percent of the business owners in New York. But it turns out that "Everybody's doing it!" is not a viable line of defense.

On $50 million in receipts over the course of five years, the state claimed to have been shorted $600,000, a little over 1 percent. Anyone else would have been assessed, not arrested.

"We can win this," Ben Brafman promised me. "I'll stick with you every step of the way. But we could go through a court battle and you'd wind up still owing the money. I have to ask if it's worth it."

So I pled out to two months in Rikers Island jail, a sojourn that could probably fill another book. Suffice it to say that, knowing how my time in MDC had gone, I reacted to incarceration with extreme anxiety. But to tell the truth, as soul crushing as the Rikers experience turned out to be, I was happy to do the time rather than face another trial. I didn't realize that when I agreed to the plea, my status as a tax felon and an immigrant would make me vulnerable to deportation. In fact, I had been assured that wouldn't be the case.

I was two years a free man in NYC, out of the clutches of the government and able to pursue my embattled business. In September 2002, the other shoe dropped. On a routine visit to the probation office, I found immigration cops lying in wait. They loaded me into a van and whisked me away. No phone call, no stopping at home to pick up a toothbrush, no nothing. It was like those cartoon images where someone is grabbed so suddenly they leave behind their shoes and socks.

I had fallen into the arms of the INS, the soon-to-be-renamed US Immigration and Naturalization Service. I had been through the mill at Rikers and the Brooklyn Metropolitan Detention Center, but I nominate the holding cells of the INS as the lowest rung of incarcerated hell. I essentially disappeared for forty hours, with no one in my family aware or able to find me.

In lockup, I started chatting with the immigration officers. "They're going to have to move you right away because this facility is full," one told me.

I looked around. I was the only one being held on the whole floor.

The INS transferred me to the Buffalo detention center in Batavia, New York. There, no one could contact me—not my lawyer, not my family. The cells were freezing and bare bones, the conditions Third World awful.

"Is somebody trying to kill you or something?" an immigration officer asked me when I arrived. "I've never heard of someone from the City winding up way up here." No writ of habeas corpus exists when the INS steps in. I was placed in quarantine and not allowed visitors.

Teeth chattering, filthy, and depressed, kept incommunicado, I recalled the words of Oscar Wilde, when he was left chained in the rain after his arrest for the high crime of loving the wrong person. "If this is the way Queen Victoria treats her prisoners," he said, "she doesn't deserve to have any."

Eventually my family and lawyer found me and I was bonded out, but in August 2003, after a torturous journey through the courts, immigration Judge Elizabeth Lamb assigned me the status of an "aggravated felon." By that time, in the wake of 9/11 and the US Department of Homeland Security reorganization, the INS had been rechristened Immigration and Customs Enforcement—the now-notorious ICE. I was once again put on ICE, so to speak, trapped in detention limbo for a month.

Throughout the process, I had become reacquainted with a grim truth: if the government ever decides to take you down, you are definitely going down, because the government will find a way. Especially if you slip through the clutches of someone like Rudy Giuliani, you can rest assured he'll come back to get you.

Giuliani wound up standing beside Donald Trump as the president's personal lawyer, pronouncing the immortal line, "Truth isn't truth." While I was being battered by immigration and city agencies, Giuliani embarked on a career as a lobbyist and corporate lawyer. Most tellingly, the same year I was busted, 1996, Rudy had begun representing Purdue Pharmaceuticals, the company that developed and marketed the opioid-based pain killer OxyContin. The company's aggressive marketing focused on denying OxyContin's addictive qualities. Giuliani brokered a deal in a crucial Florida case that allowed Purdue to continue selling the drug despite early warnings that it was incredibly addictive.

The result, of course, is an opioid epidemic that caused the deaths of thousands of people—an estimated four hundred thousand and counting. In 2017 alone, forty-seven thousand Americans died of overdose; it emerged as a leading cause of death for people under fifty, ahead of car crashes. Whatever drug use occurred in all the clubs I ever owned pales in comparison to the destruction "America's Mayor" helped unleash and directly fostered.

On September 24, 2003, I was released from custody, marched onto a plane, and deported to Toronto. I had $500 in my pocket, which Ben Brafman gave me since otherwise I was flat broke.

Out of all the direct hits and irreparable damage that I took, the reversals of fortune, the nights in jails and INS holding cells, the loss of my business, my name being smeared in the media, the worst wound was getting deported. Losing America broke my heart.

I'd been obsessed with the USA ever since I stared across the Saint Lawrence River and fantasized about the magic realm on the opposite shore. I got my green card and lived legally in America for over thirty years. I fought to keep my kids on US soil. For all intents and purposes I had become an American. I embodied the American Dream, became a success, raised a family, and made a home in the home of the brave.

I could have survived sleeping on a concrete shelf for a bed and eating shitty prison food. I could have faced being pummeled by repeated legal proceedings. But getting exiled from the land that I loved killed a part of my soul.

Nostalgia is a blade that cuts both ways. Thinking over former times, the Velvet Underground song "All Tomorrow's Parties" forms a soundtrack for my memories. They are all bittersweet.

Especially of late, I've come to believe that we have to return to the Dionysian nights when clubs were central to so many lives, the years of dance floors packed with crowds thousands strong, and remember the pure exhilaration and energy of the time. I've watched my younger children grow up in a very different world, one where social anxiety seems all-encompassing.

We need to recall the days when we were golden.

If I could go back to a single minute in my life, I'd take it standing on the balcony of Limelight, say, on some weekend night in the summer of 1995. During that period, hope rose in New York City and throughout the world. AIDS was no longer the death sentence that it had been. Magic Johnson had announced his HIV diagnosis at the end of 1991, and he went on to become the miracle man who gave us all optimism just by surviving.

We had beat the monster plague in a standoff. Nightlife started to rebound. It's hard to describe the waves of euphoria that rose off the floor when thousands of people danced to music that was loud and insane. My thoughts keep coming back to those high, fine, ecstatic moments.

They were nights of epic parties, but maybe they were something more, too. Nightlife spurred blasts of creativity that could be seen from space. The scene gave birth to music, fashion, and social trends that wound up changing the way generations saw the world.

People left my clubs and went on to rewarding careers. Names like Michele Hicks, Justin Theroux, Vin Diesel, and Chazz Palminteri might be most recognizable, but there were so many people who have built prominent lives in music, business, and entertainment. Most nightlife professionals nowadays are alumni of my clubs. Those kids went on to share a "next big thing" mentality that we fostered at the clubs.

The heyday of the digital age changed everything. Before cell phones and Facebook and Instagram, before the web went worldwide, in order to find out what was happening everyone had to get up off the couch and physically present themselves in public. To discover what people were wearing, what they were listening to, what was hot and hip and cool, you had to get out and press the flesh.

I'm haunted by the need to recreate that moment. When I sought to open a nightclub in Toronto, my old nemesis, Bob Gagne, erstwhile cowboy DEA agent, traveled to Canada and showed up to testify against me at a liquor-license review-board hearing. He arrived up north looking older but not wiser, and Ben Brafman sent him back home even older and more defeated than when he came. The new club, CiRCA, opened to massive crowds and then went on to win "Best New Venue" at the 2008 Club World Awards.

Whatever Gagne and Germanowski and Giuliani have to say, I'm still proud. Millions of people cycled through my New York City clubs over the years. We packed them in, and we maintained a crime rate so low it was almost negligible, with no major calamities.

I live in Toronto now, with Alessandra, able to spend time with my adult children and two beautiful grandchildren.

I look around today and see nothing—no European party city, no casino bacchanal—that can rival the incredible groundbreaking clubs of the '70s, '80s, and '90s. Perhaps I'm just an antiquated curmudgeon railing against "kids these days." But I've been in the big-bottle clubs in Las Vegas and elsewhere, and they can't compare with scenes I witnessed.

A blackened shroud, a hand-me-down gown of rags and silks, a costume fit for one who sits and cries for all tomorrow's parties . . . Like Lou Reed and Nico, I'm feeling elegiac for all the good times that will never be. They won't come around like they did in the golden age. I was there, and if you were there, too, you know the truth. Those were the days when the party never ended, and it was goddamn fabulous.

ACKNOWLEDGMENTS

First and forever, my heartfelt love and deepest gratitude to my wife Alessandra, who stood by me always. To my children, Jennifer, Amanda, Hunter, and Xander, who likewise were loyal through thick and thin. To my delightful grandchildren: I am so happy to share life with you. To the memory of my parents, Lilianne and Bernard: *Je vous aime et je vous honore.*

A very special shout-out goes to Benjamin Brafman, an incredible human being and brilliant lawyer whose compassion and dedication are boundless. Thank you for saving my life. Ben's wife, Lynda Brafman, and his family were welcome sources of support during challenging times.

My thanks and appreciation to Gil Reavill, who brought my words to life and made stories out of them, then helped me pull those stories together to make this book. My agents, Meg Thompson and Paul Bresnick, ushered the project through an adventuresome submission process. The team at Little A were Amazon warriors in their own right, led by Laura Van der Veer and including Emma Reh, Emily Freidenrich, Carmen Johnson, Merideth Mulroney, and Lucy Silag. Isaac Tobin created a great cover, summoning up a whole era. I have to re-mention Jen, my oldest child, for her business acumen, her blazing creativity as a film producer, and for getting the ball rolling on what eventually became *The Club King*.

To all my close friends, staff, and teams throughout the decades: I am full of appreciation and thanks for your beautiful energy and creativity. Gratitude goes out to Alan Klinger and Susan Wagner; Ben Ashkenazy; A. J. Block; Dan Lauria; Frank, Janet, Sean, Liam, and Kieran Moorfield; Yee, Jack, and Maureen Moorfield; Mark Baker; Corey Baker; Jerry Levitan; Shawn "Jay-Z" Carter; Lupe Fiasco; Larrance Dopson; Dammo the Great; Funkmaster Flex; Big Sean; David Shiller; Sean "Diddy" Combs; DJ Whoo Kid; Craig Pettigrew; Anthony Macchio; Leonardo Lubrano; Orin Bristol; Dom Faccini; Gregory Homs; Chris and Nicole Reda; Carol Hayes; Fat Tony; Mark Murray; Ashley Macintyre; Steve Eichner; Eric Goode; Serge Becker; Howard Schaffer; Justo Artigas; Kenny Baird; Christina Visca; Victor Calderone; Ethan Brown; Paul Budnitz; Paul Morris; Scotty Taylor; Michael Musto; Patricia Field; James St. James; Walt Paper; Stephen Saban; Bruce Lynn; Sophia Lamar; Russell Brunelli; Tom Doody; Nancy Dubin; Brian Rouleau; Kitty Bundy; Merryl Spence; Nichole East; Katie Longmyer; Jules Kim; Catherine Miller; Dale Araten; Jay Carucci; John Simonetti; Carlyle Mills; Ray Trosa; Matthew Banks; Mona Scott-Young; Queen Latifah; Shakim Compere; Cara Lewis; Kevin Liles; Joie Manda; Pamela Britt; Sean Brophy; Kevin; Michael Kyser; Joey Horatio; Impala; Richard; Abby Araten; John DeRobbio; Monica Michaels; Tracy Cloherty; Dino Simcoe; Erich Conrad; Jeff Mills; Junior Vasquez; David Guetta; Tiësto; Danny Tenaglia; Stretch Armstrong; Carl Cox; Joie Arias; Johnny Dynell; Lady Bunny; Kenny Kenny; Flexx Chapparo; Big Carlos; Big Candy, Mona, Diamond, and all Tunnel security personnel; John Carmen; Christopher Makos; Tracey Choi; Chi Chi Valenti; Sterling Cox; Little Candy; Ike McNamara; Tracey Fischer; Huey Morgan; Brian "Fast" Leiser; Jane, Louise, Chris, and Ray Montgomery; Pat, Rob, Louie, and Mena Fisco; Susanne Bartsch; David Barton; Gabriele Rotello; Coleen Weinstein; Tony and Posie Fletcher; Jeffrey Hacker, David Rabin, Billy and Irv Sorin, Will Reagan, Michael Francis, Sol Strazullo, and Ashok Iyer; Sertaj and the crew; David Sage; Allen Roskoff; John Dembrowski; Les Levine; Bob Silbering; Ethan Geto; Michele de Milly; Abe Backenroth; Mark Frankel; Sid Davidoff; Warren Pesetsky; Bob Bookman; and Jeff Gluck.

Too many people have left us too soon. Rest in peace to Brian MacGuigan, Sid Levinson, Chris Lighty, Tom Buckley, Mark Berkley, Tony Bongiovani, Leigh Bowery, Fred Rothbell-Mista, Gerry Snyder, Big Kap, Claire O'Connor, Arthur Weinstein, Billy Uhler, Fred Levin, and Malcolm Kelso.

ABOUT THE AUTHOR

Photo © 1992 John Bentham

Peter Gatien created, owned, and operated groundbreaking nightclubs over the span of four decades. In his early twenties, he opened his first club, the Aardvark, in his hometown of Cornwall, Ontario. He went on to helm an unbroken string of successful megaclubs, including Limelight in New York City, Atlanta, Miami, London, and Chicago, as well as Manhattan's Palladium, Tunnel, and Club USA, and CiRCA in Toronto. Gatien was also the executive producer of the film *A Bronx Tale*. Today he splits his time between Toronto and New York City, enjoying a home life with his wife, Alessandra, his four children, and his two grandchildren.